Ed Muskie

Made in Maine

Here and on front cover: Governor Ed Muskie at his desk.

Ed Muskie

Made in Maine
The early years, 1914–1960

James L. Witherell

Tilbury House, Publishers
Thomaston, Maine

Tilbury House, Publishers
12 Starr St.
Thomaston, Maine 04861
800-582-1899 • www.tilburyhouse.com

Ed Muskie: Made in Maine
Copyright © James L. Witherell
Hardcover ISBN 978-088448-351-9
eBook ISBN 978-9-88448-392-2

Design by Janet Robbins, North Wind Publishing & Design

Library of Congress Cataloging-in-Publication Data

Witherell, James L.
  Ed Muskie : made in Maine : the early years, 1914–1960 / by James L. Witherell.
     pages   cm
  Includes bibliographical references.
  ISBN 978-0-88448-351-9 (alk. paper)—ISBN 978-9884483922 (eBook)
  1. Muskie, Edmund S., 1914–1996. 2. United States. Congress. Senate—
Biography. 3. Legislators—United States—Biography. 4. Governors—Maine—
Biography. I. Title.
  E840.8.M85W58 2014
  328.73'092—dc23
  [B]   2014005769

Printed in the United States of America

14 15 16 17 18 19 MAP 10 9 8 7 6 5 4 3 2 1

Table of Contents

Preface   *vii*

Acknowledgments and Photo Credits   *ix*

CHAPTER ONE. RUMFORD BEGINNINGS   1

    An Immigrant's Son   1

    An Immigrant's Tale   7

    The Lure of Rumford   9

    A Rumford Boyhood   15

    High School Years   22

CHAPTER TWO. COLLEGE, LAW SCHOOL, WAR   35

    Bates Freshman   35

    Upperclass Years   43

    Law School   53

    Practicing Law   58

    The Navy   64

CHAPTER THREE. RISING STAR   74

    Elective Office   74

    Jane Gray   80

    First Defeat   84

    Marriage   87

    Reelection, Another War, and the Office

        of Price Stabilization   89

    A Broken Back   105

CHAPTER FOUR. IMPROBABLE VICTORY   **114**

    A Reluctant Candidate   114

    Battle Joined   129

    Building an Organization   136

    Twenty Thousand Miles on a Shoestring   143

    Debate Me, Governor Cross   168

    We Know How the Story Ends   176

CHAPTER FIVE. GOVERNOR MUSKIE   **186**

    Welcome to the Blaine House   186

    Between Sessions   197

    A Visit from the President   200

    Fall 1955   206

    Another Campaign   211

    Second-Term Governor   224

    Politics Never Stops   233

    Leaving Augusta   239

    Afterword   *246*

    Endnotes   *252*

    Bibliography   *271*

    Index   *273*

Preface

Edmund Sixtus Muskie—arguably Maine's greatest politician and statesman—would have turned 100 on March 28, 2014. A native of Rumford, as am I, he cast a long shadow in my hometown. When I graduated from Rumford High School in 1972, the ceremony took place in the school's Muskie Auditorium. Muskie had been elected to his third term in the U.S. Senate two years earlier, once again winning more than sixty percent of the popular vote in a state that had been almost exclusively Republican before 1954, when Ed and a small band of fellow Democrats set out to make two-party politics a reality in Maine.

The Clean Air Act of 1970, Muskie's signature achievement, had been signed into law near the end of his second Senate term. He had started building that legislation in 1963, putting it together line by line, debate by debate, minor bill by minor bill, brick by brick. Sustained by a clear vision of where the country needed to get, he cajoled, reasoned, and persuaded to get there, reaching across the aisle in a way all too rare today. It was said that he would compromise on anything except principle. The Clean Water Act—passed in the year of my graduation, 1972—probably had its roots in Muskie's Rumford boyhood along the polluted Androscoggin River. Before Senator Muskie there was no national environmental policy. By the time of his retirement from the U.S. Senate in 1980, an America without environmental protections was unthinkable, and Muskie was known as "Mr. Clean." As a Maine Guide, I am forever grateful of Muskie's efforts to clean up our nation's air and water.

He had been Hubert Humphrey's running mate in the 1968 presidential race, losing to Richard Nixon and Spiro Agnew. In early 1972, just months before my graduation, he was the frontrunner to become the Democratic presidential nominee before being overtaken by George McGovern. And he would become President Jimmy Carter's secretary of state following the resignation of Cyrus Vance in 1980, serving until Carter was followed in office by Ronald Reagan in 1981.

But it was the young Ed Muskie, the man forged in Maine, who most fascinated me. During the half of his life that he lived in Maine, he read and listened and thought and studied and formed steadfast opinions about how things ought to be in this state. He became a strong believer in the need to protect Maine's environment and a fierce proponent of a legitimate two-party system.

Ed Muskie was the son of Stephen Marciszewski, a Polish immigrant tailor whose dream for his son was that he one day run a tailor shop. Ed spoke only Polish until age four. He was a Catholic and a Democrat in a state dominated by Protestant Republicans. I wrote this biography to learn how the arc of his life took him from those inauspicious beginnings to the world stage. I learned that Ed Muskie was in large part his own creation. He seems to have known from boyhood that his destiny lay beyond Rumford and that education would provide the path to get there. In high school he willed himself out of painful shyness to become a champion debater.

He often benefited from being in the right place at the right time. High school teachers and administrators conspired to find him the financial support he needed to make college possible, and then a Bates College dean convinced him to attend law school. Later, during what was supposed to have been a building year for Maine's Democratic Party, he ran for governor because no one else would—and won. And after promising not to take advantage of the new four-year term he rammed through the legislature for Maine's future governors—in place of two-year terms that required a governor to begin running for reelection the year after taking office—he ran for the U.S. Senate and won again.

In common with others who achieve great things, he had the genius to recognize his opportunities and the courage to take full advantage of each one.

Facing many of the same challenges that the state still struggles with today—and against the determined opposition of a Republican-dominated legislature—Governor Muskie moved the goalposts while winning respect and admiration from both sides of the aisle. But Ed Muskie's most lasting legacy in Maine may be that, in 1954, he and a dedicated group of supporters rescued Maine from the stagnation of single-party politics.

Acknowledgments and Photo Credits

I want to thank everyone at the Edmund S. Muskie Archives and Special Collections Library at Bates College, especially archives supervisor Elaine Ardia, who often seemed to be working as hard as I was on this book.

All photos are reproduced courtesy of the Edmund S. Muskie Archives and Special Collections Library. Additional credits:

Pages 140 and 179: Photos of Frank Coffin and Don Nicoll and the front page of the *Lewiston Evening Journal,* courtesy the *Lewiston Sun Journal.*

Page 167: Photo of Ed Muskie as a candidate in Auburn by Philbrick, courtesy the *Lewiston Sun Journal.*

Page 173: The advertisement is from the *Portland Sunday Telegram.*

Page 203: Photo by Dow Air Force Base, United States Air Force.

Page 214: Photo by Alix B. Williamson.

Chapter One

Rumford Beginnings

An Immigrant's Son

Edmund Sixtus Muskie, second child of Stephen and Josephine Muskie, was delivered by Dr. William T. Rowe in the front bedroom of a first-floor apartment at 231 Knox Street in Rumford, Maine, just before 5 A.M. on Sunday, March 28, 1914. Had he a choice, Ed Muskie probably wouldn't have picked another time or place to be born. Growing up on the outskirts of town, young Ed would have the opportunity to skate, ski, fish, and play ball with his friends—when he wasn't too busy reading, that is. For any kid interested in outdoor recreation—and what kid wasn't?—Rumford was a great town.

The International Paper and Oxford Paper Company mills, the area's largest employers, were a mixed blessing. They provided the jobs that supported the workers and their families as well as all the businesses in the surrounding area—including Stephen Muskie's tailor shop—but they also poured foul-smelling pollution into the air and the Androscoggin River that flowed through town. The fouled Androscoggin planted the seed for what would become one of Ed Muskie's greatest quests, his fight to curb the pollution produced by American industry.

Ed's childhood friend Vito Puiia, who would become Rumford's cobbler, summed up his townspeople's feelings when he said about the pollution the mills produced, "From the Oxford? Didn't bother me a bit; it was my bread and butter. When them smokestacks stop, there's no money coming in." He did concede, however, that on "certain days when it was muggy and the ceiling was low, people used to stay inside and shut their windows."[1]

Anyone who has ever doubted the power of a name to affect the arc of a life should consider Ed Muskie's full name. Muskie disliked the name Edmund almost as much as he disliked Eddie, preferring to be called Ed. During his campaign for reelection to the U.S. Senate in 1970, he was displeased when the voice-over for one of his ads said, "Edmund Muskie is a great man." Muskie wanted the line changed to, "Ed Muskie is a good senator." Then he added, "And let's say Ed, not Edmund; Edmund is an odd name, it's hard to say. I like plain Ed."[2]

Edmund, he explained, had come from the respect his parents had for Edmund Rich, the Archbishop of Canterbury from 1175 to 1240, and for St. Edmund the Martyr, King of East Anglia from 840 to 870. (Perhaps the respect Stephen had for the pair had come from the few years he'd spent in England on his way to America.)

Though he thought Edmund an odd name, Ed had a bigger problem with his middle name, Sixtus. Shortly after his birth, his parents still hadn't settled on a middle name for the boy, so his father looked through the Book of Saints until he came to Sixtus. "I don't like that name very much," Josephine said.

"Sixtus was a pope, a good man," said Stephen. "We will name him that."[3] (Five popes have chosen the name: Sixtus I, who served from 115 to 125 AD; Sixtus II, 257–258; Sixtus III, 432–440; Sixtus IV, 1471–1484; and Sixtus V, 1585–1590. Named for Pope Sixtus IV, the Sistine Chapel was designed by Baccio Pontelli and constructed between 1473 and 1481 under the supervision of Giovannino de Dolci. In 1587, Sixtus V established the position of Devil's Advocate—also known as Promoter of the Faith—which was used during the canonization process. This position would be abolished by Pope John Paul II in 1983.)

Once he was old enough to have an opinion, Ed agreed with

his mother. "I found Sixtus a very embarrassing middle name when I was a youngster."[4] But it was Catholic tradition to give a child the name of at least one saint. "I was awarded two for good measure," said Muskie. "Both Edmund and Sixtus were—until I got them—the names of saints." Years later, none of Ed's own daughters was given a middle name.[5]

If the Rumford Muskies weren't the only Muskies in the United States, they were close to it. "I made [the name] up myself," Stephen Muskie said later. The elder Muskie changed his name from Marciszewski (pronounced Mar-chih-SHEF-ski) to Muskie after arriving in Rumford, probably at the urging of a town clerk. (He also considered changing his surname to March or Mack, thinking either one would sound like the first syllable of his family name.)

As it turned out, Stephen Muskie was a little late in filing the paperwork to make his new surname legal—about three decades late. Ed learned this upon finishing law school in 1939, also learning then that three of his siblings had been christened Marciszewski (though Ed had always been a Muskie). "I never made it official," Stephen told him, "in case you wanted to change your name to something else."

"Look," said Ed, "my whole life is recorded as Muskie, I have no reason to change it."[6] Soon he submitted the paperwork to ensure that all the Muskies were actually Muskies. His siblings seemed content with this, but not everyone agreed. "My mother [Mrs. Kowalzyk] would be so upset, got so upset," said Ed's friend Frances McInnis. "She said, 'How could a good Polack change a beautiful name like Marciszewski to Muskie?' And [Stephen] kept trying to tell her, he said, 'Well, you know, the plate-glass window [of Stephen's shop] can only take just so much, so many letters. . . .'"[7]

Most biographical sketches of Ed Muskie simply state that his father's name was changed in 1903 by an immigration clerk at Ellis Island, but that isn't the case. Stephen became a naturalized citizen of the United States on August 5, 1912, in Portland, under the name Stefan Marciszewski, after being married under that name the prior year. The first use of the Muskie name seems to have been when Ed was born in 1914. There seems also to have been no rhyme or reason in when Stephen used which name; birth records show that Irene, who was born in 1912, was christened Marciszewski, as were her siblings Eugene (1918) and Elizabeth (1923). Ed (1914), Lucy (1916), and Frances (1921) were all christened as Muskies.

"And if you believe in numerology," Ed once recalled, "each of my names has six letters, Edmund Sixtus Muskie. Each of them has a 'U,' which is rather odd."[8] In his native Poland, had his father not fled to England and later changed his last name, Muskie would have been Edziu Sixtus Marciszewski.

Stephen's English was certainly adequate—much better, it seems, than Josephine's—but the two appear to have spoken Polish at home, as Josephine's own parents in Buffalo had done. (To this day there are French-Canadian families in Rumford who speak only French at home.) As a result, Ed spoke only Polish until he was four, though his Polish faded when he started school and had to communicate in English with teachers and friends, many of whom were of French-Canadian, Italian, or Lithuanian extraction. Decades later, when Ed was in law school, other relatives would serve as interpreters when he spent holidays with his maternal grandparents.

Ed seemed aware from an early age that he faced an uphill battle if he was going to make something of himself. A tenement in a papermaking town nestled in the foothills of Maine's western mountains wasn't an ideal starting point for great success in life. "The fact is," he would say during his 1972 presidential campaign, "on the day I was born 58 years ago, a person like me didn't have a chance of becoming president—the son of a Polish immigrant, a Roman Catholic, from a tiny little state in the northeastern part of the country."[9] Ed knew early on that he had his work cut out for him if he was going to scale his life to his ambitions.

He had come into the world at a significant time in history. The Panama Canal had just been completed, and with it came the promise of moving people and goods around the world more quickly than ever before. But a war that would plunge the European continent into years of death and devastation was looming on the horizon. President Woodrow Wilson would be reelected in 1916 primarily because he had kept the United States out of the conflict, but America would enter the fray in April 1917 in response to increased attacks on passenger and freight vessels by German submarines. The war would rage until November of the following year.

Probably one of the first signs that Ed was not an average child came during a long train trip when he was three. While his parents had their hands full with five-year-old Irene and one-year-old Lucy (the sibling to whom he would remain closest), Ed put his arms up and asked in Polish for his father to hold him up so he could look out the window. "My arms [got] so tired," his father told the Boston *Post* years later, "they'd pain for hours. But Ed was happy, just watching the scenery as the train moved." This habit of retreating into his thoughts would become lifelong—on a bus to or from a high school basketball game or debate, or eventually staring out the window of a car or plane as he traveled on political business.

Even Ed's mother said, "He was an odd one," because, as a small child, he'd follow her around the house until she ended up in the kitchen, where he'd sit on the window seat and stare outside in silence. "She would ask what he was watching, what he was seeing, and he would smile at her and shake his head; he could not say."[10]

In his early years the behavior—which seemed introspective to some and odd to others—may have been nothing more than a manifestation of the painful shyness that would stay with him well into his high school years, when he would finally force himself to overcome it. During Ed's fifth-birthday party, which was held at the family's second apartment on Spruce Street, "I became awed by the sight of so many kids," he told the *Post*. "In fact, I became frightened. I took my ice cream and cake and went into my own room and ate it." Ed's behavior that day may seem a little less strange if some of the "friends" at the party were kids who later picked on him every day at school, calling him a "dumb Polack" and other names that drove his older sister home in tears most days. Their father told Irene not to let the name calling get to her, and to be proud that she was Polish. It didn't help much.

Ed didn't need such encouragement from his father; if the insults got to him, he didn't let it show. He battled his shyness and the bullying by sitting stoically on the steps of the Pettingill School, staring into the distance and entertaining himself with his thoughts while the other kids ran and played in the schoolyard. "I started school there and I remember very well because I was very shy. I was unusually shy and I don't think I went there more than two years."[11]

Soon Ed would be attending a different school after the family moved to the Virginia section of Rumford, just up Falls Hill. When Ed's father showed up at the school to get Ed's transfer papers, his teacher, Nellie Weeks, told Stephen that she was sad to see the boy go. When Stephen, who knew how much trouble they had getting Ed to play with other kids, asked her why, she told him that his son was one of the "best boys" in the entire school.

Maybe it was the change of schools that did it, or, more likely, early biographers just got it wrong. Whatever the case, in his 1972 autobiography, *Journeys,* Ed took issue with the characterization of his boyhood as lonely. "A few writers have suggested that as a boy I was mocked and friendless. I don't know what their sources were, but I had as healthy and happy a childhood and family life as a boy could wish."[12] He noted that his "early interests were in Boy Scouts, and 4-H Garden Club work."

After living briefly in yet another apartment on Prospect Avenue ("I guess it must have been a couple of years," remembered Ed), the family ended up at nearby 8 Hemmingway Street in 1925. Stephen Muskie, who charged about $20 for a custom-made three-piece suit, purchased a house there despite the fact that he'd planned to build one on either Knox or Franklin Street, which were closer to his tailor shop in the town's downtown "shopper's island." Josephine and Alexander Quinn, his sister and her husband, had purchased the six-year-old house in 1918 from its original owners, Willis and Una Hemmingway, by paying $25 a month on the balance of $1,200. The Quinns had recently sold their laundry business to Mrs. McLean and were leaving Rumford to run another one in the Boston area, and Stephen took the opportunity to purchase a house at what was probably an attractive price.

Stephen's family already needed more room, however, so before moving in, he added a dormer and a garage, for which he paid $2,819.46. Later Ed would recall that his father had purchased the home's furniture, dishes, blankets, sheets, and towels for around $300. "And he paid cash."

Eventually Stephen would be able to buy the house next door at 10 Hemingway Street (for which he paid cash) so he could evict the McPhees, whom he considered "bad neighbors," remodel the place, and rent it to Mrs. Anastasio, who was widowed and had eight children. Two decades later he would rent that house to Irene and Arthur Chiasson, his daughter and son-in-law, for $20 a month.

An Immigrant's Tale

The purchase of that first house on Hemmingway Street must have represented the fulfillment of the American dream for Stephen Muskie, considering where he'd started from four decades earlier. Stefan Marciszewski was born on September 1, 1884, near Bialystok, in eastern Poland, in the tiny village of Jasionowska (which means "ash-tree grove"), where his father managed an estate for a Russian nobleman. Poland then was in the midst of a long occupation by Russian troops.

Shortly after being elected to the United States Senate in 1959, and three years after his father's death, Ed would finally get to visit the village from which his father had fled nearly six decades earlier. The estate, where Ed's grandfather had once supervised workers as they cut hay, picked apples, and went about their other chores, and where he'd taught his son Stefan to fish, had been converted into a state-run farm. The once-opulent home of the nobleman was "large, white, somewhat shabby, but clinging to the shreds of an ancient dignity," Ed recalled later. It was surrounded by rotting outbuildings.

There, in what the country's deputy foreign minister described as "the saddest part of Poland," Ed was struck by the bareness of people's lives, and he realized how much he owed to the decision of his grandparents, Stefan and Tekla, to send their son from home as a teenager to seek a better life far away—and to his father's courage to go. "But for my father's dream of freedom and opportunity," he said, "this would be my life—the life of my children."[13]

In his father's hometown, Ed was able to locate just one Marciszewski. An elderly woman of uncertain relation, she was living in a meager dwelling that was "dimly lit and sparsely furnished. She opened the trunk and reached in and drew out some pictures my father had sent years and years before," remembered Ed. "It was a moving experience to see him there, in this way." As his visit neared its end, Ed went to the local cemetery that his father used to talk about. "When we looked to see if we could find any family tombstones, we found just one with the name on it. It was on its side."[14]

Apprenticed to a tailor in Bialystok in 1896, when he was twelve, Stephen ate and slept at his workbench. In 1900, by the time he'd reached age sixteen, he was a master tailor. It was around this time that his father sent him to London to avoid being conscripted into the occupying Russian army. (During World War I, Poles in various parts of the country were conscripted into both opposing armies—Russia versus the Central Powers—and made to fight each other.)

During Ed Muskie's failed presidential run in 1972, a wealthy McGovern supporter named Stewart Mott would demonstrate just how long memories can be in politics, issuing "a 23-page pamphlet attacking virtually every aspect of Muskie's record—from his past support of the [Vietnam] war to his compromises on environmental legislation. Mott devoted a page to 'Muskie's Ancestors: Draft Dodgers.' In it he noted that the 1903 flight of Muskie's father from Russian-occupied Poland to the United States [*sic*] occurred when he was 17, the conscription age."[15]

Stephen spent three years working for a Jewish tailor in London, who not only let the young man live in his home but also taught him how to make bagels, which Stephen would later whip up from time to time for his family in Rumford. Or perhaps Stephen wasn't in London the entire three years. An intriguing entry in the 1901 census of England and Wales lists a Stefan Marciszewski who was born in "Russian Poland (Russian subject)" in 1882, living in Leeds, England.[16] (Stephen's naturalization form lists his nationality as Russian.)

Most accounts of Stephen's early life have him leaving England for America in 1903, but Ed recalled later that his father left England on the day of Edward VII's coronation, which was August 9, 1902. Like millions of other immigrants looking for a better life, he entered the United States through Ellis Island, but he soon ended up in the Scranton, Pennsylvania suburb of Dickson City, a coal-mining town, where he stayed until about 1907. He was eventually followed to the United States by his sister. (He also had at least one brother, possibly two, who probably stayed behind in Poland.)

Stephen's migration northward began with a move of about 200 miles northwest to Buffalo, New York, where he felt at home among the city's large Polish population. There he met Josephine, the third of eleven children born to Antoinette Czarnecka and her husband, Theodore, who worked for the railroad. Stephen visited Josephine at the family's home on Goodyear Avenue, and the two agreed to try dating to see if it would work out. It did, and on February 27, 1911, just before her twentieth birthday, Josephine married twenty-seven-year-old Stephen Marciszewski at St. John Cantius Church in Buffalo.

"Right after the wedding, the next day, we came to Rumford, Maine," Josephine Muskie told the Polish Service of the Voice of America Radio when her oldest son was running for vice president in 1968. "That was supposed to be our honeymoon. My husband promised that he would bring me back to Buffalo, but here it is fifty-seven years have gone by, and I'm still in Rumford, and my husband is gone, too."

The Lure of Rumford

What was it that made Stephen Muskie want to move to Rumford with his new bride? Could it have been the town's great waterfall, which reminded him of Niagara Falls? The main attraction was

probably that his sister and brother-in-law were operating a successful steam laundry business there and told him about the town's
booming growth, which included recently opened paper mills along
the Androscoggin River (whose name is from the Algonquin "Ama-
raskahgin," meaning "turbid, foaming, crooked snake"), and a modern high school.

Historian George Varney called Pennacook Falls "the grand-
est cataract in New England," and these magnificent falls, which
run alongside Falls Hill, made Rumford what it became. The area
was first settled in 1782 by Jonathan Keyes and his son Francis,
who moved there from Shrewsbury, Massachusetts, and the town
was incorporated eight years later. Like the Keyeses, the settlers
who came after them for much of the next century made a living off
the land in one way or another, and it wasn't until 1882 that Hugh
J. Chisholm (1847–1912) first laid eyes on the falls and saw their
potential as a source of cheap, plentiful power.

According to John Leane's *History of Rumford, Maine, 1774
–1974:*

> Normally about 33,000 cubic feet per second gushes
> down the river at Rumford during the spring run-off.
> In one disastrous flood, the rate was clocked at 77,400
> cubic feet per second.
>
> In the early summer the river subsides and set-
> tles back to a slower pace until the rainfall of late fall
> months brings it back to a more normal level.
>
> Along the course of the Androscoggin there are
> many waterfalls and rapids. The most powerful and
> most spectacular falls are at Rumford, where the river
> surges over three rock barriers (97 feet, 59 feet, and 30
> feet), dropping 177 feet in one mile. This is the biggest
> fall of any river east of Niagara.

Hugh Chisholm was born in a small town in Ontario, Canada.
His father died when he was thirteen, and the youngster went to

Work being done on Congress Street, which would become Rumford's main street, more than two decades before Stephen and Josephine Muskie arrived in town.

work selling newspapers to passengers on the Grand Trunk Railroad alongside another ambitious lad named Thomas Edison. While Edison would continue with the experimenting he did in the train's baggage car, Chisholm decided to make his mark in business and industry, and before long he and his brother owned a newspaper distribution company. By the time of his first visit to Rumford, he was already a giant of American industry with interests in banking, railroads, electric power, and paper mills. He built three mills in Rumford—International Paper, the Continental Paper Bag Company, and the Oxford Paper Company—between 1892 and 1896.

When it came to environmental issues in the early 1900s, Hugh Chisholm was ahead of the times in one respect and a product of them in another. Realizing that the need for pulpwood for the paper mills of Maine and New Hampshire alone had the potential to decimate the forests of western Maine, he implemented what was probably the country's first forestry management plan to ensure a sufficient supply of wood for the papermakers. But as for the discharge from the mills' papermaking process, the accepted way of dealing with it was to pump it directly into the river. At the time there were no laws prohibiting the practice; the Clean Water Act, championed by Ed Muskie, was still seven decades in the future.

One area in which Hugh Chisholm excelled was taking care of his workers. Having seen firsthand the condition of the tenements in which factory workers in places such as Lowell and Lawrence, Massachusetts, lived, he spared no expense to ensure that his employees would enjoy a high standard of living. The community would be called Strathglass Park, after Strathglass Carries of Scotland, where Chisholm's father was born. (If you're ever in Rumford and you happen to overhear someone say, "I live in the park," it means that they live in Strathglass Park, and not that they're occupying the village green.)

"We will build of brick, and stone, and slate," Chisholm proclaimed, "and we will provide not merely for a house, but for comfort, elegance, and social gratification." And he kept his word. To design Strathglass Park, which would eventually consist of 186 units spread among 51 duplexes, four single-family homes, and nine brick apartment buildings, Chisholm commissioned renowned architect Cass Gilbert. For nine dollars a month—plus one dollar to Rumford Falls Power Company, which was also owned by Chisholm—his employees and their families could enjoy a standard of living that many of them could previously only have dreamed of. For decades, workers at the mill could feel like one of the town's successful bankers as they walked to work. (The Oxford Paper Company's ownership of Strathglass Park would last until 1948, when the company, though still highly successful, evidently decided to focus on its core business and sold the homes and duplexes to individuals for between $3,400 and $3,900.)

In just four short years (1906–10), Rumford's property valuation jumped from $3 million to nearly $4 million, and between 1900 and 1910, its population nearly doubled to around 7,000, as people who were willing to work hard for a living were drawn to the town by the mills' generous wage of ten cents an hour. The town would keep growing, exceeding 10,000 citizens by the start of the Great Depression. With executives, salesmen, and accountants from the mills and associated businesses needing nice suits, Rumford looked to Stephen like a place where he could realize his dream of raising a family in a house of his own.

Ed's childhood friend Frank McInnis remembers that Stephen was brought to Rumford by a tailor named Adam Jugelevich. Perhaps Stephen's sister and her husband had arranged for the two to work together. Soon, though, Stephen was working with another tailor, James Shea, who operated his Fine Custom Tailoring shop at 29 Congress Street and may have had an association with a local department store, C. H. McKenzie. The two men partnered until at least 1922 but then evidently had a falling out, and Stephen opened his own shop at 69 Congress Street, downtown Rumford's main thoroughfare.

Stephen was politically opinionated, and his shop became one of the town's centers for discussing the issues of the day. Coincidentally, he had arrived in Maine, a GOP stronghold, during the only period between the 1850s and 1964 when both houses of its legislature were controlled by the Democrats. This once-in-a-blue-moon legislature, which had been elected only because of a rift between conservative and progressive Republicans, ratified the Sixteenth Amendment, helping to establish the federal income tax. Years later, Stephen's son would become just the second Democratic governor elected in Maine since the First World War,

Customers could expect two things from Stephen Muskie: fine clothing at reasonable prices and strong opinions on a wide range of subjects. The shop opened promptly at 8:00 A.M. and closed sometime between five and six o'clock in the afternoon, depending on how busy it was—or how heated the discussion had become. Ed remembered his father as a "closet Democrat" who voted in the June primaries but never in the general elections. The managers at the Oxford Paper Company were all Republicans, and they "all bought their suits from my father," said Ed, "because he was the only custom tailor in town. And by God, they had to sit and listen to his political

Rumford cobbler Nicola Bevalaqua stands in front of his shop, which was located directly beneath Stephen Muskie's tailor shop on Congress Street. In 1933 a fire that started in the shoe shop would burn the building to the ground.

views when they came to have their try-ons and all the rest of it. They respected him that much, too."[17]

There's at least one story about a mill executive who spent several hundred dollars a year at the shop until he finally got tired of listening to his tailor's views on the issues of the day, then took his business elsewhere and never spoke to Stephen again. He was the first person to offer condolences to the family when Stephen died, however. "A man might spend $500 or $1,000 a year with him," remembered Ed, "but if my father disagreed about politics, war, peace, prices, taxes, or whatever, they had it out. His opinions were worth more to him than his income."[18]

Before wedding Stephen, Josephine had "made it clear to him that she couldn't cook," said Ed, "and she couldn't sew. . . . [M]y father made it clear to her that she would learn. . . . [S]he became superb in both departments."[19] The first sewing machine Stephen bought for her was an inexpensive model that wouldn't work properly. He returned it and bought her a much nicer one, which she used for the rest of her life.

Josephine became good at cooking and sewing because she had to, and quickly. Almost as soon as Stephen and his young bride arrived in their first apartment on Knox Street, he informed her that he had taken in two boarders to help meet expenses. Josephine suddenly found herself responsible for feeding three other people. The sewing she learned from her husband. The cooking she figured out on her own.

A Rumford Boyhood

Stephen and Josephine had been living in Rumford fourteen years and had six children when they moved into the house on Hemmingway Street in 1925. The house brimmed with life. Ed shared a bedroom with his brother, Eugene, while the four girls shared another bedroom. "[A]s I think back," said Ed, "these younger sisters and brothers just appeared, and I can't remember a day when they didn't exist. . . ." There was one unfortunate exception. "The only one I remember was one child that did not survive. I didn't even know whether it was a girl or a boy. And it was the last child born, I'm certain of that."[20]

Though Ed and Eugene (born in 1918) were brothers, "Eugene was altogether different than Ed," says childhood friend Phil Anastasio. "Altogether different, I mean like night and day. [Eugene] was a fellow that didn't, he didn't care what happened, you know."[21] "Gene was more of a, well he was always raising the devil a lot," said Ken Bosworth, another childhood friend of the Muskies. "He wasn't what you'd call a studious homebody."[22] Years later, when Stephen told Eugene he should try to be more like his brother, Eugene snapped, "Be like Ed! Be like Ed! I don't want to be like Ed, I want to drink beer."[23]

Gene, who grew to be as tall as his big brother and much more ruggedly built, "worked in the [paper] mill, working the rewinders," remembers Frank Anastasio. "In the rewinders, yeah, they liked him. But he was strong, boy, yeah, yeah, yeah. Funny as the devil, laughing all the time."[24] After training at Fort Devens, Massachusetts, Gene would go to Arlington, California (which is now part of Riverside, west of Los Angeles), during World War II, and the last time anyone around town can remember him coming back to Rumford was in 1968, when Ed was running for vice president.

Perhaps it was because Eugene seemed more like a normal kid that even their mother once admitted favoring him over his better-known brother. "Frank responses and appraisals are a family trait. Sample: Asked about her Senator son, Mother Muskie replied, 'I liked Eugene (Edmund's younger brother) better.'"[25] (In his autobiography, Ed explained that much of what his mother said needed to be taken with a grain of salt, and what she really meant by the remark was that Eugene was the jollier and more outgoing of the two boys, and more fun to be around.) As he got older, Ed outgrew his need to follow his mother around and grew closer to his father, with whom he'd have long conversations, often about politics. When the two weren't occasionally screaming at each other over political topics in the spotless living room, "They *whispered* to each other," Josephine said.

Josephine took her responsibilities as housewife and mother seriously, and the rest of the family's three-bedroom, three-story

A Muskie family picture, probably taken during the mid 1930s, shows Elizabeth, Francis, Lucy, and Gene in front of Irene, Ed, and their parents, Stephen and Josephine.

home (including attic) was just as tidy as the living room, which was on the left as you entered the house. Past the living room were the dining room and then the kitchen, where Josephine spent so much time cooking. She had housework down to a science. In addition to her daily chores, she did the laundry on Monday, ironed on Tuesday, and so on. "In fact," recalled Kenneth Bosworth, "you'd go in that house, I think you could eat off the floors anywhere."[26] In the back yard she tended flower and vegetable gardens.

Strict rules also helped keep the home tidy. "There was none of this kicking around, you sat down," said Frank Anastasio, "the furniture was nice. . . .[A]nd I think they had a piano. Irene played the piano, which I thought was a great thing. I wish I could have had a piano, and things like that."[27]

Actually, it was Lucy who played the piano—but not for long, it seems. "Ed used to get mad at me when I was playing," she said. "I was making too much noise. Then they gave the piano away."[28] But music remained in the Muskie home, occasionally filling it from one of the first Victrolas in town. "I can see it coming in the door now," said Ed, "that big console with the picture of the dog listening to 'His Master's Voice.'"[29] The family "set it up in the living room," said Ed. "[Y]ou had to hand-crank it, and quality, well, it sounded like heavenly music to us." The record player had one drawback: "You had to crank the damn thing after every record."[30]

Later, the family got a radio "with wet batteries to power it." Ed recalled listening to the Rose Bowl football game on the machine, which had three dials that had to be synchronized in order to receive a station. Each time the family discovered a new station, they wrote down the setting of each dial so they could find it again.

They ate in the dining room until they acquired a kitchen set, a hand-me-down from newlywed Irene after she'd won a new one in a contest. After that the Muskies ate their meals in the kitchen, except on Sundays and holidays, occasions when the Muskie men did the dishes. (According to Irene, the table and chairs she'd given to her parents turned out to be much sturdier than the ones she had won.)

In the rush of weekday mornings, the family had cereal for breakfast, but on the weekends it was bacon and eggs, Grape Nuts, or popovers. Other breakfast treats included fresh doughnuts and, during the colder months, homemade oatmeal. And, of course, bagels.

As Christmas approached, Stephen would wait for the right Sunday afternoon to grab his ax and set off up the hill across the street in search of the perfect tree. By Christmas Eve the splendid tree would be set up in the living room, nearly ablaze with what Ed estimated must have been a hundred candles. The table groaned beneath the weight of a feast that included a turkey and pies, puddings, and cakes. Christmas gifts included new games, which the parents played with the children, and new sets of clothes made by Josephine for her girls' dolls. "And books! They always bought us books," said Ed, "because we all loved to read."

Ed showed up at the town library on his birthday when he reached the age (ten or eleven) at which he could get his own library card. "I was just determined to read everything I could get my hands on," he said. The librarian joked that he must have read every book they had and that she had to tell the youngster to visit the library more often when the number of books he was borrowing at one time reached the limit of eight.

He also received a lot of education by listening to his father at the tailor shop, where Ed spent many hours "because he had me learning his trade in Rumford to be a tailor." Father and son didn't see eye-to-eye on everything, and other lessons came in the form of discipline, as Ed and his siblings could occasionally expect to receive swift punishment for misbehavior. Ed remembered one occasion, when he was about eight, on which his father became so upset with him that "he took off his belt and strapped me with it, and it was only after he'd hit me several times that he realized he was hitting me with the buckled end."[31]

When he realized what he'd been doing, Stephen immediately stopped and turned pale. "And he never spanked anybody again after that." That event left a lasting impression not only on Ed, but also on his father; nearly three decades later, just after his son's first inauguration as governor, Stephen Muskie would look at his daughter Irene and say, "See how smart Ed is? I should have licked the rest of you more."[32]

During the summer of 1927, the Muskies piled all their kids into Stephen's Cadillac and headed to Buffalo to attend the wedding of one of Josephine's brothers. Along the way, the family stopped in Boston to visit Stephen's sister, and after the wedding they drove to Dickson City, Pennsylvania, where Ed flew kites with his cousin, John Wilczewski, and waited in the car for what seemed like hours while his father caught up with an old coworker.

The stop in Boston made such a strong impression on Ed that he'd still remember it as he was preparing to run for president forty-five years later. "My first view of Black ghetto life in America," he'd recall, "came when, as a child, I visited my aunt and uncle in South Boston, on West Brookline Street, close to Roxbury, where much of the Black population lived. I was too young to get a clear picture of the relationships between the groups there, but I had some sense of the tensions that existed."[33]

Stephen had previously owned a Chevrolet—one of the first new cars in Rumford—and then a Durant, both of which had side curtains for windows and had to be hand-cranked to get them started. Though the thrifty tailor bought it used, the seven-passenger Caddy was in excellent shape—just the right vehicle in which to take the entire family on a long road trip. But the thrill of traveling in style wouldn't continue long. When the effects of the Great Depression reached Rumford, Stephen did not want to be seen driving a luxury car, even a used one, by people who had fallen on hard times, so he put the Cadillac up on blocks in his garage and never drove it again. And he continued to walk to work, up and down Falls Hill, a mile each way, as he'd always done.

Rumford was a great place to be a kid during the 1920s, and when the wind was blowing the smoke and smell of the mills away from town, and the air was clear, it was even better. Besides the steam laundry, the Virginia section of town featured a large sawmill just upriver from the falls, to which "long logs would come floating down the river," remembers Ken Bosworth. "And that was a big mill,"[34] which made it a great place for Ed and his pals to play, pushing the log carts up and down the tracks until they were chased off by the watchman.

"[He] spent many hours fishing and sitting beside the Androscoggin," says historian David Sargent. "It already was becoming polluted, and swimming was off-limits, except for surreptitious dips by youngsters when adults were not looking."[35] The river was becoming polluted even before it reached the falls and the two paper mills because there were other mills far upriver in Berlin and Gorham, New Hampshire.

In 1930, Cornell University (where Ed would attend law school) conducted the first major study of the Androscoggin River and found it to be "heavily polluted," but concluded that the river's situation "was not serious." Still, people had realized for some time by then that there was something wrong with the Androscoggin; the city of

Lewiston had switched to nearby Lake Auburn as the source of its drinking water in 1901, after people had complained about the taste of the water coming from the river.

"[W]e played baseball, football, skied in the pasture on barrel staves [with his friends Elmer McQuade and Johnny Bartash], went fishing, roamed over those hills in back of the house, played cowboys and Indians," said Ed. "We skated on the river in the winter and built bonfires on the shore. How can you grow up in a town like Rumford and not have fun? You step out your back door and go tree-climbing, building tree houses, picking strawberries in the summertime, oh, so many things we did—we were busy all the time. "[36]

Before he gravitated toward basketball in high school, Ed loved to ski. But it wasn't downhill skiing or even cross-country gliding that attracted the youngster; Rumford had one of the first ski areas in the East to have a good ski jump. And Ed loved to jump. He loved it so much that he would go out before breakfast, and then he'd go again in the evening if there was enough moonlight. But there were a few activities Ed wouldn't engage in with his friends. He wouldn't gamble with them when they played card or dice games, and he wouldn't go with them when they went off to steal apples. He already knew that he had an image to maintain—that of a good student and a good boy.

Not all of Ed's childhood adventures were with his friends from the neighborhood. Every Wednesday when the weather was nice, area merchants would take the afternoon off and go to nearby Roxbury Pond or Worthley Pond in Peru to swim or take part in other activities. And every summer the family would rent a camp at Roxbury Pond for two weeks. Stephen liked to swim, but he liked to fish more, and often he and his friend Alfred Gagnon would take their sons Ed and Robert to one of the area's many ponds and streams to spend the afternoon wetting their lines.

One of the group's favorite outings, in which they included another father and son, was an annual camping trip to Four Ponds, just south of Rangeley. To get there, they rode in the caboose of the Rumford Falls & Rangeley Lakes Railroad train that went to

Mooselookmeguntic Lake, but got off the train in Township D at a stop called The Summit, just a couple miles beyond Ten Degree. (A bridge and much of the railbed would be washed away during the Flood of 1936 and never rebuilt.) Ed remembered the hike in to Long Pond from The Summit as being about four miles, with a spring about halfway. Today the Appalachian Trail skirts the northern edges of Four Ponds.

The party carried in enough food and clothing to sustain them for a week of fishing on the interconnected ponds. Long Pond, which is as big as the other three combined, and tiny Moxie Pond offered the best fishing, said Ed, while Round and Sabbath Day ponds seemed to be better sources of mosquitoes than trout. "If we wanted trout for breakfast," he said, "we just got up fifteen minutes early and went down to the lake and caught them."[37] The six fishermen took this trip for three successive summers just before Ed started high school.

High School Years

Ed began his freshman year at Stephens High School in 1928. "Some of the boys, they took college [preparatory] courses," said Vito Puiia. "Ed was one of them. Well, he was so much smarter than most of us anyway, he knew he could swing it somehow on scholarships and all of that."[38]

The once-modern high school named after prominent Rumford citizen John E. Stephens had been built in 1911 on eight acres of land donated by the Rumford Power Company and had been expanded in 1915 (a west wing) and again in 1917 (an east wing). Some 126 pupils had attended Stephens in 1911, but by the late 1920s it had begun to show the wear and tear of nearly two decades of use and had yet again become too small to handle comfortably the town's ever-increasing high-school enrollment. Another remodeling was clearly needed.

The wheels of government moved no more quickly in Rumford than anywhere else, and the time needed for the approval and construction of the school's additions would surprise no one, today or then. Upon its completion the remodeled Stephens building would once again be up to snuff in every way, with the $71,000 project adding another wing to each end of the existing school and increasing its number of classrooms to twenty-two. On the third floor were two large classrooms that were usually used as study halls, and the basement boasted a new cafeteria, where Mrs. Dunton and her staff could feed forty-eight students at a time at eight large tables. For the first time, the newly expanded building also boasted a gymnasium.

The problem for Ed Muskie was that the bigger, better Stephens High School wouldn't be finished and dedicated until January 8, 1932—just five months before he graduated. This meant that throughout Ed's high school years, the Stephens Panthers basketball team had to play its home games at the Mechanics Institute on Congress Street in downtown Rumford.

Yet another of Hugh Chisholm's community-improvement projects, the Mechanics Institute had been built in 1907 and dedicated as a social and recreational center in 1911, the same year Stephens High School was built. The institute, which is now called the Greater Rumford Community Center, is listed on the National Register of Historic Places and still gives Rumford residents free memberships. The purpose of the Mechanics Institute was—and remains—to improve the physical and mental well-being of the townspeople, as seen in its mission statement, which consists of one run-on sentence:

> The primary object of which is to develop the physical, mental, and moral qualities of the citizens, and by literary and social intercourse, friendliness and a better acquaintance between employer and employee, to so regulate and control those two great economic forces, capital and labor, that no misunderstanding may hamper the growth and welfare of the community.

As a high school freshman Ed was still painfully shy, especially around girls. The one extracurricular activity that might have had him interacting with young ladies was the school's Latin club. Although he was only five foot four at the time (Ed would grow a foot during high school), he also went out for the freshman basketball team, and in the spring he ran track and was a strong half-miler. He would stick with basketball and running all through high school. (In his senior year he also tried the high jump during one track meet, and won the event.)

Ed's courses that first year were English, Latin, elementary algebra, and ancient history. From interviews of his old friends, one could easily get the impression that Ed earned straight A's all through high school, but that wasn't the case. It wasn't that he was a bad student—or even average—but he seemed to do better in the sciences than in language arts and history, in which he managed "only" B's. And he loved math. "I liked math and was good at it," he said. "Math was probably the best subject I ever had . . . because it involved the exercise of mental discipline, and order, and organization, and so on."[39]

As Ed began his second year of high school in 1929, the country was beginning its plunge into the Great Depression. For the first six months of President Hoover's term in 1929, investors had been bullish on the stock market, pouring in as much money as they could, even if they had to take out loans or mortgage their homes to do it. But investors started selling in the second half of the year, a trend that continued until the devastating October crash. Those who'd invested unwisely lost everything, including their homes.

Soon shantytowns called Hoovervilles, after the man who said the country could get out of the situation if people just helped one another, started to spring up around the country. Flimsy shacks were inhabited by destitute people who covered themselves with "Hoover blankets" (newspapers), repaired their worn-out shoes with "Hoover leather" (cardboard), and flew "Hoover flags" (empty pockets turned inside out).

As a sophomore Ed Muskie added student council to his outside activities and added an elective, biology, to his required courses of English, Latin, French, and plane geometry. He continued to compete in track meets and participated in basketball. High-school basketball had always been popular in Rumford, and a lot of towns-people got to see Ed play—at least once in a while. Because he grew tall in high school, "They tried to make him a basketball player," said Frank Anastasio, but he had to work at it. "[H]e was never a star, you know, I mean never. Although in basketball he was a substitute center one year. I don't think they played him that much, but he did play—he went out. When he was asked, he went out."[40]

"Back in those days there was no finesse in basketball," remembers Austin McInnis, "it was just another football game. And he could handle himself, you know, with that. He took some bruises, but he also handed some out, I figure."[41]

"When I graduated from high school I weighed about 155 pounds, six feet four," said Ed, "and I just couldn't last a full game, so I was a substitute."[42]

"I guess he just wanted to do something," said Ken Bosworth, "or they wanted him to do it—and he'd give it his best."[43]

At times, Ed probably frustrated his coach, Bertram Faulking-ham, who was also the school's submaster and athletic director. According to one story, the coach had to look for Ed during his junior year because he wasn't on the bench at the start of a game. He was sitting in the locker room, reading. Ed disputed that story, however. "I don't know where the story came from," he said. "I very much wanted to make the team. I was off practicing, as I recall."[44]

After a game he went right back to the books, reading on the bus ride home while his teammates horsed around or tried to sleep. Once, after the Panthers won an early-round game at a tournament in Lewiston, they stayed overnight instead of traveling back to Rum-ford. While his teammates ran up and down the halls of their hotel yelling and cheering, Ed sat on his bed studying.

A couple years later, when Mr. Faulkingham, who was also the school's chemistry teacher, was unable to make it to school, Ed filled in for him and, by all accounts, did an excellent job teaching the class. "Any time a teacher was absent," remembers classmate Vito Puiia,

*This 1932 Stephens High School
yearbook picture shows how
Ed slicked back his unruly hair at
the time.*

"they never had a substitute teacher. [They'd] put Ed Muskie in, [he] ran the class better than the teacher. [H]e could run that chemistry class better than our chemistry teacher, Mr. Faulkingham." And when Ed taught class, he was serious and demanded respect. "Oh, there was no fooling around," said Puiia.[45]

Ed's last two years at Stephens are perfect examples of his ambition coinciding with being in the right place at the right time. Stephen's tailoring business had become busy enough that he'd hired a second assistant named Vito Umbro, meaning that maybe, just maybe, he could afford to send his oldest son to college—if Ed continued to keep his grades up. "[T]his little Italian kid came over from the old country," remembers Vito Puiia, "couldn't speak a word of English, and he happened to be taking up the tailoring business. He'd been an apprentice in the old country, and he came here to Rumford. Old Steve took him in."[46]

Though his academic pattern would remain the same—A's in algebra, chemistry, and science and B's in English and French—Ed was determined to break out of his shell by becoming involved in more activities. "In high school I was intent on becoming involved in school activities," he said, "because I wanted to get over my shyness. So I went out for sports, I went out for debating. Because I was a good student, I worked hard at my homework, I really did. I didn't need to because the studies were easy, but I did."[47]

"He was a good bookworm in high school," remembers Anastasio. "Oh, yeah, he was a regular bookworm. He studied, and studied, and studied."[48]

Beginning with his junior year, however, Ed had a lot less time for studying because he added six more extracurricular activities to the four in which he already participated. He became a member of the "R" club, an organization for students who'd earned their varsity letters, and joined the athletic council, of which he was elected secretary. He also joined the school's science and drama clubs and even landed the position of general manager of the school fair. (One biographer says Ed was the president of his class at Stephens, but he wasn't. That position was held by Elizabeth Spinney all four years. Ed would be president of his class during his last two years at Bates College.)

When they talk about Ed's high school days, nearly every one of his old classmates credits a certain teacher with transforming the young man into the fine thinker and public speaker he became. Ed himself remembers that she "finally ran me down my junior year, talked me into trying out for the debating team and I enjoyed it."

Celia Isadora Clary was born in Waldo, Maine, and graduated from Colby College. At Stephens she taught English, coached the debating team, and advised the drama club. She taught only until she married Barry Fossett in 1932, when she left to help him run a small department store outside Waterville.

Four decades later, when Ed was considering a run for the presidency, his former teacher would deflect much of the credit she'd been given for molding him into a skilled public speaker, saying, "He was interested in all manner of school activities, and being the scholarly type that he was, he would just naturally drift to debating. And he was a good debater; he was good at anything he undertook."

And she added, "If he says that I was the one that got him interested in debating then I thank him for that."[49]

(She also advised the drama club, which probably explains Ed's sudden "interest" in the performing arts. And at least one former classmate thinks that Celia Clary may also have had something to do with Ed being accepted at Bates College. "Sometimes the right counseling means a lot, too," said Diana Anastasio. "And . . . Miss Clary probably had a lot to do with it.")[50]

Ed's own recollection was that he had to be persuaded to join the debating squad, and he agreed only after Celia Clary had asked Principal Lord how she could get Ed to be less of an introvert. "She should have been a track coach," he said, "because she ran me down, chased me, caught me. For days I had tried to escape her [by checking the hallway for her before dashing from one classroom to the next], but she thought I was a prospect for the debating team she was trying to put together. I was glad, eventually, that she did catch me. But getting up to make my first speech was a painful experience," he recalled, "for me and the audience."[51]

"She was a very good teacher," said Ken Bosworth. "She was nice, friendly. Fact is, when I had that class reunion in '82, the fiftieth, she was there."[52]

Ed was "a damn good debater," according to Frank Anastasio. "That's where he got his stuff as far as being a public speaker, and as far as getting down and figuring out what he's going to say when somebody else was talking," he said. "Miss Clary, she picked that up, she sensed it, I think, when she got hold of this guy."[53] According to his classmates, Ed held his own against debaters from Wilton Academy and Portland High School, and even against freshman teams from Bowdoin and Bates colleges.

Being on the debating team did put Ed in one predicament when he found out he had to attend a formal dinner and that he'd be seated between two distinguished women from the community. Afraid that he wouldn't have anything to talk about with them, he asked one of his teachers for advice. "Just ask them if they're married and about their children," he told Ed. "Once they start talking about their families, you'll be able to eat your meal in peace."

The evening of the dinner, Ed found himself exactly where he thought he'd be, so he decided to take the teacher's advice. Turning to the woman on his left, he asked her if she was married. When she said that she wasn't, Ed asked her if she had any children. When his second question was met with an angry glare, he decided to try a different approach with the lady to his right. This time he asked her first if she had any children. When she replied that she had two sons, he asked her if she was married. Ed may have failed at his attempt to get the women to do all the talking, but at least he no longer had to worry about making conversation.

During Ed's senior year he bloomed into a class leader and was elected president of the student council and to the National Honor Society as well as the National Athletic Honor Society. A piece in the November 10, 1931, edition of the *Broadcast,* the school's newspaper, after enumerating the young man's achievements, concluded with, "When you see a head and shoulders towering above you in the halls of Stephens, you should know that your eyes are feasting on a future President of the United States."

He was again a member of the drama club, but he did not take part in the senior play, *Adam and Eva,* which was performed on Thursday, May 19, 1932, and described as "a three-act comedy drama." Ed was pursuing other extracurricular interests—unsuccessfully, it would turn out. "In the spring of my senior year in high school," Ed would write in his diary a year later, "I imagined myself madly in love with a pretty girl named Dorothy Poulin." She was a fellow member of the debating team (which also included: Adelaide Foster, Pearl Harvey, Bernard Goodfellow, and Avid Hines), and he mustered the courage to ask her to the senior prom, where he danced awkwardly with her based on some pointers his sisters had given him. "She had auburn hair and blue eyes. This infatuation lasted a year. I even contemplated marrying her someday. However, she didn't care for me and, in time, my ardor cooled."[54]

The following year, Dorothy, who was still living in Rumford, would have a change of heart and would hint to the young college man that he should ask her to the movies at the Strand Theater during his late-summer visit home. But by then Ed had also had a change of heart, and he ignored her suggestion; he was now pining for a slightly older coed he'd met at Bates and socialized with during the summer.

That last year at Stephens, Ed would be fortunate enough to have Lucille F. Hicks as his American history and English teacher. Lucille had been born in Rumford and graduated from Bates College in 1927, where she had been a member of the debating team. Like Celia Clary, Lucille Hicks would also leave the teaching profession shortly after having Ed as a pupil; in 1934 she would marry Warren S. Abbott[55] ("a staunch Republican," according to one of his sons), and the couple would raise three boys on a farm just outside town. One may wonder how differently Ed Muskie's life might have turned out had he not been taught by Misses Clary and Hicks.

The approach Lucille took toward teaching was unconventional, at least in her American History and Current Events class. She "taught a surprisingly unstructured class that ostensibly covered history and government but more accurately dealt with the changing institutions of the United States and may have been one of the true starting places in Muskie's life," according to a biographer. And she "remembered four decades later his 'logical, orderly way of thinking,' and said with unusual penetration, 'He was just an average boy who was much more than average.'"[56]

Ed would later recall that Miss Hicks was interested in politics, though probably only as an observer, not an active participant. One former classmate recalled how the future governor "leaned forward in his seat, holding onto the back of the chair in front of him as he listened intently to Miss Hicks talk about the need to strengthen the Democratic Party in Maine."[57] Five or six pupils, said Ed, "used to meet in her room after classes and discuss the current political scene, which was 1932, before that convention which nominated FDR."[58] Less than a decade later Ed would return the favor of captivating Stephens' students when he'd work there briefly as a substitute teacher.

Besides Lucille Hicks's American history class, Ed's senior course load consisted of solid geometry and trigonometry, physics, and senior review math. It also included English, which she also taught, and that may be the reason he worked to bring his grade in that subject up to par with the rest of his marks.

Or maybe he worked even harder because he wanted to please his father. One thing that used to bother Ed in high school was the fact that no matter how well he did, his father never praised him. Stephen "expected his children to do well and saw no reason to compliment them when they met his expectations. 'Well,' Muskie said much later, 'he didn't believe in showing affection very much except in the things he did for us. . . . He didn't believe in praise, and I thought I did very well in high school and I rather resented—oh hell, I really knew, I was just being petulant . . . feeling sorry for myself.'"[59]

Though his academic achievements may not have impressed his own father, they got the attention of Stephens High principal George E. Lord and his staff, who named Ed the valedictorian of the class of 1932—eventually. "[W]hen it appeared briefly, through some administrative slip, that the . . . honor would go to another [Pearl Harvey], Muskie literally was sick with disappointment, sick, pale. When word came of the error, he erupted with joy."[60] On Students' Day, May 16, Ed was chosen to serve as "Superintendent of Schools."

Most of the letters Ed received congratulating him on his achievement were addressed to him at the home of Charles Taylor in the Frye district of Roxbury, just north of Rumford. There were no school buses from Frye to Rumford, so the children of the three families who lived up there "rode down on the train that came from Rangeley, oh I'd say about, early in the morning. And of course a lot of those trains were bringing wood from Rangeley to the mill, but they had a passenger car or a caboose on the end of it . . . and their children all came to the high school on the train in the morning. And I can remember seeing them, they'd walk up from the station, up through [Strathglass] Park to go to the high school. . . ."[61] Since there's no indication of any problems at the Muskie home in Rumford, perhaps Ed just enjoyed the relative peace and quiet he found at the home of his classmate with whom he worked on the school newspaper. The two young men were good friends and would be roommates at Bates College that fall.

Graduation for the Class of '32 was held on Thursday, June 16. An article in the following week's edition of the local newspaper described the proceedings as follows:

A class of 104 received diplomas at the Commencement exercises of the Class of 1932 of Stephens High School, held Thursday night in the auditorium at the high school before an audience of parents, relatives, and friends that jammed the big assembly room. Exercises were held at 8:00 P.M.

The Processional opened the program, music being played by the high school orchestra under the direction of Harry J. Cohen. Prayer was offered by Rev. Fr. D. J. Hegarty of St. Athanasius church, following which musical selections were sung by the Senior girls' glee club.

The Salutatory was delivered by Miss Pearl Harvey who spoke on the subject "Thought." The First Honor essay, the subject of which was "Deeds," was delivered by Miss Avis Hinds, following which a selection was played by the high school orchestra.

The Second Honor essay was given by Miss Phyllis Carroll, who spoke on "Habits," and the Third Honor essay was delivered by Miss Christeen Howard, whose subject was "Character." Musical selections were sung by the senior boys' quartet, following which the Valedictory was given by Edmund Muskie, whose subject was "Destiny."

Diplomas were presented to the Seniors by L. E. Williams, superintendent of schools, after which the Class Ode, written by Miss Barbara Howard, was sung by the class. Benediction was given by Rev. C. E. Brooks, pastor of the Methodist Church, Rumford.

All parts given on Commencement night were given according to rank and the subjects of the addresses were based on the class motto.[62]

> Sow a thought and reap a deed
> Sow a deed and reap a habit
> Sow a habit and reap character
> Sow character and reap destiny

An early draft of Ed's address, "Destiny" reveals that it started out as a four-page, double-spaced essay written by Ed and edited heavily in blue pencil by Lucille Hicks. "I remember that my high school valedictory speech," he would write forty years later, "was keyed to the Kellogg-Briand Pact,[63] the treaty that was to end all war. And all the while we worried about peace and our domestic economy pressures were building in Europe and in Asia that would engulf all of us. I had barely established my law practice when the Japanese attacked Pearl Harbor."[64]

Next to his yearbook photo Ed Muskie is called "A public man of light and leading." And, as it turned out, he was also a man with good timing. If he had to leave Rumford, he'd chosen the right time to do so. During Ed's last three years in high school, the Great Depression had taken its toll on the Oxford Paper Company; the mill's annual output had dropped from 102,000 tons to just 64,000, and the average number of days worked per laborer had plummeted from 360 to 191. By the time he would graduate from Bates in 1936, the Continental Paper Bag Company, which had purchased the International Paper mill in 1923, had gone bankrupt.

Perhaps the most popular song of the Great Depression had been written in 1930, with lyrics by Hip Yarburg and melody by Jay Gorney. "Brother, Can You Spare a Dime?" was included in the 1932 musical *Americana*, and recordings of the song were number-one hits for both Bing Crosby and Rudy Vallée that year:

> *They used to tell me I was building a dream, and so I*
> *   followed the mob,*
> *When there was earth to plow, or guns to bear, I was*
> *   always there right on the job.*
> *They used to tell me I was building a dream, with peace*
> *   and glory ahead,*
> *Why should I be standing in line, just waiting for bread?*

The best-known Hooverville of all was thrown up in Washington, D.C., in the summer of 1932 by 15,000 veterans of the First World

War, many suffering from what doctors then called "shell shock" but is now known to be post-traumatic stress disorder brought about by the war's brutal trench combat. Congress in 1924 had overridden President Coolidge's veto to pass the World War Adjusted Compensation Act, which promised a payment of $1.25 for each day a veteran had served overseas in the Great War—a $2.4 billion commitment—but the certificates issued to the veterans were not redeemable until 1945. Now those veterans, many of whom had been struggling through the 1920s, flocked to Washington by train, thumb, car, and truck, families in tow, to demand immediate payment of a bonus they felt they had earned. Calling themselves the Bonus Expeditionary Force, they squatted at Camp Anacosta, as they called their Hooverville across the Anacosta Bridge from the Capitol, and their numbers swelled to 25,000 while they waited to see what Congress would do. But legislation for immediate payment of the bonus failed in the Senate, and when D.C. police failed to disperse the Bonus Marchers in July, President Herbert Hoover called out the army to get the job done.

Army Chief of Staff General Douglas MacArthur led the assault himself, ignoring the objections of his aide, Major Dwight D. Eisenhower. Major George S. Patton, commanding the 3rd Cavalry Regiment, pushed the Bonus Marchers back to the bridge with six tanks, then MacArthur cleared out Camp Anacosta with infantry using tear gas and fixed bayonets. The shanties were burned, and the BEF dispersed. Fifty-five veterans were injured and 135 were arrested. It was a public relations disaster for Hoover, and he would lose the presidential election in November by a landslide to Democrat Franklin D. Roosevelt, who promised the country a New Deal.

Chapter Two

College, Law School, War

Bates Freshman

Despite the ever-worsening effects of the Great Depression, late 1932 must have looked pretty good to Ed Muskie. Not only had he made it into Bates College in Lewiston, but Louis J. Brann would soon become the first Democrat to be elected Governor of Maine since World War I. (The next one would be Muskie himself, in 1954.) The election of Franklin Delano Roosevelt as president must have made Ed happy, too, especially since one of Roosevelt's New Deal programs would help the young man pay for his college education. "[I]f it hadn't been for those New Deal programs, you know, assistance to students and all the rest of it," he remembered later, "I probably would have had a helluva hard time in graduating from college."[1]

Roosevelt's New Deal consisted of broad economic and social policies that modified the United States free-enterprise system in an effort to help the country recover from economic depression and to prevent such economic crises from occurring in the future. Some of the programs FDR established during his first term included the National Labor Relations Act, the Social Security Act, and the Rural Electrification Administration. The president would easily win reelection over Kansas Governor Alf Landon in 1936. Indeed, the only states Landon would carry were Maine and Vermont, giving rise to the wry twist on an old saying, "As Maine goes, so goes Vermont."

Even with the government's help, Ed had a difficult time paying for his education. Eight cents bought a loaf of bread or a quart of milk in 1932, and a wage-earner at the Oxford Paper Company earned $10.80 for a 54-hour week. Even though Bates was thought of as a poor-man's college at the time (there was a saying that you could tell a Bates man by the patch on the seat of his pants), it still cost more than $700 a year to attend.

Given his record of achievement at Stephens, one might assume that Ed received a full scholarship to Bates and could spend his hours immersed in study and academic clubs, but nothing could be further from the truth. While his $250 scholarship helped a lot ($125 was earmarked for each of his term bills, which were due in November and March), Ed still had to work hard to pay his way through school. Nearly every fall, the young scholar would be left wondering if he'd be able to afford another year at the small college in Lewiston—and sometimes he didn't know whether or not he'd be returning to Bates until days before the start of the school year. Ed's scholarship to Bates looked like a home run to most people in Rumford, but in truth it was more like a walk to first base.

The summer before starting college, Ed earned ten dollars a week for ten weeks at the Narragansett By The Sea resort in Kennebunk Beach, where he worked as a dishwasher. "I had a wonderful time and made many new friends," he'd write in his diary. "It was a poor season for the hotel due to the Depression, but I was assured a job for [1933]." By the summer of 1935, he'd work his way up to a better-paying bellhop job, to which he'd return every summer until he graduated from law school.

Ed's father even took out a life-insurance policy for him to borrow against. But even that usually wasn't enough, and almost every semester, when Ed received his term bill, he'd have to write and ask his father for a few dollars. As the Depression dragged on, those dollars became harder and harder to come by, and things would become even more difficult for Ed during the latter part of his senior year.

His journey to Bates College had begun, probably unbeknown to him, about halfway through his senior year in Rumford. In November 1931, Stephens principal George Lord had written a letter to Bates president Clifton Gray recommending two of his students for admission. On December 1, Lord received the following reply from the college's dean of men, Harry Rowe:

> Thank you for writing us about Henry Giroux and Edmund Muskie. We are going to write to them and will send them a catalogue and some literature. We will appreciate your good offices in helping line up these boys for Bates.
>
> Beginning next year we start on a somewhat different policy in regard to assistance for freshmen from what we have had previously. Freshmen will be expected to take care of themselves fully for at least a semester. Campus work, scholarship aid, and loans will not be available until after at least a semester's residence. In effect, this will mean that freshmen who establish themselves and make good records will be taken care of during the second semester.
>
> If it happens that Muskie is one of your high-ranking students, it is possible that we might include the Stephens High School in our school list of School Scholarships with the idea that you would nominate him for the award. In this group we wish outstanding scholars, men of promise with capabilities for general participation in college activities. A man might or might not be a good athlete.[2]

Once the ball started rolling, things happened quickly. In March, Ed received the Bates application he'd been urged to request. (He also received an application to Bowdoin College in Brunswick, but never filled it out.) The same month he also received a letter (which was addressed to "Edward Muskey") and a debate booklet from Brooks Quimby, who coached the team in the Eastern Inter-collegiate League. In April Ed received another letter from Dean Rowe, this one telling him he'd been accepted for the fall term and reminding him to send the ten-dollar deposit for his dorm room— and a current record of his vaccinations.

Dean Rowe's rule about granting no campus work for first-semester freshmen wasn't set in stone. Around Labor Day Ed received a letter informing him that all freshman men were required to report to Chase Hall at exactly 7:30 P.M. on Monday, September 26. Soon after his arrival at Bates, Ed went to discuss his financial situation with Rowe and Norm Ross, the school's bursar. "Norm made suggestions about places in Lewiston where I might go looking for a job. And I remember spending a day trying to, around the streets of Lewiston looking for a job without success, and, so finally they, Bates, offered me a job at the Commons waiting on tables."[3] The Commons was located in John Bertram Hall, which was commonly referred to as "JB" on campus.

In hindsight, Ed realized that the college's administrators weren't about to let a student of his caliber get away. "[I]f you had something," he said, "they'd do something for you. Norm Ross could have given me that job at the college Commons when I first went to him, but he wanted to see whether I had the guts to go downtown and hunt for a job."[4]

While Ed's new job in the Commons allowed the shy young man to meet and interact with his fellow students, none of them were female. This was because all the male students ate in JB, while the young women of Bates dined across campus on the second floor of Rand Hall. The only exception to this rule was the one time each semester that the senior men were allowed to dine with the women.

The school's origins helped explain why the rules were so strict. Bates College had gotten its start after the Parsonfield Seminary, which had been founded in 1832 by Free Will Baptists, burned in 1854. The following year Dr. Alonzo Garcelon convinced the seminary's founders, Reverends Oren Burbank Cheney and Ebenezer Knowlton, to relocate to Lewiston, where the school was called the

Maine State Seminary. One year after receiving its college charter in 1863, the school was named for its biggest supporter, local industrialist Benjamin E. Bates. At that time the college consisted of just Hathorn and Parker Halls and fewer than one hundred students. By the end of Reverend Cheney's tenure in 1894, the Bates campus had grown to six buildings on fifty acres. The college became nonsectarian in 1907 in order to qualify for funding of its professors' pensions by the Carnegie Foundation.

"I can remember [Bates President Clifton Daggett Gray] saying once to Ed, 'Well, here's the only Democrat in the college,' which, of course, was not true,"[5] recalled one former classmate. While it is true that Ed was in the minority politically speaking, he fit right in at the then-conservative college—beginning with its longstanding religious traditions, which, at the time, were as regimented as its dining rules.

After the day's first class, which ran from 7:40 to 8:40 A.M., all 550 Bates students headed to the chapel, where everyone sat in alphabetical order so that English professor Robert Berkelman could tell from the empty seats who was missing. "It was very unreligious," remembered one former student; usually they listened to a talk by a professor or a college administrator. On Tuesdays and Fridays, the choir performed. The students were released at 9:00 A.M., and classes started on the hour for the rest of the day.

The school's religious traditions were not a problem for Ed. He automatically knelt and prayed beside his bed as soon as he got out of it every morning, said his roommate, fellow Stephens graduate Charlie Taylor, who was also attending Bates. Upon their arrival at the college, Charlie and Ed were assigned to a room in Roger Williams Hall, which was known around campus as "the Bill." The building's first floor was home to the dean's office, the president's office, and the business office. A photograph shows the freshman pair studying in their dorm room beneath pennants reading "Rumford, Me," and "Bates." While Ed would graduate in 1936, Charlie wouldn't be as lucky.

During Ed's first year at Bates, the only club he joined was the debate team. His studies included three math classes (algebra, trigonometry, and plane geometry), two classes each in English, German, and chemistry, as well as introductory courses in public speaking, social sciences, and biology. Ed reported in his diary that his grade averages were 91 for the first semester and 86 for the second semester. He also notes that he twice ran for class president his freshman year, finishing second both times.

Early in Ed's second semester, fire consumed his father's tailor shop along with several other businesses on downtown Rumford's Congress Street. Many area residents who later recalled the blaze—including Ed himself—thought it had started in the shop that Stephen rented at 69 Congress Street. Perhaps an iron had been left on and ignited some cleaning fluid, they thought.

But a newspaper account of the Sunday morning fire contradicts those recollections and supports the memory of Ed's then-sixteen-year-old sister Lucy, who recalled that "there was a shoe shop down, a shoe-shining place and repair downstairs, and my father was upstairs. Irene [who was twenty-one] and I had gone to church, and we got to the top of the hill, and we looked down and I said, 'Gee, look, there's a fire down there, and why don't we go down, and if it's cold, we can always go into the shoe shop and get warmed up.' So we went down and that was the place that was burnt."[6]

According to the *Rumford Falls Times*, the February 12, 1933, blaze started around 7:30 A.M. in Nicola Bevalaqua's shoe repair shop, downstairs from Muskie's business and the barber shop of Ralph DeSalle, which were located four steps up from street level. Firefighters from Rumford and Mexico battled high winds, freezing temperatures, and thick black smoke as they trained ten hoses on the fire for more than five hours. The building, which was owned by Lucy Abbott and valued at $7,000, was a total loss.[7]

The Lamey-Wellehan shoe store located in the building owned by Minas Rallides was heavily damaged, while the J. J. Newberry store and Elks room on the corner of Congress and Exchange Streets sustained slight damage, as did another barber shop and a women's-wear shop in the McKenzie Block. Total damages resulting from the fire were estimated at about $22,000; all the business losses were covered by insurance. Thinking that Ed's studies might suffer if he found out about the fire, his family didn't break the news to him until much later.

After Stephen received his $1,550 insurance check (to cover his $1,800 loss), he relocated his business across Congress Street at 35 Exchange Street, about a hundred yards from his previous shop. Accompanying Muskie to his new location were his two helpers—and the shop's safe, which had been recovered from the cellar hole. (When Senator Muskie stopped by his father's old shop during a visit to Rumford in 1978, then-owner Vito Umbro proudly pointed out that the safe was still in use.) The site of the newer tailor shop is now home to the River Valley Grille.

Ed went out for the track team in the spring of his freshman year, concentrating on the high jump. As with anything to which he applied himself, he did well in the event, getting up to about six feet and taking first place in several freshman meets. But it would be his only season of track. After summer vacation, Ed returned as a sophomore who had decided to concentrate on his studies and on extracurricular activities of a more cerebral nature.

Toward the end of his first year at Bates, he got to see one of his idols perform in person when Rudy Vallée broadcast his WEAF radio program live from the Lewiston Armory, which was (and still is) nearly across the street from the college on Central Avenue. Vallée, who grew up in Westbrook, Maine, drew nearly 4,000 people to his May 24 performance, which was held as a fund raiser for the New Auburn fire relief fund, established to aid the victims of one of the worst conflagrations the state has ever seen. On May 15, much of New Auburn had been destroyed by a fire set by "a mentally deficient eleven-year-old boy." Fueled by dry conditions and a north wind, the inferno burned an area 600 feet wide and half a mile long, stopping only when it reached the Oak Hill Cemetery. By the time it was over the fire had consumed 249 buildings—half of them wood-framed tenements—as well as two schools, a synagogue, and several businesses. More than 2,100 people were left homeless.

During his second summer of dishwashing at Kennebunk Beach

in the summer of 1933, Ed kept a diary that sheds light on the hopes and fears—and daily life—of a financially struggling college student during the Depression. The nineteen-year-old made it clear that he was crazy about Marjorie Goodbout, a twenty-year-old German major from Lisbon Falls who'd just graduated from Bates. Marjorie made it clear that she wanted to be just friends, however, and as if to emphasize the point, her former boyfriend showed up occasionally to take her out. Although he played tennis and went swimming with her several times a week, Ed realized that his chances of becoming Marjorie's steady boyfriend were slight.

Making no effort to hide his despair—what's a diary for, after all—Ed wrote frankly of his fears for his future as well. "I am a mere sophomore in college with a very slim chance of returning to college, although I have won a $125 scholarship," he said in one entry. "What will I do after the few short weeks remaining of summer are over? Go back to college? A very slight chance. Stay at home? Most likely. But what will I do at home?"[8]

But as the summer progressed, Ed's situation gradually improved, at least financially. The Narragansett Hotel hosted nearly twice as many guests as it had the previous summer, and Ed and Charlie Taylor had their dishpan hands full almost all the time. Business was so good that there was talk of hiring another dishwasher, and Ed was asked to write to his sister Lucy in Rumford and tell her to come to hotel, where she'd have a job waiting on the bellhops in the side hall. (After the summer, Lucy would work in Boston for a while before returning to Rumford, where she'd attend beauty school.)

By mid-September the amount of Ed's scholarship had been increased slightly, and the prospects of his returning to Bates had improved considerably. "I forgot to mention," he wrote in his diary, "that I was promised a $150 scholarship and a [waiter] job for board for half a year by Mr. Rowe. Therefore, I am going back to Bates."[9] He also mentioned that "I applied for the Elks Fraternal Foundation scholarship of $300. I hope I got it." It's unclear whether or not he did.

Ed's diary also contains several entries that won't do anything to endear his memory to Maine's myriad Red Sox fans. On July 19 he

Ed and his sister Lucy in front of the Narragansett By The Sea hotel, where he worked his way up from dishwasher to bellhop during college and law school summers.

wrote, "The Yankees now top the American League. They won as the Senators lost. Good work, Yanks!"[10] But the Red Sox were having a terrible season, and Ed's parents had moved to Maine from New York. (For the record, New York had won its ninth straight game, beating the Chicago White Sox 9-4 to improve their record to 54-30, while the Senators lost to the last-place St. Louis Browns 4-3. That same day Boston lost to the Cleveland Indians and dropped to 35-49.)

Upperclass Years

Back at Bates for a second year, Ed took English, German, history, physics, and math (analytic geometry and calculus) both semesters. He was elected to the student council and joined the Spofford

Literary Club—although at least one of the club's members couldn't remember him ever attending a meeting. And he returned to debating under the tutelage of Professor Brooks Quimby, who had been the head of the history department at Deering High School in Portland before coming to Bates in 1927.

Though he was unaware of it at the time, Professor Quimby—and before him, Celia Clary—were providing Ed with skills he'd need to succeed in politics. And Ed wouldn't forget the potential his old professor had unlocked in him; during his 1968 vice-presidential run, Ed would repeatedly call Quimby, who was dying of cancer, and the two would talk for an hour at a time.

"[Brooks Quimby] emphasized substance. Of course presentation, speaking ability, yes that was important," said fellow Bates alum Vincent McKusick, "but he also drilled in the necessity for research and preparation in the subject matter, and that careful preparation is awfully important."[11] (McKusick would become a lawyer and go on to serve as Chief Justice of the Maine Supreme Judicial Court.)

"The thing we learned in debating was to document everything," confirmed Bates classmate Ruth Rowe Wilson. "You never assume, and you always look it up and check it out. . . ."[12] According to biographer David Nevin:

> The footing Quimby gave Muskie in debate is fundamental to his career. It had many effects on him, but one of the clearest was that it gave him a structured forum in which to escape his shyness. It gave him a reason to stand up and talk and a forum for doing so. The rules of debate forced him into channels with the rest of the contestants, and once he was moving, his quick mind and his developing ability to cut to the heart of an argument were free to rove across the problem and bring up his capacities.[13]

Ed was certainly getting his money's worth from his classes at Bates, but funds, as always, remained tight. In a letter to Lucy, he told her that he was going to need more than the usual ten dollars from their father to help cover his March 1934 term bill. Ed owed the college $4.50, plus six dollars for two textbooks (German and calculus) and other incidentals, and was afraid that he'd need to ask for as much as twelve or thirteen dollars from his folks in Rumford.

During the summer between Ed's sophomore and junior years, his financial situation became even bleaker than it had been a year earlier. A flurry of letters between Dean Rowe and Ed during the first three weeks of September cast his return to Bates very much in doubt. At one point Ed even believed he'd been told not to show up at the Lewiston campus. Rowe informed Ed that the previous year he had received $385 in financial aid from the college—more than any other student—and suggested that he find work until he could save up enough money to pay for his education.

But Dean Rowe was in almost as big a bind as his cash-strapped student. In March, Ed had been elected class president and secretary/treasurer of the student council for his junior year, so it would have been awkward had Ed suddenly disappeared from campus life. In a letter dated only a few days before the start of the fall term, Rowe explained that he hadn't meant Ed shouldn't return, and that if Ed showed up at Bates he'd have a job as a headwaiter in the Commons at least through football season. Rowe reminded Ed that once football was over and the regular headwaiters returned to their jobs, his work status would be up in the air, so he'd better do his best to make himself indispensable in his new position.

Ed had once again managed to return to Bates, but this time with a different focus. By the end of his sophomore year, he had decided to change majors from mathematics to government and history. Though he loved the rules and logic involved in solving mathematical equations, he found himself increasingly drawn to the social and political issues he argued as a member of the debating team. Math classes disappeared from his junior-year transcript, which consisted of three history courses; two classes each in economics, government, and psychology; and studies in Greek and public speaking.

He continued to do well in his studies and extracurricular activities, but he wasn't earning such high marks for social life. With Marjorie no longer at Bates (though Ed would see her again the next summer at Kennebunk Beach), his fancy turned to two other coeds, Betty Winston and Dot Staples, both of whom seemed happy to have him as a friend with whom to take in a movie or go to church—but nothing more. Some of Ed's problems were of his own doing. Telling the college newspaper that he found the school's coeds "to be either frankly insincere or insincerely frank" cannot have done anything to endear him to the ladies.

To this day it remains common for college students to find their future spouses among members of the student body, but that was especially true several decades ago. (Many young women of the time joked about going to college to earn their "MRS degrees.") And Bates was an especially fertile meeting ground during the Depression for three main reasons. First, the students' nearly complete lack of access to automobiles kept them more or less on campus almost all the time. Second, they knew their peers well—especially the ones who sat near them alphabetically at their daily chapel sessions. And finally, chaperoned Saturday-night dances at Chase Hall provided a venue for young men and women to mingle and dance to the music of the eight-piece Bates Bobcats band.

Betty was in the same financial boat as Ed. Her father worked for the post office, and she too had to work her way through college. During her sophomore and junior years, the South Portland English major worked as an *au pair* for a Bates Shakespeare professor who, according to her, was almost universally disliked by the students. Betty's job took care of her room and board while a scholarship paid for her tuition, leaving her parents to cover just the cost of her textbooks—about seventeen dollars.

"By the time [Ed] was a junior," she recalled, "he'd blossomed out considerably and a lot of his shyness was gone, although he was always shy with females."[14] Maybe Ed felt comfortable around her because they were both Catholics and always went to church together. Ed started to develop feelings for her, but only a week or so into the school year he could see the writing on the wall. He wrote to his sister Lucy that Betty had been promised to another young man, even though she wouldn't cool their friendship for another two months.

By early November Ed would be writing Lucy that none of the young ladies he liked seemed to like him as much as he liked them. He was done with women, he said, and was going to spend his time concentrating on his studies—just as soon as he got back from his date that evening.

Letters preserved in the Muskie Archives show that Dot Staples and Ed corresponded on a regular basis for several years after college, with Dot even telling him in one letter that she'd attended Betty Winston's wedding to John Levinson. Though all these letters make it appear that Ed was closer to Dot than Betty, this seems not to have been the case. Between his election in 1954 and his swearing-in in 1955, Ed would visit Betty and her husband in Chicago. Later she would accompany Ed and his wife, Jane, on all their travels during his 1968 vice-presidential run.

As the fall semester drew to a close, Ed owed the college $8.50 and was still unsure whether or not he'd be demoted back to a regular waiter from his headwaiter position. But he was excited about how well his debating activities were going; he'd been assigned three freshman debating teams to coach and was looking forward to an upcoming "radio debate." His debating club was also arranging a contest with the University of Puerto Rico for the following February, in which he would discuss the dangers of fascism.

Given his change of major, Ed must have met Professor Raymond R. N. Gould in or prior to his junior year. While a few of the students referred to the professor as Railroad Gould, everyone else just called him Pa. "Pa Gould," recalled Robert Wade, "was a tough marker, and an awful lot of people avoided him because he was tough."[15]

Gould, who taught American history and government, was a fixture at Bates, having arrived there in 1911. "He was the one," said fellow student Robert York, "who kept emphasizing to us, 'You should get involved in the affairs of your community, you should take a stand on the issues of justice and right and things like that, and don't just be a passive onlooker, but get yourselves involved.' And he was also a strong partisan of the view that Maine badly needed an effective two-party system."[16] Just as Lucille Hicks had done a few years earlier, Pa Gould was instilling in Ed's mind the need for a strong Democratic Party in the state.

Following the March 18, 1935 student elections for the following school year, Ed wrote to Lucy, "I was fairly successful. I was reelected president of my class and, in your senior year, that is the biggest honor you can get as far as offices go. In addition to that I was elected vice-president of the Student Council."[17] Ed neglected to mention that he had defeated Edward Wellman for class president by a single vote.

In another letter a few weeks later, Ed told his sister of the duties he was required to perform in his headwaiter position, which he had indeed retained after the football season. "I have to keep the books, hire substitute waiters, make out the payroll, supervise twenty student workers, and other miscellaneous functions." For once Ed's compensation for his job at Bates had kept pace with his expenses, and he was able to tell Lucy, "I guess my term bill this semester pleased father a lot. It was the smallest one I have had in college. The college had to pay me $1.10."[18]

One of those "miscellaneous functions" was keeping a group of hungry young men in line—literally—or at least trying to. The Commons, where the men ate, was run at the time by Miss "Ma" Roberts, a strict authoritarian who is said to have kept the same weekly menu six weeks in a row. One day she decided she didn't like the way the fellows were rushing into the dining room at mealtime, so she told her headwaiters, Ed and Joe Biernacki, to make them line up outside the room's two entrances and wait to be escorted in small groups to their tables.

It didn't take long before the guys in Ed's line figured out that they had strength in numbers and began to shove their way past him. Ed was the second tallest person in his class but very thin, and he was powerless to stop them. Realizing his friend's plight, Joe, a former football player, yelled at the students in his line to stay where they were, and rushed over to help Ed restore order.

Ed went on to tell Lucy that he had just been elected to the Bates Politics Club ("for those majoring in government, and getting an A or high B") and to Delta Sigma Rho. The latter, he explained, "is the national debating society, and to be elected to it is one of the biggest honors a student can get." And there was more. As Stan Franczyk wrote:

> Scholastically May 22, 1935 was probably was one of the most important days for Ed Muskie at Bates. It was on this day that Dr Walter A. Lawrence, chairman of the honors committee, announced a list of nineteen students who qualified for the Honors Study plan. Eligibility prerequisites were: a minimum average of eighty percent, and an average of at least eighty-five percent in the student's major subjects for the first three years of college work. A recommendation from the student's major professor was also required.
>
> Ed Muskie was one of three qualifiers in the history and government section.[19]

As his junior year wound down, Ed looked forward to returning to Kennebunk Beach, where he was in line for a promotion at the Narragansett Hotel. Anticipation was tinged with trepidation, however, because his old interest Marjorie was also returning to the resort town for another summer. "Betty is quite sure of going back too," Ed wrote to Lucy. "I can smell war in the air."[20]

Before leaving for his working vacation, Ed had a weightier problem to deal with. Every June the junior class hosted the college's Ivy Day activities, for which two men in the class were appointed to be marshals. At the time the student body, which had grown to around seven hundred, included two African-Americans, Jim Carter and Owen Dodson. Both were well liked and accepted among the members of the campus community, but when it became known that Carter was going to be one of the class marshals, the event's planning committee received an anonymous letter "protesting his appointment and threatening to make an issue of it."[21]

"We had a meeting of our small committee and decided to stick to our guns. It was a small matter, in today's context, but it wasn't inconsequential then, and certainly not to Jim Carter,"[22] Muskie would write in his memoir, *Journeys*. Carter would go on to become a Chicago City Commissioner and a member of the Illinois legislature, and Owen Dodson would become a poet and playwright, teaching at Howard University and the Harlem School of the Arts.

Back at the Narragansett for his fourth summer, Ed was promoted from dishwasher to bellhop, a position that paid five dollars a week with room, board, and uniform included, plus about thirty dollars a week in tips—three times what he'd earned washing dishes. One of the better tippers Ed waited on that summer was Louisiana Senator Huey Long, who stayed at the hotel briefly in early August before heading to Canada. Long would be assassinated four weeks later.

The wished-for war between Marjorie and Betty seems not to have transpired. Both wanted to remain friends with Ed—but apparently nothing more.

At the end of August, about a week before he left Kennebunk Beach for two weeks back home in Rumford, Ed received a letter from Dean Rowe informing him that he would be working as the proctor of East Parker Hall during his senior year in addition to his duties as a headwaiter. (Ed's buddy Joe Biernacki would be looking after West Parker.) These new proctor positions were federally funded by one of FDR's New Deal programs.

With his financial situation under control at least for the first semester, Ed returned to Bates for his senior year. To his ever-growing list of activities he added honors work in history and government, ensuring that he'd graduate Phi Beta Kappa. He also became a member of the Freshman Week Committee and of another committee that oversaw the enforcement of such rules for freshmen as not dating, not smoking on campus, and wearing the freshman cap.

Ed's selection of senior-year classes seems to indicate that he was considering a career as a high-school teacher. (At the time, Bates was known for turning out graduates who became "teachers and preachers.") Besides two courses each in history, government, public speaking, and economics, he also took classes in the history of education and the principles of secondary education. Had he become a high-school teacher, it would have been easy to see him teaching history and government—and coaching debating.

Ed took seriously his duty of enforcing the recently reestablished freshman rules. Once, he and some other upperclassmen confronted three freshmen who weren't wearing their freshman caps in downtown Lewiston. The frightened young students were told to report to the committee the following day to learn their punishment. When they showed up, they were put in a car and driven five miles from campus, where they were dropped off and told to walk back.

Feeling the pressure of all he'd taken on, Ed confided to his sister Lucy about how busy his life had become. Classes, honors work, and studying—not to mention his obligations to debating, the student council, "and a million other little things that are always popping up"—had to be scheduled around his daily five hours of work as a headwaiter. The one thing that didn't require a lot of time, Ed wrote, was his position as a proctor in Parker Hall. All that involved was carrying around a master key in case students locked themselves out of their rooms and seeing "that they don't get too wild."[23]

One reason Ed found the proctor job easy was Joe Biernacki, who recalled handling one sticky late-night situation himself. "So [there was] a lot of noise, and then a little more noise, and the first thing you know there's, they're yelling out, and then there's pushing going on." Joe jumped out of bed, got half dressed, and ran down the hall to find that the commotion was being caused by three "pretty drunk" guys, including two Bates football players who'd recently graduated. "I got down there, and I got into the middle of it, and I clobbered a couple of them with my fist, actually. I don't, that's one of the, probably the only time I ever hit anybody that way."[24] With order restored, Joe went back to bed.

On his way back from breakfast the next morning, Ed encountered Dean Rowe, who mentioned the previous night's dust-up. "What was that?" asked Ed. Only when Rowe told him did Ed learn what had gone on. He'd slept through the whole thing.

Life got even busier for Ed and classmate Irving Isaacson in mid March when the two of them represented Bates on a whirlwind debating tour around the Northeast. (Isaacson, who would become a prominent Lewiston attorney, described himself and the lanky Ed as a real "Mutt & Jeff" pair.) They appeared first at the Cambridge Forum before moving on to Brooklyn College, New York University, Rutgers, and finally Lafayette, where they rendezvoused with the rest of the Bates team for a regular league contest.

During that week the conditions that would cause the Flood of 1936 were building to a head. It had rained or snowed seventeen times during the first three weeks of the month, and by March 18 the Androscoggin had swollen to twenty times its normal volume and had flooded Bethel, Hanover, and Rumford—including Prospect Avenue in the Virginia neighborhood, near the Muskie home. Ice floes and thousands of cords of pulpwood from the Oxford Paper Company smashed into the Ridlonville bridge just outside Rumford, sweeping the wreckage five miles downriver, where it smashed into the Peru-Mexico bridge. Farther south, the Turner Center bridge was wiped out and much of Lewiston and Auburn were flooded.

By the time the debating team got back to Maine, the Flood of '36 was well underway, and the students couldn't get back to Bates. The destruction was general, but one of the complications was personal. "I was going to the senior prom with Ed," said Betty Winston, "and he was off on a debating trip, and when they got back to Auburn we were having a flood, and they couldn't get across the river. So he called a friend who came and picked me up and took me, and he did get there before it was over."[25]

Toward the end of his senior year, Ed's money problem once again reared its ugly head. "Ed ran out of money the last semester of his senior year," said Ruth Rowe Wilson. He took his problem to her father, Dean Harry Rowe, who told him, "You just go back to class and don't worry."[26]

Rowe approached Bates treasurer George Lane (who'd started out as the janitor at the Lewiston Trust Company and worked his way up to president) with the situation. Before long Lane had given Ed the money because he liked to help out "worthy students," said former bursar Norm Ross, who added, "We didn't go to the well too often."[27] Lane solved Ed's latest financial problem by giving him a $7 weekly stipend. At the urging of his father, Ed accepted the money, but only as a loan. He then went to a local restaurant, where he made a deal to get all his meals for $6 a week. (Ed paid back the money while working as a substitute teacher after law school.)

Later in 1936, President Franklin Roosevelt would win reelection in a landslide over Governor Alf Landon of Kansas, a moderate Republican. Roosevelt's New Deal (including Social Security) was proving widely popular, and his vote margin was the second largest since 1820; even Kansas swung to Roosevelt. Landon won only two states: Vermont and Maine.

Law School

While fully aware of the positive influences exercised by high-school teachers and college professors on his academic pursuits, Ed seemed consistently surprised by the help he received from the heads of those institutions of learning. The unexpected scholarship that had made it possible for him to attend Bates had been the doing of Stephens principal George Lord, and now, just a month before Bates' June 15 commencement exercises, he was approached by college president Clifton Gray with a similar proposition.

"When I graduated from Bates, it never occurred to me to be a lawyer, that wasn't in my field of vision at all. But President Gray called me over to his office one day during commencement time, and he said that Cornell Law School, because of the excellent record that Bates graduates had made at Cornell, was making a scholarship available to anyone of his choosing, and he asked me if I wouldn't like it."[28] Ed asked the dean if he could have the summer to think it over, and eventually he decided that a law degree would be a good stepping stone to the career he really wanted and now dared to dream of, one in the diplomatic field.

But the proffered $400 scholarship covered only the cost of admission to the prestigious school, and Ed would have to find a way to pay the remaining $700. He knew he wouldn't be able to attend unless something suddenly changed—and it did. Later in May he wrote his father saying that "there is a possibility that I can get board and room free in addition to tuition. If that is the case, it certainly looks as if I might be able to pull through next year."[29]

Ed was referring to one of six "guestships" offered annually by the Cornell branch of the Telluride Association, for which he'd applied during his fifth summer at Kennebunk Beach. Unfortunately, there were far more qualified applicants than openings, and he wasn't selected. When his request for a waiter job at the school didn't pan out either, Ed once again had to turn to his father for help. In the end he rented a room in a private home at 105 Catherine Street in Ithaca, just a couple blocks south of Myron Taylor Hall, where most of his law classes were held.

His landlady, Mrs. E. A. Beddoe, remembered that she immediately liked her new boarder. "'They don't come any nicer than Ed Muskie.' Mrs. Beddoe recalled the time she first met Muskie. 'He was a good six foot five, and he took the smallest room I had. I offered him a larger one, but he said someone was helping him through school and he didn't think it would be right to spend more money than was absolutely necessary.'"[30]

Since money was tight and travel expensive (it cost almost $21 for Ed to get to Rumford from Ithaca), he spent some holidays with his mother's relatives at Goodyear Avenue in Buffalo, to which he could travel for only $3.60. "There wasn't time to come back home to Maine when I was in law school, so we went to Buffalo. That's when I really got to know my mother's family, which is a larger one." Communication with his grandparents, who spoke no English, was "no problem" with the kids translating.[31]

Though he'd been an academic star at Stephens and Bates, Ed had no such luck at Cornell. Shortly after finishing his first semester, he received a letter from the school's secretary, William Farnham, telling him that since his grade-point average for the first term had been less than 1.75, his scholarship was unlikely to be continued for the second year unless the quality of his work improved. Ed's grades for his first full year (1936–37) included B's in torts and actions; C's in contracts, property, criminal law, and equity; and a "pass" in agency law.

Whatever the reason, no scholarship was offered for Ed's second year, and his prospects of returning to Cornell in the fall looked bleak. "By that time there was a lot of slack to pick up because my summer job as a bellhop didn't provide enough. My father carried me through the first year at Cornell, but now my father and I had come to the end of our rope. There wasn't any way that we could see of doing the rest of the job."[32]

As the summer progressed, Ed's options dwindled. In early July he wrote to the school to ask about financial aid and a job as an assistant librarian, but nothing was available. The school's administrators suggested that he take a year or two off and try to save some money. By early September he seems to have accepted that he wasn't going back to law school anytime soon, and he applied for a teaching position at Mars Hill High School.

Two days later Ed heard about an eccentric millionaire whose name appeared as William Bingham, II on his letterhead, and who made a habit of lending money to deserving college students. With nothing to lose, Ed wrote to him asking for money, and was quickly contacted by Bingham's lawyer. While Mr. Bingham summered in Bethel, his agent, George Bourne Farnsworth, M.D., lived on Harbor Hill at Christmas Cove in South Bristol. As Ed recalled in an interview years later, the long drive to Christmas Cove was well worth the effort:

> [Mr. Bingham] was a very rich man and he made it,
> he had a hobby of helping people who had started school
> to finish school. He wouldn't help them get started, but
> he'd help them finish. And when I heard of him, he
> was helping about fifty students a year, and he worked
> through a doctor who lived at Christmas Cove—aptly

named—a Dr. Farnsworth, and so I wrote Mr. Bingham a letter. The very next day I got a call from Christmas Cove. Dr. Farnsworth asked me if I couldn't come
down the next day [September 15, 1937]. Of course law
school was about to start in a week or two, second year.
So I went down, my brother-in-law drove me down, and
I spent several hours with Dr. Farnsworth. He told me
in a letter he wrote many years later . . . really the reason
he gave me the help was because he liked my smile.

I'm sure he was pulling my leg a little bit. In any
case, he was, you know, finding out who I was. When
I left that afternoon I had a check for nine-hundred
dollars in my pocket, and he said, "Next year you come
back again."[33]

And Ed would. The terms of the loans were ten years with no
interest, but as it turned out, Ed wouldn't have to repay them at all.

Dr. Farnsworth wrote the letter to which Ed referred in early
February 1943. Not only does it support the story about his smile,
it also explains a small mystery about the way Ed signed the IOU.
"I recall so well the day you first came to see me," wrote Dr. Farnsworth, "and the genial grin that spread over your face when I asked
you what your real name might be. You and I both understand the
wisdom of cutting off unnecessary syllables."[34] In light of this part
of their conversation, Ed signed the note "Edmund S. Marciszewski
(Muskie)."

With funding for his second year unexpectedly secure, Ed
returned to Cornell. His grades that year remained unremarkable:
B's in equity II, sales, and constitutional law; C's in insurance, nego-
tiable paper, trusts, property II, and evidence; and a "pass" in procedure II.

Late in his second year at Cornell, Ed knew that his grades,
while not stellar, were good enough to graduate the following year
if he could get the money to pay for it. On May 8 he wrote to Dr.

Farnsworth mentioning that "I have done nicely" with the $900 from the previous year but thought that he ought to request $1,000 this time around to help with the extra expenses of graduation and job hunting.

A few days later Ed received a reply from the doctor in which he expressed reservations about the extra hundred dollars:

> I admit the validity of graduation expenses, but "job hunting" makes me scratch my head a bit.
> This I can say however, unless we have a revolution or something by September, you may count on your final grant of $900, the other $100 will bear talking about.
> Please get in contact with me in early September, preferably by telephone at South Bristol 212, to make an appointment.[35]

Always prompt, Ed showed up at Christmas Cove on September 2 and left with a second check for $900, which he combined with his summer savings of $116 and a small scholarship he'd received. Maybe it was at that meeting or maybe later on, but at some point Ed persuaded the doctor to kick in the final hundred dollars. The check, which Dr. Farnsworth mailed in February from his winter home in Miami Beach, came with a note to let Ed know that this was going to be the final loan. (Working for William Bingham, II, appears to have been a good job; other letters Ed received from Dr. Farnsworth bore return addresses such as "aboard the *Sally II*, off Boothbay Harbor," and "The Ritz-Carlton, Boston, Mass.," where he was staying after coming down with the flu on his way to Miami.)

In spite of a heavy course load during his final year at Cornell, Ed managed to keep his grades at an acceptable level, achieving an A in business regulation; B's in business associations (first term) and in trusts and estates; C's in future interests, property III, and procedure II; and "satisfactory" in conflict of laws, business associations (second term), security transactions, municipal corporations, and administrative law. The "satisfactory" grades were based on a comprehensive exam given at the end of the year.

Late in the school year, with graduation in sight, Ed's letters home began to sound more like the ones he'd written from Bates, telling his folks that he had been elected president of the Wilson Chapter of Phi Alpha Delta (a law fraternity) and had been awarded an additional scholarship. (He failed to mention that it was for $100.) He also wrote that he'd had a "prize-winning letter" published in the fraternity's journal, the *Reporter*.

But Ed's final year at Cornell wasn't all work and no play. "I didn't see much of him after college," said his old friend Betty Winston, "although New Year's Eve '38-'39, another couple from Bates and Ed and I spent New Year's Eve at the Ritz-Carlton dancing. Where they got the money, Roger [Ed's Bates classmate John "Roger" Fredland] and Ed, to pay for it, I don't know, although I'm sure it doesn't cost so much now as it did then."[36] Perhaps Ed viewed the occasion as an early graduation celebration, secure in the knowledge that that extra hundred dollars would soon be on its way from Florida. The following summer, two weeks after announcing her engagement to someone else, Betty met a young lawyer named John Levinson at his family's summer home in Kennebunk. The couple married in late September and moved to Chicago.

Practicing Law

After receiving his LL.B. from Cornell on June 1, 1939, Ed looked for work that would at least bring him back to New England, interviewing at places such as The Travelers Insurance Company in Hartford, Connecticut, and the Farm Credit Administration in Springfield, Massachusetts. But the economy was still bad, and when he wasn't able to procure a position at Robinson & Richardson in Portland, Ed spent yet another season working as a bellhop at the Narragansett By The Sea.

In early fall he passed the Massachusetts bar exam and was admitted to practice as an attorney in the Commonwealth on October 25, 1939. It's unclear why he didn't practice law in Massachusetts. Maybe he couldn't find a position that suited him, or maybe he just wanted to stay in Maine. Whatever the reason, he returned to Rumford, where he picked up substitute teaching jobs at Stephens and Mexico high schools while studying for the Maine bar exam. Though Ed was probably "the only unemployed college graduate in Rumford" at the time, he made out quite well for himself; since he was the only substitute for both high schools, he was assured of making five dollars a day, every day. The only drawbacks were that he didn't know from one day to the next where he'd be teaching, and—he'd later admit—he sometimes found himself teaching subjects he had never studied.

"I was in high school at the time," said Frances McInnis. "And he taught English, he took Frances Martin's place, she had a breakdown or something, and he took her place for a year. And I remember coming home and he'd be sitting in the kitchen talking with my mother. And I'd be so embarrassed because there was a teacher sitting, you know. . . ."[37]

Don Nicoll, who would become instrumental in Ed's 1954 gubernatorial campaign, recalled a story about the time Stephens principal Lawrence Peaks saw a group of students standing in the hall after the period had started. When he asked them why they weren't in their classroom, they told him that the previous class was still going on. When he looked inside, he saw Ed sitting on the front of his desk talking to the students, who appeared to be mesmerized.

Ed's return to Stephens High School may have had another effect on his alma mater, the revival of the debating team. There's no mention of the club in the school's 1939 yearbook, the *Tribute*, but the 1940 edition not only mentions the debaters, but calls them one of the school's most successful teams. It's easy to imagine Ed's influence in the organization's formation, though the coach is listed as "Mr. Thomas"—probably because Ed was a substitute teacher who would, as it turned out, leave before the end of the school year.

On January 2, 1940, he applied for permission to take the Maine bar examination. The test was given on February 7 and 8 in Bangor City Hall, and Ed achieved an average score of 72. On March 5 he was "duly admitted to practice as a counselor and attorney" in the State of Maine, but jobs for young lawyers in western Maine remained scarce. He wouldn't have long to ponder his fate, though; upon learning that Ed was now qualified to practice law in the state, Rupert F. Aldrich, an acquaintance who was also the Oxford County clerk of courts, told him about an opportunity that had recently become available a couple hours away.

The reason for the sudden opportunity was the passing, at age fifty, of Waterville attorney Carl A. Blackington. Aldrich took Ed to check out the practice, which Blackington's widow, Doris, and her elderly attorney, Harvey D. Eaton, were offering to sell for $4,000. The terms called for him to pay Mrs. Blackington $1,000 up front and the remainder over three years. Just one thing stood between Ed and his own law practice, and once again it was money.

During the negotiations with Mrs. Blackington, which seemed to be going nowhere, Ed came up with the idea of once again approaching his old friend Dr. Farnsworth about another loan from William Bingham, II. It appears that Ed made his case in a March 22 letter, arguing that Mr. Bingham had previously made loans to people who were starting businesses. But Ed had gone to the well once too often, and a few days later he received a letter from Miami Beach that included the following:

> In the first place, Mr. Bingham does not lend money to start businesses (whatever he has done in the past has no relation to the present and future).
>
> In the second place, considering your record, your innate ability, and what you may reasonably hope for in the future after you get over the first hard sledding, I should not consider myself morally sound in enabling you to sink your brains in a collection business.
>
> And so, after much thought and consultation, I am obliged to refuse your request.[38]

In the end Ed borrowed the down payment from people who knew him well; half of it came from his father, the other half in the form of two $250 loans from his godmother, Mrs. Kowalzyk, and Anthony Banoch, a family friend.

Just before signing the papers to make the deal official, Ed had an idea he thought might save him some money. He asked Mrs. Blackington if she'd accept $3,000 in cash for the practice if he could come up with the balance fairly quickly. She agreed, and gave him six months to get the rest of the money. "So five months plus after I moved into the office, I went to the [Federal Trust Company in Waterville] and borrowed $2,000."[39] The note was marked "Paid In Full" on November 1, 1940, six months to the day after it was issued—quite a coup for a man who was just scraping by. "It was probably the only financial brilliance I have ever shown," Ed said.[40]

As the young lawyer was getting his new practice on track, forces were at work to reroute his future and those of millions of others around the world—the Second World War was looming on the horizon. FDR, who'd be elected to a third term in 1940, was already preparing the country for the inevitable—being dragged into the war. To get the United States ready for the ordeal, President Roosevelt had called for the nation's first peacetime draft with a goal of amassing an army of 1.2 million men and women. He had also allocated $18 billion for the construction of a navy capable of taking on any other navy in the world. In a few years, Ed would find himself serving on one of those new ships.

Based on the value of Ed's new law practice, which was located in Waterville's bustling downtown at 120 Main Street, he had made out well. While his practice would never come close to challenging the powerful Waterville firm of Perkins & Weeks, Ed's new office did include an up-to-date law library worth about $2,500 as well as hundreds of stamped envelopes and other supplies. Most importantly, Ed inherited the practice's existing clients, so he had a ready-made business. "[Blackington] did a lot of collections," said Ed. "He had small probate court cases and small criminal cases, but he did very well."[41]

The problem was that most of his business was based on collecting outstanding debts, the very part of the job Ed disliked the most.

"I didn't like the fact that I couldn't pick my cases on the basis of interest," he said, "but had to pick them on the basis of money, those that would pay a fee. It's a matter of people's troubles translated into dollar signs, and that's kind of distasteful."[42] "You have to be a mean stinker to be good at collecting," said Aldrich. "Ed was really deeper in the law than that. He was well educated and he liked complicated legal problems; he was interested in constitutional matters."[43]

Though bigger than Rumford, Waterville had a lot in common with Ed's hometown. Both were bustling mill towns located on a river—in Waterville's case, the Kennebec. Both were full of friendly, hardworking people and featured thriving downtowns. Though Colby College had outgrown its space in the business district and was beginning the move to its present location on Mayflower Hill, the area was still a beehive of activity located within walking distance of several mills and the Hathaway Shirt Company. "It was also probably the only city in America with a Chinese restaurant named The Jefferson which was run by a Jewish family and featured strawberry shortcake."[44]

Ed wasted no time in getting to know the people of his new hometown, especially the ones who traveled in the social circles to which he aspired. He introduced himself to the city's thirty or so Democratic lawyers and began attending Democratic meetings— at first just as an interested citizen. He also got to know the Blackingtons' daughter, Martha, quite well, although exactly how well remains unclear.

"[U]ntil I moved to Waterville," he recalled, "I had never entertained the idea of running for public office."[45] But that idea would have to wait, because, aside from the aforementioned books, supplies, and clients, Ed's new law office came complete with Carl Blackington's seasoned secretary, Blanche Nadeau, and Blanche came with strings attached. She "was a great collections secretary," he said, but "she was a tough old biddy. She made me promise never to run for public office before she'd sign on with me."[46] So, for the time being at least, Ed stayed out of politics.

"The only damned thing that saved me from her was that when the war came on and I had to—you know—I had to go into the service, well, she wasn't interested in holding my office open going through however many years the war lasted. So she left me, and I was able to pick up somebody else." That new secretary was Mrs. Marjorie Hutchinson, a bright, personable young woman who would fill in at the position "temporarily" and remain in Ed's employ for several decades. Marjorie was the daughter of Deputy Sheriff William Sterling, one of Ed's first close friends in Waterville, and, like her father, was "a red-hot Republican." Their disparate political views were never a problem in the office, however, and she would become one of the first Muskie Republicans, voting for him in every election.

Though it would be more than a year before the Japanese attacked Pearl Harbor, everyone knew by mid 1940 that it was only a matter of time before the United States became involved in the war. In late June, President Roosevelt authorized the United States Navy Reserve Midshipman's School, popularly known as the Navy College Training Program V-7. Initially the program had been aimed at getting college juniors and seniors into ordnance and gunnery, seamanship, navigation, and engineering programs, but it would be amended in 1941 to include any single male college graduate under the age of twenty-eight who'd taken plane trigonometry plus some additional math courses.

Ed registered for the draft in mid October 1940, about a month before receiving a letter from his friend Roger Fredland, who wanted to make sure that Ed was aware of the V-7 program, telling him that "you make $150 a month or so as an ensign, and you don't have to sleep in mud holes."[47] Ed would later take his friend's advice.

But for the rest of 1940 and the following year things were pretty much business as usual at Ed's little law practice, as he continued to weave himself into the fabric of Waterville. He was admitted to practice in United States District Court on April 1, 1941.

Almost exactly two years after he'd started his law practice, Ed enlisted in the United States Navy Reserve, signing up for training as a deck officer on March 26, 1942, two days before his twenty-eighth birthday. Since he showed almost no mechanical ability, the Navy naturally assigned him to its V-7 diesel engineering program. "Within a week after I enlisted in the Navy, I don't know how he learned about it, I got a letter from Dr. Farnsworth enclosing the first note canceled. He said 'I don't think you ought to go into the service with this burden hanging over you,' and he said 'Next year, we'll return the second,' which he did."[48]

The Navy

The following summer probably seemed to fly by as Ed sensed his call to active duty drawing nearer. In early June he was told to report (at his own expense) to the District Medical Officer at 150 Causeway Street in Boston for a physical, and on August 12 his call-up became official, and he was ordered to report to the United States Naval Academy at Annapolis, Maryland, on or before September 11, 1942.

A week before his reporting date, Ed spent a day putting his affairs in order. He drafted a four-page document including a complete list of assets and debts, as well as instructions to sell his law practice to Rupert Aldrich for $3,000 should he not return. (Ed decided to keep his practice open while he was gone. Not only would it give him something to return to, but "I felt it was important," he said, "to keep my name active in Waterville.")[49] He sent the document with a letter to his father.

> Dear Father:
> I am enclosing, for your convenience, and for my convenience, a list of the property I now own, together with a list of the debts that I owe.
> You will notice that the total assets, not including the life insurance policy, amount to about $5,000.00, and that the total debts, including Mr. Bingham's note [of

$900.00], which I don't expect to have to pay, amount to about $3,500.00.

I am also enclosing my will to be in your care.

The debts do not include such current bills as I have outstanding, and which I will take care of as soon as possible.

In the event that anything should happen to me, Mr. Aldrich has agreed to do everything in his power to help you straighten out this business down here, and all of the information you will need will be found in the office safe. I thought it would be best to leave it right here where it should be safe, and where it will be all together. I certainly don't expect that anything will happen to me. I have the feeling that I am going to live to a ripe old age, but as someone has said, "God is firing every bullet in this war," and since He does not see fit to let us know all His plans, we should make every provision for the future.

I look forward to enjoying this new work that I am going into—happy in the thought that I will be doing as much as I can to bring about the right result, and anticipating a peace in the not-too-distant future when I can return and take up my work again.

I leave all my love with you and Mother and the family.[50]

Ed's meticulous planning included instructions for the care of his car, a "1942 Studebaker Commander Skyway sedan, serial number 4218283. Purchase price, $1,465.00."

LIST FOR MY BROTHER WHEN HE COMES AFTER THE CAR

1. You will find wedding gift for [his sister] Frances in the car.

2. You will find wedding pictures in the glove compart-
   ment.
3. Directions for care of car:
      (a) Be particular about keeping the inside clean,
          and vacuum the rugs.
      (b) Drain the Prestone. Flush the water system
          and put more Prestone in to bring it to winter
          strength.
      (c) Keep the tires at 32 lbs.
      (d) Rotate the tires, starting immediately, and after
          5,000 miles thereafter, as follows:
              Spare to the right rear;
              Right rear to left front:
              Left front to right front;
              Right front to left rear;
              Left rear to spare.
          Before doing so, however, check cuts in the
          spare for nails, glass, etc.
      (e) Change oil every 6,000 miles with new filter
          cartridge. Grease car on 1,000-mile marks. Use
          #10 oil.
4. The key to the tire locks is in the tool chest.
5. Make [the last fourteen] car payments, starting
   with payment due Oct. 27, through my office. They
   amount to $50.00 a month, with interest.
6. The automobile insurance policies are in the office safe.[51]

Ed's training at Annapolis lasted sixteen weeks. In his first
month he was an apprentice seaman at a pay rate of $20 a month,
and for the next three months he was a midshipman, which doubled
his pay. It wasn't much, but his room, board, and uniforms were paid
for, and at least he didn't have to worry about paying for school.

Crammed into a four-man room with two sets of bunk beds, Ed
and the others were rousted into the wide hallways of Bancroft Hall
at 5:30 each morning for calisthenics. The new recruits were tested

During the war, Ed and his brother, Gene, who was in the Army, got to spend some time together, probably in New York.

with a stressful, fast-paced schedule governed by bells. They were given twenty minutes to eat, and a bell would tell them when it was time to go make their beds. Another bell then told them to muster again.

A week after arriving at the Naval Academy, Ed finally had the time to send a postcard back to his family. Fittingly, it showed the scale on which he and thousands of other young men were being processed, with a picture of the hangar-like Bancroft Hall mess hall on the front and the following description of it on the back: "Length: 523¾ ft. Width: 73 ft. Maximum seating capacity: 3,500. Mess attendants: 245. Largest mess hall in the world."

Ed made it through his first test in the military and became Ensign Edmund S. Muskie on January 5, 1943, during commissioning exercises held in Annapolis' Mahan Hall.

After leaving the Naval Academy, Ed took about a week and a half of leave, which he spent in Rumford. Besides enjoying a late Christmas, he arranged for the payment, with interest, of the $250 loans he'd gotten from Mrs. Kowalzyk and Mr. Banoch in 1940, repaying each River Street resident $265.

While returning to duty, Ed ran into Annapolis classmate Francis Mascianica at South Station in Boston, and the two traveled together to Penn State, where they were to attend sixteen weeks of diesel engineering school beginning on January 16, 1943. (The starting and ending dates of many of Ed's assignments are approximate due to travel times, periods of leave he may have taken, and the fact that the dates on which military orders are issued often differ greatly from the dates on which they take effect.) Getting there was a battle in itself, remembered Mascianica.

> So we got on the Federal Express at eleven o'clock at night. And it was in the wintertime, colder than hell, and we got on the train, and we got out at Philadelphia at, oh, well about two-thirty in the morning. . . . [A]nd we got on another train, and, to Altoona, I think, PA. And we had to stand I remember, and hotter than blazes in the train, and we stood up for two or three hours.
>
> Got out of there at about five-thirty in the morning, and now we're supposed to be on . . . another train into State College, PA. So we got out, and I'm just looking around, colder than blazes, and then I went up to an old conductor and I says, "How long a wait for the train to State College, PA?" He says, "There it is. It'll be leaving in about four or five minutes, you might as well get on it." I says, "Where?" He says, "On the caboose."
>
> So Ed and I ran to the caboose, pot-bellied stove in the middle of the caboose, and we were the only live individuals there in the back, I remember. And we hit every little stop along the way, and we staggered into State College, PA, I don't know what time it was, about eleven-thirty in the morning.[52]

Francis and Ed would be roommates at the Nittany Lion Inn for the next four and a half months while they studied diesel engineering nearly every waking hour. There they absorbed instruction on the care and feeding of several types of diesel engines that powered the Navy's wartime fleet. Classes covered every aspect of how to maintain the massive power plants, from lubrication and electrical systems to fuel injection. "And, in fact, you had homework, you know. It was school, school, school, school, and that was it." It didn't matter that money was tight, because so was the time to spend what little they had. "And for entertainment we'd go to the Radskill and had probably a beer at night," said Mascianica. "And at about nine-thirty or so that was the end of that. . . ."[53]

Once the engineering phase of his training was complete, Ed was ordered to report to the Commandant of the First Naval District, Boston, for duty "afloat in such diesel-powered local defense vessel as he may designate." Since his training had been in the operation and maintenance of diesel-powered ships, the Navy naturally assigned him to the USS *YP-552* (the ex *Taormina*), a gasoline-powered ship, on which he'd serve for about a month.

On June 1 he was ordered to report to the USS *YP-556* (ex *Fantasy*), a diesel-powered ship. His new duty was indoctrination at Fort Schuyler in the Bronx, New York. Built on Throgs Neck shortly after the War of 1812, the initial purpose of the irregular-pentagonal fort had been to protect New York City from enemy ships coming down Long Island Sound. Over the years it had undergone several renovations, the most recent of which had been in 1939. Before that, recruits had had to sleep on folding cots on a barge that may or may not have had hot water in the mornings. Now the trainees had rooms and showers that were much more livable, at least by military standards.

On November 11, having recognized Ed's potential, his commanding officer wrote a letter of recommendation for Ensign Muskie in which he stated that the "subject officer, having served aboard this ship since 29 May 1943, has demonstrated that he is qualified for the duties of a deck officer, and he is recommended for the additional classification D-V(g)."[54]

Ed's next sixteen weeks of training were broken into two blocks. On October 21, 1943, he received orders to report to the Submarine Chaser Training Center at Pier 2, Miami, Florida, on or before November 27. There he lived for eight weeks at The Venetian BOQ (bachelor officers' quarters). By early February 1944, Ed found himself in Columbus, Ohio, where he completed eight weeks of "recognition" training at Ohio State University, meaning that he learned how to distinguish enemy ships and aircraft from those used by the Allies.

On March 1, while still stationed in Ohio, Ed was promoted to the rank of Lieutenant (junior grade), an achievement he probably celebrated with a young woman he met there. After he'd left for the West Coast in early April, the woman, who signed her letters "Vi," wrote Ed several times (he kept more than a dozen of her letters) asking him to stop in and see her the next time he had a chance. It appears that Vi was a divorcee with a young son, and that she and Ed had dated while he was in town. It's obvious that she cared for him, even after their break-up—which she characterized as the gentlest one she'd ever been through—but it doesn't appear that her repeated requests for a reunion ever resulted in one.

Those early April orders required Ed to report to the "Commandant of the Twelfth Naval District in San Francisco for temporary duty pending transportation to a port in which the USS *Bracket* may be."[55] The USS *Bracket* (DE-41), was an Evarts-class destroyer escort that had been launched on August 1, 1943, at the Puget Sound Navy Yard in Bremerton, Washington. It was named in honor of Lieutenant Bruce Godfrey Bracket, a patrol plane pilot who'd been posthumously awarded the Silver Star for gallantry for actions before his death in the Solomon Islands on December 16, 1942. The *Bracket*'s commander, Lieutenant John H. Roskilly, Jr., was in charge of fourteen other officers and 183 enlisted men assigned to the 289-foot, 1,450-ton ship, which completed its shakedown cruise and repairs in time to leave San Francisco for Pearl Harbor four days before Christmas 1943.

The *Bracket*'s primary mission was to protect convoys between the Marshall and Gilbert Islands from Japanese submarines and aircraft, which it did from February until early May 1944, when its starboard propeller shaft was damaged. During the *Bracket*'s six-week

Ed in his U.S. Navy officer dress whites.

repair back at Pearl Harbor, Roskilly was relieved of duty by Lieutenant Commander A. C. Reed, Jr.

Ed finally made it on board the ship during the summer of 1944. At first, things didn't go as he had hoped. "[M]y first assignment on board a ship was as a supply officer on a destroyer escort. I had some training and experience in the engineering department, so I asked the captain if I could get back into engineering, rather than supply. He took me off supply."[56]

During his time in port, Ed had a chance to practice law again, at least briefly:

While the ship was in the Navy Yard for repairs, we had the usual disciplinary problems. One involved a steward's mate, who was Black. The complaining officer was, as it happened, from Maine. The steward's mate had been charged with disobeying an order and was to be given a court-martial, and I was assigned to him as counsel. I was more than willing but the prosecutor was more than able. There was a board of three officers and they found the mate guilty. I got the distinct feeling that the decision was controlled more by the sense that an officer was the complainant than by a balanced view of the rights of the enlisted man.[57]

Throughout the second half of 1944, the USS *Bracket* escorted ships in the areas of Saipan and the Marshall Islands, with big excitement on July 28 when the ship's crew dropped depth charges on a suspected enemy submarine (though there's no evidence that they hit anything). Ed did remember that his ship was hit once by enemy fire, but it sustained only light damage in the encounter. The *Bracket* sustained heavier damage, he said, when it was caught once in a typhoon.

Toward the end of September, Ed received a mimeographed letter from Brooks Quimby at Bates addressed "to all Bates debaters in the service." As expected, this form letter updated its recipients on events at the college, and the debating team in particular. Quimby added a personal postscript saying, "Thanks for the good letter and check. Maine is still so Republican that I feel lost in this Democratic county."[58]

In early January 1945 the *Bracket* fired on and destroyed a Japanese gun emplacement on Taroa Island. In early February the ship returned once again to Pearl Harbor, where the crew had a month-long rest. Around this time Ed was awarded another advancement in duty, if not in pay grade, prompting a buddy to write, "Chief Engineer—that's quite a large order, isn't it? Even for a lawyer! Knowing as little as I do about you, I'll still bet my bankroll that you can handle the job—without strain."[59]

Following four more months of escort duties, the *Bracket* arrived in San Francisco in mid July for an overhaul at the Mare Island Navy Yard. Before he'd even arrived in port, Ed put in a request for three weeks of leave from July 29 through August 20. When he notified everyone back in Maine that it had been approved, one person took particular interest in Ed's impending visit—Martha Blackington.

In late July, Martha, who was living in Estabrook Hall while taking summer classes at the University of Maine at Orono, wrote a letter to Ed that seems to suggest the two were something more than casual acquaintances. "I've been anxiously waiting for your return for so long," she wrote, "that now I'm afraid the next few weeks won't go by fast enough." She signed it, "Love, Martha."[60]

The *Bracket* was still undergoing its renovation when Japan surrendered on August 14, 1945, and Ed wasted little time in writing a letter to his superior officer stating his case for a discharge from the service. In the letter dated September 8, he noted that before entering the service, he had engaged a fellow attorney "to give as much attention to my affairs as he could spare from his own considerable practice and business interests," but that business at his law office had dwindled to the point where it was now "barely covering expenses."[61]

The Navy being the Navy, it required Ed's continued presence on the USS *Bracket* until the ship's decommissioning was completed on November 23. (The *Bracket* was sold to the National Metal and Steel Corporation on May 22, 1947, and was scrapped.) True to its word, the Navy let Ed go home on November 24. (He probably took a "terminal leave," meaning he was home on leave until his official discharge date of December 18, 1945.)

Ed received credit for thirty-six months of active duty, including one as an apprentice seaman, three as a midshipman, and thirty-two as a commissioned officer. He was now free to return to Waterville, where he could enjoy life as a civilian once again—and set about rebuilding his law practice, which had survived thanks to the efforts of Marjorie Hutchinson, her father, and Rupert Aldrich, Ed's Republican friend, who drove from South Paris to Waterville (eighty miles each way) twice a week to help run the practice. After the war, Aldrich refused to accept a penny for his services. "That's what friends are for," he said.

Chapter Three

Rising Star

Elective Office

The story goes that during his first day back in Waterville after the war, Ed was visited in his office by former Waterville mayor F. Harold Dubord, a Democrat, who asked him to consider running for a seat in the state legislature. Dubord's timing was good. After more than three years away, Ed had returned to a law practice that was in dire need of revitalization, and what better way, he figured, than by cultivating some political connections? (At the time, his social life consisted mostly of activities at the city's new AMVETS post. AMVETS, or American Veterans, had been funded just over a year before by returning World War II veterans and in 1947 would become the first World War II organization to be chartered by Congress.) He was interested in the idea because of his father's strong political views. "And the whole New Deal period had coincided with my own personal life and problems," he said later. "But it had never occurred to me to get into politics until Harold Dubord came to my office and asked me."[1] He saw the possibility of two years in the Maine House of Representatives as an excellent opportunity to learn and sharpen his political skills.

The timing was good in another respect, too. Maine might not be quite ready yet for a bona fide two-party political system, but the

Republican stranglehold on elective offices was loosening just a bit, and change was in the wind. Mainers returning from the war, Ed noted, were comparing the state to other places they'd seen around the country—and the world—and finding its politics wanting. They were beginning to feel that Maine should have a more competitive political system. So Ed told Dubord that he would seriously consider running as the date of the primary drew closer.

But the primary wouldn't be until June, and in the meantime Ed was going to try to grow his law practice. He shared his plan for that with his parents in a January 1946 letter:

> First of all, I have located offices in an excellent location across from Day's Jewelry store, and almost across the street from my present location. They are in a wooden building, but the landlord is going to install imitation brick-asphalt shingles which will make it very attractive. There are four large rooms and a bath which are grouped together in a very good arrangement for a law firm. I am getting a five-year lease with an option for five years more. The rent is $60.00 a month, which is about $20.00 to $40.00 less than the real value of such large rooms in that location, but I have to paper, paint, and alter them at my own expense. In the end, of course, I will save money; and I am very enthusiastic about the layout. I expect to be able to move in by the 1st of March.
>
> The second piece of news is that I am forming a law firm with a fellow by the name of James Glover, the firm to be known as "Muskie & Glover." It isn't going to be a partnership, but just an arrangement whereby we will share offices and share expenses and keep our own individual business. If it works out well we may eventually form a partnership, but that is all in the future. Glover is a local boy who is well known and well liked, and who has a lot of connections locally. He is a year younger than I and worked for another local law firm

before the war. Since he returned from the Merchant
Marine, he has opened his own office. Although he
doesn't have much of a practice right now, he is very
much a politician and I don't see how I can lose since
I won't have to share my present practice with him. A
firm name adds prestige and also attracts the business
of out-of-town concerns like insurance companies, etc.,
who like to feel they will always have a lawyer on hand
to do their business.

Still no word on a car. Marden says he thinks he
will be able to let me have the second Commander
he gets. So far he has had about five Champions, but
I'm not interested in them. It shouldn't be too long, if he
keeps his word, before I'll have a car, as Studebaker is
still in production.[2]

The address of the new office was 131 Main Street, and the
cost-sharing arrangement with James Glover seems to have lasted
about five or six years before Glover sold the business he'd started (the
Waterville Credit Bureau) to his secretary, Yvette Roy, and moved to
Massachusetts to pursue other opportunities. Not only would Ed let
Mrs. Roy continue to use his office rent-free until she located her own
space, he even lent her a desk to replace the dilapidated one she'd
been using. (Ed would keep his law office open until he was reelected
governor in 1956.)

As Ed's practice began a slow growth—he became a justice
of the peace in early March—his interest in politics was gradually
becoming keener. In late March he attended the state Democratic
convention in Portland, where the speeches no doubt included the
now-familiar rallying cry that Maine was ready for a real two-party
system and that, since the old Democrats were suffering from stagnation and had been reduced to fighting over the same small piece of
the pie, the state's recently returned veterans were the logical choice
to lead the fight. The strategy of running veterans in the upcoming elections would be firmed up in mid May, when the Demo-

cratic establishment realized that they had no candidates for many offices—and time was running out.

A week later Ed attended an AMVETS convention in Portland, where he took the lead in developing resolutions and programs calling for a bonus for veterans along with medical care, revenue for a state fund for GI loans, and property tax exemptions for the homes and businesses of veterans. Though he was still a few years from becoming the polished public speaker people now remember, Ed's personable style and closely reasoned arguments went over well, and it was probably around this time that fellow Democrats convinced him to become a candidate for the Maine House of Representatives.

It was also around this time that Ed decided he wanted a place of his own. After returning from the war he had rented a room from the Blackingtons, and then, in the spring, shared an apartment with a Waterville optometrist. Maybe he wanted a break from all the meetings and conventions in which he'd suddenly become involved, but more likely he just wanted a quiet place of his own, a place where he could sit, read, and collect his thoughts while gazing into the distance as he had done all his life. Maybe he'd finally been able to purchase that Studebaker that would make living outside town feasible. Whatever his reasons, on May 22, Ed used his GI benefits to purchase a small camp on the east side of China Lake for about $3,500—fifty dollars down and fifty dollars a month.

He bought the camp about ten miles from Waterville, from the Augusta plumber who'd built it. The tap water came from the lake through a hose, and wasn't drinkable. The interior was sheathed to hide the studs, and the tiny kitchen had a propane stove. There was also a small dining room, and at one end were two small bedrooms with a john in between, "but no bath. There was no shower, no tub, or anything of that kind."[3]

Waterville's district sent two representatives to the Maine House of Representatives. Ed and Democratic incumbent Roland Poulin ran unopposed in the June primary, garnering 122 votes and 156 votes, respectively, and both earning the privilege of running

Ed owned this tiny camp on the east side of China Lake for fourteen years, selling it after being elected to the U.S. Senate in order to buy a bigger one at the southern end of the lake.

against Republican incumbent William A. Jones and another GOP contender in September.

One day during the campaign, Ed ran into fellow Democrat Dick McMahon at the post office. McMahon, an ex Marine, wanted to know what had possessed Ed to run as a member of the minority party. "In those days," said McMahon, "being a Democrat in Maine was a lot like bumping your head against a stone wall."

"'Well, if I lived down south I'd probably be a Republican,' Muskie replied with a smile. 'Somebody has to do it.'"[4]

One of Ed's priorities during the campaign was the bonus for Mainers who had served during the recent war. He favored a $500 bonus plus the other previously mentioned benefits, while Republican Governor Horace Hildreth envisioned a much smaller award, about $130. Ed, who thought his plan could be funded by revenue from horse racing, opposed the governor's plan because it would have required the implementation of a state sales tax.

Once the results of the September 9 election were tallied, the results showed Roland Poulin with 2,678 votes, Ed with 2,635, and William Jones with 2,111—Ed had defeated the Republican incumbent by 524 votes. "I ran, and I was elected. No one was more surprised than I,"[5] Ed would later write in his autobiography. He became one of only 24 Democrats opposed by 127 Republicans in the House of Representatives in Maine's 93rd Legislature, while the GOP outnumbered Democrats by thirty to three in the Senate. (The Democrats in Augusta used to joke that there were so few of them, they could caucus in a phone booth.) The scale was tilted even further by the reelection of Governor Hildreth, U.S. Senator Owen Brewster, and Maine's three (at the time) U.S. Representatives—all Republicans.

In exchange for serving at the State House for six months every other year, plus special sessions, Ed was given an annual stipend of about $800 to cover the cost of his meals and lodging in Augusta. Fortunately he had to concern himself only with wear and tear on his car, since he lived close enough to commute between the State House and home. As a freshman in the minority party, Ed found himself assigned to two minor committees, Federal Relations and Military Affairs, on which he labored in relative obscurity. He said later that, during his first term, "eighty-five percent of the legislation came from committees on which Democrats were not permitted."[6] As was his habit, Ed thought things through before he spoke and took care to get along with all his colleagues, which impressed everybody—including Republicans.

In the wee hours of October 17, 1946, the law offices of Muskie & Glover was struck by a fire that probably started in the wiring of the intercom system in the firm's reception room. The blaze, which was largely confined to that area, resulted in $2,300 in damage to office furnishings, according to an inventory compiled by Ed's insurer, Macomber, Farr, & Whitten. According to the *Waterville Morning Sentinel,* three other businesses in the two-story building— Mansfield Insurance, jeweler Lionel Tardiff, and the clothes-pressing business of building owner Peter Pericles—suffered a further $2,700 in smoke and water damage. Muskie & Glover was soon back in business at the same location.

Jane Gray

By late 1946, Ed's fondness for Martha Blackington had abated, and he began dating Waterville native Jane Gray—but only after she and her boss had invested considerable effort in getting him to notice her.

Born in Waterville on February 12, 1927, Jane Frances Gray was the youngest of five children born to Myrtie May (Jackson) Gray and Millage Guy Gray, who worked as a watchman at the Hollingsworth & Whitney mill (later Scott Paper Company) just across the Kennebec River in Winslow. Her father's daily walk to work from School Street took him across the Two Cent Bridge (which was the footbridge's actual toll) until he became unable to work. "[H]e unfortunately had one stroke after another," said Jane, "and then he died when I was ten."[7]

Her father's death left her mother to raise Jane and her siblings, Lerlene (Lee), Howard, Jackson (Jack), and Virginia, on her own. Through hard work and determination, Myrtie Gray kept her brood together, supporting them by working as a cook and pastry chef. "We had a big house on what was called College Place," recalled Jane, "on . . . the then property of Colby College."[8] There her mother and two assistants fed sixty young men who were attending the school. Mrs. Gray also worked at the Pie Plate restaurant, where she made the doughnuts on Saturday mornings, and as a pastry cook at resorts around the state during the summer. One of those summers Jane spent with her mother in Rangeley, where, as a fourteen-year-old, she was put to work washing dishes. She remembered the experience being "awful," but then added, "It didn't kill me."[9]

Even at an early age, Jane was as outgoing as Ed was introspective. She later recalled that her first time in the limelight was in 1931, at age four, "playing the piano in a big store window in Waterville for a special radio broadcast."[10] Years later, when her husband was running for vice president, she'd tell a reporter, "As I look back now on that occasion, when the whole town was staring through the window, I realize the event [was] prophetic."[11] And it wasn't just

*Jane Gray's high school
yearbook photo.*

her outgoing personality that attracted people to her; when she was a senior in 1945, the slender, brown-eyed brunette was voted the prettiest girl in her high-school class.

Jane got her first after-school job at fifteen, selling dresses at Montgomery Ward. To celebrate her new position, her brother Howard, who had overcome polio to become general manager of the *Waterville Morning Sentinel*, bought her a thirty-nine-cent hat at a local dime store. "I was prouder of that hat than any I've ever owned since,"[12] said Jane, who was earning $3.94 a week at the time. After she graduated from high school, Jane's fortunes would change when she was offered (and quickly accepted) a job at Waterville's most exclusive women's store.

Alvina Lewia and her sister Delia Bouchard owned and operated a downtown store that most local ladies considered so classy and high-end they dared not go into it. Alvina's half of the store carried the latest fashions and furs, while Delia specialized in expensive handmade hats. At the time they hired Jane, the women also hired another young woman, Florette Hebert, whose mother had served in the WAC (Women's Army Corps) during the war and belonged to the local AMVETS chapter with Ed.

Though she'd been hired to work in sales and as the bookkeeper, Jane quickly took on all the related duties required of anyone who works in a small business. She would later remember that she "did all kinds of things: selling, buying, paying people their salaries, and jack of all trades. Ed used to laugh because he kept telling people that I was a model. I think I was in two of [Alvina's] style shows, but anyway that didn't exactly describe me as a model."[13]

Alvina was a determined matchmaker, but arranging a meeting between Ed and Jane wasn't easy. "Alvina used to take me to the Templeton for lunch so that I could meet Ed. That wasn't my desire, that was her desire."[14] But before long, Jane was fully on board with the plan and let Alvina, who didn't have any children of her own, dress her in the finest fashions so she'd look great in case Ed glanced out his window as she walked by on her daily trip to the bank. "I was the first one in Waterville to have long dresses when they became fashionable," she said. Once she even went as far as "accidentally" running into him as he was leaving the Templeton. Jane said "Excuse me." Ed looked up from his newspaper long enough to say "Certainly," and continued on his way. (The Templeton Hotel would burn to the ground in April 1955.)

By late summer 1946, when Ed was running for the Maine House, Jane found herself telling her staunchly Republican mother, "I see this guy at the Templeton when my boss takes me there for lunch, and he's so nice. I really think you ought to vote for him." (Mrs. Gray never told anyone how she voted, but it seems unlikely that she voted for Ed—at least that first time.)

Eventually Alvina's matchmaking efforts paid off, but not without help from Florette and her mother, who asked Jane to accompany them to an open house at the AMVETS center, which was located up over Preble's Studio on Main Street. When they got there, the crowd was small, so they sat in the front row where they could better hear the commander of post number 4, Ed Muskie (he was also the judge advocate for the Maine AMVETS department). After the meeting Ed offered a ride home to anyone who didn't have a car, and Jane was one of those who accepted. Ed quickly devised a route that would drop off all his other passengers first, and when he stopped the car in front of Jane's house, she wondered what he was up to. What he was up to was screwing up the courage to ask her to accompany him to the legislative ball in Augusta the following month. The next day he asked her to lunch, and they lunched together for the next year and a half.

When Jane told her boss about being invited to the ball, Alvina "went down to Boston immediately to buy me a wardrobe of evening clothes. So you see, I had chosen the right person to work for."[15] (Apparently Alvina and her sister were also able to fix up Florette with a guy, because twenty years later she'd tell a reporter, "We did better for the girls who worked for us than we did for ourselves. My sister and I both stayed widows.")[16]

Though she'd soon come to like Ed and accept that he was dating her baby sister, Virginia at first told their mother that Jane shouldn't be going out with an older man. Well aware of the thirteen-year difference in their ages, Ed did everything he could to show that the couple wasn't trying to hide anything from anybody. "At night they went to political and civic meetings, at which she was expected to be quiet and ornamental. They bowled and went to the movies and talked. Did they laugh, dance, and play? 'No, not really. He was always enjoyable to be with,' Jane said, 'but he wasn't what you'd call a live wire.'"[17]

But Mrs. Gray seemed to be fine with the pair dating; he was friendly and intelligent, and she also liked the fact that he was tall enough to change light bulbs without a ladder. But she did have to draw the line somewhere. In the spring of 1947, when Ed said he planned to spend a couple weeks at his camp on China Lake and that Jane ought to join him there, Jane told him she couldn't. Ed said that he was going whether she accompanied him or not, and Jane told him to go ahead but not to expect her to be waiting for him when he got back.

As fate would have it, a former boyfriend of Jane's who was studying medicine at Columbia University happened to come home that same day. To get back at Ed, she walked down Main Street hand-in-hand with the boy, making sure everybody saw them. Her timing was perfect, as Ed drove past just in time to see them together. He became so angry that there was probably more smoke coming out of his ears than out of his Studebaker's tailpipe. (Jane's mother had earlier warned her about marrying a doctor, telling her they're never home. Evidently she hadn't said anything about politicians.)

Before long Jane would be spending a lot of time at China Lake with Ed, not because her mother had a change of heart but because Ed's father had recently retired. He had sold his Rumford tailor business to Vito A. Umbro, Jr., on March 3, 1947, for the price of its equipment ($483.61) plus a percentage of the unfinished suits. The sales agreement also stipulated that Umbro must make it clear that Stephen Muskie was no longer the owner or a part owner of the business. With Ed's parents now spending a lot of time at his camp, Jane's mother allowed her to stay there—as long as they were around. She and Ed's family got along well; she felt so at ease around them that she even painted Stephen's toenails bright red once while he slept in a rocking chair on the porch.

First Defeat

On April 24, 1947, members of the legislature decided to relieve stress by holding a mock session. The Republicans made Ed governor for the day, a position that came with the admonition, "Well, if you were one of us, Ed, we'd make you governor; you'll never get anywhere as a Democrat."[18]

About that time Ed helped draft a zoning ordinance for Waterville, and it was probably due to this involvement in the city's affairs (along with his recent political success and his bipartisan "support") that Ed was asked later in the year to run against Waterville mayor and local bank president Russell M. Squire. Since Ed's practice, which still relied heavily on collections for its income, was still slow, he agreed to enter the contest.

The months leading up to the December 1 mayoral election saw Ed being pulled in several directions at once. In early October he drove a carload of local members to the AMVETS national convention in Columbus, Ohio, where he was selected as a national executive committeeman. (He reportedly sang Rudy Vallée songs the whole way. He would remain a fan of the crooner until early 1968, when Vallée considered running for mayor of Los Angeles. The singer, who had attended Suffolk University Law School in Boston in 1937, was quoted as saying, "Something should be done about the property tax. I don't think a man like myself, with no children, should be required to pay the same school tax as a man who is the father of nine.")[19]

By the end of November, Ed was even busier. On November 27 he gave a campaign speech on local radio station WTVL in which he took Waterville's current administration to task while managing a little backhanded commentary on women's fashion that would play well with male voters:

> We are told by the present city administration that, during the past two years, there has been a "new look in city affairs." We are told that this "new look" consists of nonpartisanship in the conduct of the city's business.
>
> I think you will agree, after careful analysis, that, as in the case of the latest women's fashions, this "new look" means simply this—"everything under cover."[20]

"The city," he went on to say, "is being run by a mayor, a treasurer, a clerk, an overseer of the poor, a street commissioner, and other officials who are all members of one party."

He spent the following weekend in Bangor as chair of the platform committee and keynote speaker at the state's Democratic preconvention conference. There he gave what had become the customary speech about how people were growing tired of a one-party system, and that the time had arrived for Democrats to grab a bigger piece of the political pie:

We think that, as a result of the actions of the Republican Party in the 93rd Legislature, there is cause for serious dissatisfaction for the people of the state. We think there is reason to believe that a united, revitalized, and dynamic Democratic party can take advantage of such dissatisfaction to score a victory in the 1948 elections.[21]

The Monday after his attempt at rallying the troops in Bangor, Ed received 2,853 votes in the Waterville mayoral contest—434 fewer than Mayor Squire. Ed had won only the Sixth and Seventh Wards, while the incumbent had carried the other five. Though he'd done reasonably well (Squire would be reelected by 1,400 votes four years later), a defeat was a defeat, and the reasons for it depended on whom you asked—and when.

One theory held that he hadn't been accepted by the Franco-American voters who lived in the Democratic wards known as the Plains along the Kennebec River. "There was a rumor the day before the election that Ed was Jewish and that hurt him,"[22] said Dick McMahon. In another interview around the same time (fifteen years later), McMahon told a different writer that Ed lost because he'd befriended "'an old [French-Canadian] bum, a man whom the French wards despised,' for reasons that now retreat into the past. Muskie refused to repudiate the man—'Goddammit,' he told McMahon, 'I'll pick my own friends!'—and the French wards went against him."[23]

To Ed the reasons were more straightforward. There were no big issues on which he could attack Squire, and besides, he wondered, "Who in the heck is going to vote for me when I got him for collection?" Years later, Jane would say that the defeat was "probably the best thing that ever happened to him." Ed learned the hard way that campaigning meant trying to appeal to as many voters as possible—and that he couldn't take anything for granted. Undeterred by his setback, Ed would serve as chairman of the platform committee at the Maine Democratic Convention the following March.

Marriage

In late 1947 and early 1948 Ed made two major purchases. He took on the payments for a new four-door Studebaker Champion that cost $1,763 with defroster and Climatizer heater, and he purchased an engagement ring for Jane.

> When he finally presented her with an engagement ring and proposed [in March], he told her that he had been carrying the ring around in his pocket for quite a few months but hadn't wanted to give it to her until it was paid for. "That was just about the most honest statement I'd ever heard and I said yes immediately," Jane Muskie recalls.[24]

The nuptials were scheduled for late May, leaving some of Ed's out-of-state friends, such as his Bates College buddy Joe Biernacki, scrambling to make arrangements to attend; Joe's letter congratulating Ed on his engagement didn't reach Waterville until ten days before the wedding. (Though the wedding was quickly planned, it was not an emergency; the couple's first child, Stephen, wouldn't be born until the middle of the following March.)

A couple of issues needed to be worked out before they could marry, however. The matter of religion was resolved when Jane agreed to convert from First Baptist to Catholic, but almost as important as religion in Ed's firmament was the question of political affiliation. There too Jane accommodated her fiancé's beliefs, agreeing to become a Democrat. "'I guess he figured if he was going to try to rejuvenate the Democratic Party in Maine,' she said, 'rejuvenation would have to begin at home.'"[25] She also wryly noted, "We weren't married until I was twenty-one. He certainly would not have married anyone who couldn't vote."[26] According to the comma-happy announcement:

> The Sacred Heart Church, Waterville, was the scene of a pretty wedding when Jane Frances Gray,

Waterville, became the bride of Attorney Edmund
Muskie, at 4 o'clock, Saturday, May 29. Reverend John
Holohan, of that church, performed the double-ring
ceremony, which was witnessed by the groom's father,
Stephen Muskie, Rumford, and the bride's brother,
Howard Gray, Waterville, who gave them in marriage.[27]

Jane's sister, Lerlene Powers, of West Hartford, Connecticut, was the matron of honor, and Ed's associate, James Glover of
Waterville, served as best man. The reception was held in the Blue
Room of the Elmwood Hotel. Among the presents on the gift table
were two wool blankets from fellow Democrat Dick McMahon, who
worked in a local woolen mill. (Five weeks later, McMahon and his
bride, Nellie, would receive a clock as their gift from the Muskies.
He always suspected that Ed and Jane had received two clocks as
wedding gifts.)

Following the reception, Ed and Jane left for a weeklong honeymoon in Rangeley with a brief stop in Rumford. They were accompanied on the first leg by Joe Biernacki and his wife, Bernice, who
stayed in the next cabin at the Rumford motel. Two years earlier,
Joe and his bride had spent part of their honeymoon tracking down
Ed and five local businessmen who were fishing at a nearby lake
and had spent a night in a room set aside for them in the otherwise-
stag cabin before leaving the following day. ("In other words," said
Biernacki, "Ed was on our honeymoon as we were on their honeymoon, and we always got a big charge out of that.")[28]

In Rangeley the newlyweds were alone at last, and the only news
of their week on the lake came on the back of an early June postcard
to Ed's father: "Weather beautiful—having a grand time, plenty of
rest. Our camp looks out on the island you see here. Expect to go
through Rumford on Sunday, and will stop in to see you. Love to all,
Jane and Ed."[29]

The area probably brought back happy memories for Ed, who'd
fished there with his father as a boy, but it's easy to imagine Jane
remembering the summer seven years earlier she'd spent washing

dishes in Rangeley. (In another seven years, when Ed, as newly elected governor, was asked to pose for a picture helping his wife with the dishes, Jane informed the photographer that the last time Ed had done that was during their honeymoon. Maybe he got his fill during college summers in Kennebunk.)

After the honeymoon, the couple spent the rest of the summer at China Lake, then got an apartment in Waterville when the weather turned cold. The Muskies would go on to spend summers at China Lake even after Ed became governor. Their first two children would have their own little bedrooms, and when more kids came along, Ed converted the glassed-in porch to a bedroom. In January 1960, about a year after being sworn in as a U.S. senator, Ed would sell the first camp and pay Charles Skogland $9,500 for a bigger one at Birch Point, on the south end of China Lake.

Reelection, Another War, and the Office of Price Stabilization

Later in 1948, Waterville-area voters gave Ed another term in the House. "I was elected House Minority Leader. It was a post without much power. The majority made all the committee assignments and they were careful to keep the Democrats off most of the important committees."[30] One of the few exceptions was Ed himself. The Republicans appointed the thoughtful young attorney to the prestigious Judiciary Committee.

At around that time, Ed sought an appointment from Governor Hildreth to the Public Utilities Commission, probably more for the income it would have provided than for political reasons. Fortunately for Ed, the governor passed him over and selected Bridgton attorney Edgar Corliss for the seven-year appointment. If not for that disappointment, Ed wouldn't have been available to stand as the Democratic Party's candidate for governor six years later.

Erroneous banner headlines notwithstanding, 1948 was a good year for another Democrat, Harry S. Truman, who defeated Republican Thomas E. Dewey (as well as Dixiecrat Strom Thurmond and the Progressive Party's Henry Wallace) in that year's presidential contest. Since becoming president following Franklin Roosevelt's death in April 1945, Truman had presided over the end of the war in Europe on May 8, 1945. He had made the highly controversial decision to drop two atomic bombs on Japan in order to induce Japan's surrender (on August 14, 1945) without the necessity of an invasion that might have cost 250,000 to 500,000 American lives. (Truman never regretted that decision, and it probably hastened the war's conclusion for hundreds of thousands of American service men and women, Ed Muskie among them.) He had overseen the difficult return of the American economy to a peacetime footing, and he had vigorously supported the GI Bill—a rare social program favored by conservatives as well as liberals. (Passed in 1944, the GI Bill aimed to prevent a repetition of the Bonus March of 1932, when the country had seemed close to falling apart.) He had been a strong supporter of the United Nations, which officially came into existence on October 24, 1945. He had initiated the Truman Doctrine in 1947 to contain the spreading influence of the Soviet Union and the Marshall Plan in 1948 to rebuild war-shattered Europe and, again, counter Soviet expansion. And to overcome a Soviet blockade of West Berlin, he initiated the Allied forces' Berlin Airlift on June 25, 1948, the success of which contributed significantly to his reelection.

Truman favored, among other things, civil rights legislation and the abolition of the poll tax, views that had almost cost him the election. During his first and only full term, he would be able to expand the federal housing program, secure increases in the minimum wage and social security benefits, and abolish segregation in the military. Although his Fair Deal legislative agenda was largely defeated in Congress, he prevented the rollback of major New Deal programs. One program that he unsuccessfully lobbied for was government-sponsored health insurance.

Ed and Jane's first house at 17 Silvermount Street as it looked in 1951. Two years after this photo was taken, Ed would fall and break his back while remodeling the upstairs.

In most articles, interviews, and books (including Ed's 1972 autobiography), the Muskies seem to say that they bought a little house in Waterville shortly after getting married. In fact, documents indicate that the couple's first house was purchased toward the end of 1949. An income tax return filed four weeks after the birth of Stephen Oliver Muskie on March 18, 1949, shows the family residing at 25 Winter Street, which was probably the apartment they'd rented since leaving China Lake in the fall. According to the deed, the Muskies secured a $10,000 loan for an $8,000, 1½-story cape located at 17 Silvermount Street on October 22, 1949. At the time, Ed's annual income was about $5,000 from his practice plus another $800 for his time in Augusta.

Ed remembered the house as being ideal for a young, growing family provided he could become a home handyman and undertake renovations as needed. Despite work and family obligations, he made time later in the year to stay involved in his party, acting as chairman of the platform committee at the 1949 Maine preconvention Democratic conference.

Not even a snowstorm could keep the faithful from attending the Maine Democratic Convention on March 24–25, 1950, in

Lewiston's City Hall auditorium. National Committeewoman Lucia Cormier and her party arrived from Rumford, saying they had found the traveling conditions to be excellent. Victor Hunt Harding, executive director of the Democratic National Congressional Committee, arrived from Washington on the 1:12 P.M. train. After a late lunch, Harding, who was scheduled to address the group that evening and again at the Saturday night banquet at the DeWitt Hotel, pointed out to reporters one of the problems Maine Democrats faced:

> [Maine's] September election, he said, "complicates the whole situation." Maine holds its election before "the machinery has been all set up," so that assistance from the national committee is made much more difficult.
>
> In spite of this, however, the Democratic National Congressional Committee plans an "intensive campaign" in Maine this year. "The Second District especially looks very promising," Harding declared.[31]

Although Ed was chairman of the platform committee, he was not one of the convention's scheduled speakers; speeches were to be given by Harding, by John F. Jacques of Portland, and by newcomer Frank M. Coffin of Lewiston. Coffin stole the show with his pull-no-punches address. "I'd done a number of talks being highly critical of the party and its tendency to shoot itself in the foot and be content with just being a series of tribal chieftains in the mill cities of the state," he said later.[32] He told the gathering:

> [I]n the past three state elections, if we had elected every candidate whom we had placed on the ballot, if we had batted one thousand, we should still have been very much the minority party . . . . How many Democrats have had to play tic tac toe in the voting booth for lack of anything else to do?[33]

He went on to suggest that "nothing snowballs so fast as a political movement sparked with sincerity. . . . Like so much sticky snow the independent voter lies waiting to go along with anyone who rolls a decent snowball."[34] Even the political reporter for the right-leaning *Bangor Daily News* gave the young Democrat a glowing review:

> Where have the Democrats been keeping that bright and magnetic fellow? They better get him out of hiding pronto! He is the best soldier I have seen break through the tent flaps in many years, and when he gets into battle, he will be a powerful and dangerous foe—if I am not mistaken. Young, level-headed, and clear-thinking, he really is terrific.[35]

Also impressed with Coffin's talk was twenty-four-year-old Shepard "Shep" Lee, who was working at his father's local automobile dealership. "[I]n 1950 Frank gave the keynote address at the DeWitt Hotel," said Lee, "to—was it the Democratic Convention? I remember being so impressed I wrote him a letter and said I would like to do some work for the Democratic Party. And everybody in Lewiston-Auburn knew Frank, knew him by reputation. He was *summa cum laude* from Bates. Bright young lawyer and all of that. So I knew who he was and got involved in that way."[36] Shep Lee would remain a staunch supporter of the Democratic Party, becoming close friends with Coffin, Ed Muskie, and several other party stalwarts along the way.

Coffin shared much in common with Muskie, who was four years his senior. Frank had graduated from Bates in 1940, served as a U.S. Navy ensign in the Pacific Theater in World War II, earned a law degree (Harvard) in 1947, returned to Maine to practice law, and become active in Maine's Democratic Party. He would later serve Maine's Second District for two terms in the U.S. House of Representatives (1957–61) before losing the 1960 race for Maine's governorship to the Republican candidate, former Aroostook potato farmer John H. Reed.

One person who wasn't all that sure of his future in politics in 1950 was Ed Muskie. On the one hand, he felt the need to tend to his family and his law practice, both of which continued to grow slowly. On the other hand, he felt an obligation to the voters who had twice elected him to the Maine House. "Finally I went to see an older Republican friend and counselor, Harvey Eaton [who a decade earlier had represented Mrs. Blackington in her sale of the law firm to Ed]. He heard me out, looked me in the eye and said: 'If you're going to be in this world, Muskie, you might as well be a part of it.' I decided to run."[37]

The September 1950 election brought a GOP sweep of the major offices and a squeaker for Ed. "I won by one vote in that third election," remembered Ed. "By one vote."[38] In fact, though he did beat Republican runner-up A. Perley Castonguay by a single vote, his margin of reelection was eight. The top two vote getters would be going to the Maine House, and Ed outpolled the third-place finisher, a young GOP attorney named John Thomas, Jr., who'd advertised heavily, 2,957 votes to 2,949. After being sworn in again, Ed would be reelected minority floor leader.

Between election day and his swearing-in, Ed busied himself with other causes, both local and national. In late August he chaired a three-man committee to plan a fundraising campaign for the Ticonic Boy Scout District. A few weeks later, Sister Hortense, the superintendent of Sisters' Hospital, announced that he had agreed to organize a junior advisory board to teach these young men about the facility's resources and administration and the growing needs and demands of the "highly specialized" patient care offered there. Ed's work with AMVETS took him to Washington, D.C., and Boston between December 11 and Christmas.

Two days after Christmas, Ed accepted the position of temporary National Executive Director of AMVETS, taking on the task at the request of National Commander Harold Russell following the resignation of Elliot Newcomb, who'd quit to become secretary-general of the International Federation of World's Veteran's Organizations in Paris, France. Ed told a reporter that he'd accepted the post for "two or three months" until a permanent successor to Mr. Newcomb could be found. Had he taken the job permanently, Ed would have had to relocate to Washington, D.C., instead of making occasional trips there.

Fighting had been raging on the Korean Peninsula since mid 1950 when the North Korean People's Army, backed by China and the Soviet Union, invaded South Korea. By September the KPA had overrun South Korea and pushed all the way to Pusan in the southeast corner of the Korean peninsula. The Truman Administration saw in Chinese and Soviet involvement a repeat of Hitler's European aggressions of the 1930s; a failure to respond, Truman and Secretary of State Dean Acheson believed, would repeat Britain's failed policy of appeasement and would jeopardize Japan, now viewed as a U.S. protectorate and the prize of Southeast Asia. United Nations forces (eighty-eight percent of whom would be American) deployed to Pusan under the overall command of General Douglas MacArthur (commanding mostly from Tokyo) beginning in July, and in September began a counteroffensive (supported by an amphibious landing at Inchon) that pushed the North Koreans all the way to the Yalu River border with China in November. Chinese forces crossing into North Korea turned the tide of conflict again, forcing the U.S Eighth Army back across the thirty-eighth parallel by mid-December.

By July 1951, the war would devolve into protracted trench combat with fierce fighting in and around the Iron Triangle region (straddling today's demilitarized zone), including the battles of Pork Chop Hill, Heartbreak Ridge, and Bloody Ridge. The jet age would officially begin when American F-86 Sabres of the Fifth Air Force tangled in dogfights with Mikoyan-Gurevich MiG 15s (which were given the NATO codename "Fagot") in "MiG Alley" in northwestern Korea. And President Truman would relieve Douglas Mac-Arthur of command in April 1951, replacing him with General Matthew Ridgeway. MacArthur had crossed the thirty-eighth parallel in the mistaken belief that the Chinese would not enter the war—or at least that was what he assured his commander-in-chief. He had promoted a plan to attack airbases in China despite Truman's rejection of it, had claimed decision-making authority over the use of nuclear weapons in the war, and had publicly threatened to destroy China unless it surrendered. MacArthur would be hailed as a hero upon his return to the U.S., giving a speech to a joint session of Congress that Truman called "a bunch of damn bullshit." Congressional hearings in May and June would determine that the general had defied his commander-in-chief's orders in violation of the U.S. Constitution.

By the time the fighting would end in July 1953, nearly 34,000 Americans had died. Military expenditures would double as a result of the conflict, and the cost of living would increase five percent during the first six months of the hostilities—and Ed would get his next job as a direct result of this.

On February 8, 1951, Ed resigned his position in the House to accept a new appointment. House members on both sides of the aisle lauded the tall, lanky Democrat for always being fair and reasonable and for the well-considered arguments he always made, no matter the subject. Ed returned the compliments to his fellow legislators. His letter to the 95th Legislature's Speaker of the House William Silsby read "Dear Sir":

> On January 29th last I was assigned as Acting District Director for Maine of the Office of Price Stabilization. [The "acting" would be changed to "indefinite" on April 20, 1951.] I have been acting in that capacity without a formal appointment. Pending clarification of my status with the Federal Government I have not previously taken any action with respect to my position in the Legislature.
>
> Today I have taken and subscribed the formal oath of office as Acting Director. I cannot, therefore, under the provisions of our State Constitution, continue to hold office as Representative to the Ninety-Fifth Legislature from the City of Waterville. Consequently, I tender my resignation herewith. I take this step with regret. No other experience has been more interesting and more enjoyable than my terms in the House.
>
> Respectfully yours,
> (Signed) Edmund S. Muskie[39]

Upon Ed's departure from the House, the position of minority floor leader passed to newcomer Thomas E. Delahanty, a Lewiston lawyer who'd been elected Ed's assistant. (In 1958, in one of his last acts as governor, Ed would appoint Delahanty to the Maine Superior Court.) Ed also resigned as acting AMVETS national executive director after only about a month on the job. He accepted the OPS position at the end of January, but decades later claimed to still be in the dark as to how he'd been chosen for it. "I don't know who pushed the buttons to get me appointed OPS director, but that happened when the Korean War started."[40]

But Milton Wheeler, who had been involved from the start with the Maine branch of the OPS, would later recall that he had been appointed director of the Maine office by national director Michael V. DiSalle in mid January. Wheeler told DiSalle that he would accept the position as long as the organization's main office was located in Portland, where he lived. Then, two weeks later, DiSalle called Wheeler back to tell him that the Democratic National Committee wanted Ed to be the director, and Wheeler agreed provided two conditions were met. "We can handle it this way," he said. "I'll defer to Muskie to take the job as director, [and] I'll take the job of enforcement director for the same money, providing the office remains in Portland."[41] The deal was struck. Both men were hired at the GS 14 pay grade (about $8,000 a year at the time), and the office stayed in Portland.

Ed's appointment may have come at the urging of Democratic National Congressional Committee Executive Director Victor Hunt Harding, who had addressed the Maine Democratic Convention the previous March. Harding would have wanted to help Ed establish a solid base on which he could build in any future campaigns.

Initially the new OPS headquarters were located in a two-room suite over the Langley Restaurant in the post office building on Congress Street—where the phones, furniture, four clerk-typists, and 16,000 price-regulation booklets arrived all at once in a flurry of activity—and then at the old Falmouth Hotel on Middle Street. From those offices the two set about recruiting the forty or fifty staffers, including many fine attorneys, they'd need to carry out the office's mission. Ed even offered an assistant U.S. attorney position responsible for OPS litigation to his friend Frank Coffin, but Coffin declined the position to concentrate on his growing law practice—and other matters that would soon arise.

Even while he was busy setting things up in Portland, Ed was traveling around the state giving talks, not all of which were related to OPS matters. Two weeks after leaving the state legislature, Ed posted a letter to Mrs. Beverly Jones Lohfeld of the Bates College News Bureau letting her know that the subject of his upcoming talk to Dr. John C. Donovan's citizenship laboratory would be one close to his heart, "[t]he responsibilities of the majority and the minority parties in government." "The minority party has the duty to observe and to criticize the mistakes, the failures, and the neglect of the majority party," he wrote. "It has a duty to provide a positive program and qualified candidates to put that program into effect. The minority party cannot ask for a change just for the sake of change, it must offer a constructive change."[42]

Once the OPS office was set up, Ed stayed in Portland during the week and returned home on weekends. To make that commute and the long road trips to speaking engagements around the state more tolerable, in March he traded in his 1948 Studebaker for a used 1949 Lincoln Cosmopolitan Sport Sedan equipped with a radio, heater, and hydromatic transmission. The Portland car dealer allowed Ed $750 for his old car, leaving him a balance owed of $1,245 on the Lincoln. Ed could drive around the state in what was then considered the lap of luxury.

But her husband's weekly absences were nerve-racking for Jane, who delivered her second child, Ellen, on September 22, 1951. She feared the worst, saying, "I hated that he was in Portland all week and I was there in our little house, scared to death that somebody was going to break in, take my babies."[43] And Ed's ten-dollar-a-week room in Maine's largest city would soon land him in trouble with the taxman.

His wife was far from the only one with whom Ed's new job ran the risk of making him unpopular. The OPS was modeled after the Office of Price Administration in World War II, and its purpose was to establish a ceiling on prices and thus limit wartime inflation. Disagreements with businesspeople were more or less inevitable. Ed tried to make it clear to Maine business owners that dealings with the OPS need not be adversarial. "We are trying to stop almost overnight a flood of rising prices. It cannot be done that easily."[44] And while he promised to crack down on violators, Ed also wanted people to know that "we hope you will look upon us as people to whom you can come for advice and assistance."[45]

"My two guiding principles as OPS director," Ed said later, "were fairness and reason. If government is neither fair nor reasonable, no amount of power or enforcement personnel will make the system work effectively for very long."[46] A system that people feel is unfair, he thought, leads only to token cooperation. This philosophy played to one of Ed's strong points, the one he'd learned in high school and college debating practice and honed during his years as a lawyer and politician—the art of persuasion.

To spread the word about the OPS and its mission, the state was divided into eight districts, and two-man teams were sent out to every city and town, no matter how small or far flung, to meet the owners of businesses of every type and size. The operation was a huge success, far exceeding its 300-towns-in-thirty-days goal by making 3,052 business contacts in 344 towns in just eighteen days.

Ed and his staff weren't compliance minded to the point of harming businesses, especially large ones. Ed himself helped carve out some leeway for farmers growing one of Maine's largest cash crops. Floyd L. Harding, who was then the assistant general counsel of the Maine Potato Growers, later remembered a meeting he had with Ed about price controls:

> And he says, "Well, you know, it's a matter of the war. And you know when we create a war, we've all got to do our part." And I said, "Well Mr. Muskie, there's price controls that you've imposed on potatoes that are fresh fruit and vegetables." And he says, "That's right." "But on seed potatoes . . . Mr. Muskie, on seed

potatoes there are no price controls, right?" He says, "No, no, that's not a necessity." I said, "Isn't it going to be difficult to tell whether these potatoes are sold as seed or as table stock?" He said, "You see an opening there, don't you?" So for some reason from then on, we had the largest export of potatoes I believe in Aroostook County for seed than we'd ever had in any other year.[47]

More than two decades later, Michael DiSalle would write an open letter to President Nixon citing Ed's work with potato growers as an example of how price restrictions could slow the inflation of food prices. "The only way to get food prices down," he wrote, "is to keep them down on the farm once they've seen parity." As prelude, DiSalle asked rhetorically, "What did happen [when restrictions were implemented]? In 1952, instead of becoming scarce, potato production went up, and potato prices went down. Was the action a— pardon the expression—political hot potato? Certainly not."[48]

By 1952, change was in the air. In early April the *Bangor Daily News* ran a short article in which an unnamed political reporter claimed that Democratic leaders had blown a chance to get Ed to run for governor. According to the report, he had made "a proposition embracing several thousand dollars" for the support of his family while he was out campaigning. Desperate though they were for an electable candidate, party leaders took too long to come to a consensus and "let him slip away" when he made up his mind to stay at the OPS.

In mid June Ed nixed the idea of a write-in campaign in the June primary, even though the Republicans suddenly appeared vulnerable because of an ongoing probe into the state's liquor sales. In a letter to the *Lewiston Evening Journal,* Ed explained his decision:

I want to thank you for the friendly and complimentary way in which you discussed the possibility of my candidacy for the Democratic nomination for governor in the coming primary election.

It is true that many people over the state have been kind enough to suggest that I seek the nomination via the "write-in" method. However there is no indication of such widespread, spontaneous interest as would produce the necessary votes without considerable organized effort. Such an effort would be difficult at best in the few days that remain prior to the primaries. It is made almost impossible by reason of the fact that many party leaders whose cooperation would be essential to success previously have committed their support.

I gave serious thought to seeking the nomination prior to the filing deadline in April and decided against it. It would be most unfair to those of my friends who already have committed their support to change my mind at this eleventh hour for what obviously would be interpreted as reasons of expediency. To force my candidacy under such circumstances might well destroy all possibility of party unity at a time when such unity is of utmost importance to the people of Maine.

As you know, I have in the past fought to implement my belief that we can best promote and ensure competence, efficiency, and honesty in government when we have a strongly competitive two-party system. That goal, not the candidacy of myself or any individual, is of primary concern to me as a citizen in this important election year.

For these reasons I have not made and will not make any effort to seek the Democratic nomination for governor at this time.

With warmest personal regards, I am sincerely yours, Edmund S. Muskie.[49]

Just prior to this, the *Lewiston Evening Journal* had run the headline, "Liquor scandal gives Dems hope." The state's Republican governor, Frederick Payne, was being investigated by the Legislative

Research Committee because of accusations by Gardiner wine distributor Herman Sahagian that the Maine Liquor Commission had accepted bribes when deciding which brands to stock in the state-run liquor stores. In order to rise above the partisan bickering, Payne, who was involved at the time in a U.S. Senate primary challenge against incumbent Republican Senator Ralph Owen Brewster, chose Democratic lawyer Frank Coffin to defend him against Sahagian's charges of discrimination.

"[Coffin] was all intellect and legal knowledge," said former UPI reporter John E. "Jeb" Byrne, "and not worried about some of the niceties," such as shining his shoes.[50] And he did his job well, convincing the committee that the distributor's setbacks were due to regular business trends. "The Legislature cleared the Governor and the Commission, confirming Coffin's observation before the Committee that the accusations against the Governor amounted to 'a case of very sour grapes.'"[51]

Coffin and Payne became friends during the hearings, and Coffin even endorsed Payne in radio ads during his successful primary challenge of Brewster, whose career in Maine politics had been long and checkered. Brewster, a radical conservative, had been elected governor in 1925 with Ku Klux Klan support, clashing with such moderate Republicans as U.S. Senator Clyde Smith (husband of Margaret Chase Smith) and Percival Baxter. Serving in the U.S. House of Representatives from 1935 to 1941 and the Senate starting in 1941, Brewster became a close associate of Joseph McCarthy after World War II and an ardent supporter of McCarthyism, earning himself the vocal opposition of Margaret Chase Smith. He had also smeared Howard Hughes during the war, and Hughes bankrolled Payne's campaign and helped bring about the rare defeat of a Republican Senator in his own primary. Six years later, Payne would lose his bid for reelection to Ed Muskie.

Coffin also got to know another Republican at the time, one who would become a big asset to the Democrats shortly after the 1954 election. "I had relied on one of the Governor's friends," said Coffin, "Maurice Williams, who was in the finance department, to prepare data and charts, and Maurice [later] agreed to work with Governor Muskie to advise him [on budget matters] . . . ."[52]

If fellow Democrats had wanted to consider Frank Coffin a traitor for defending Governor Payne, all they needed to do to renew their faith in his fairness was to recall the election held in Lewiston a few months earlier. A blizzard had hit the state on February 17, the day of the election, and since it was obvious that nobody was going anywhere in all that snow, Coffin, who was the city's corporation counsel, and City Clerk Lucien Lebel decided to postpone the voting for a week. To say that the decision didn't sit well with Republican Mayor Ernest Malenfant, who was running for reelection, would be a huge understatement:

> He was furious. His principal base of support was in the central city and those voters could and would walk to the polls. His anger accelerated after the rescheduled election, when he lost. In complaining about his defeat, which he attributed to the delay, he referred to the corporation council as "that dirty double-crosser, Frank Coffin."[53]

The plot thickened on July 18, 1952, when Ed resigned his position at the OPS. Among his reasons for leaving, he cited the time he'd had to spend away from his family, the government's weakening of the price control laws due to the resistance of businesses, and "public apathy." Ed noted that he'd been considering leaving the post for a while, but had decided to wait until Congress had acted on the program. The OPS would be dismantled a year later with the ending of the war.

Though Ed had been on the job only eighteen months, he'd accomplished a lot, both in OPS regulation and in furthering his political career. His OPS coworker Milton Wheeler remembered that Ed traveled statewide addressing civic organizations, and "he learned, he became a very good speaker, and he spoke on the theory of compliance with the law. And he apparently was very well liked because he was invited all over the State of Maine to make speeches. And he did, and that's where he made a lot of his contacts, which later helped him when he ran for governor."[54]

Ed would later agree that the traveling helped him politically. "Yeah, it really did," he'd say. "There were so many small businessmen that appreciated the fact that we were not enforcement minded. We were compliance minded. So we sent teams of people around the state to help them meet the reporting requirements. And we handled each of those cases as an individual case. It did an awful lot of good."[55]

And there was yet another perk from Ed's time with the OPS. "[T]he staff we set up," said Wheeler, "became the organization for his first trial as governor subsequently, later. We used to meet at the Pagoda Restaurant across from the office, Chinese restaurant. The Pagoda was run by Henry and Danny Wong, who were clients of mine, so we'd go over there and conspire to set up a political team for Muskie. That was even before he was considering running for governor. So we had many meetings over there."[56]

But no good deed goes unpunished. Shortly after Ed's stint with the government ended, he found himself in a disagreement with the Internal Revenue Service over the validity of one of the deductions he'd listed on his tax returns. The $450 Ed claimed for gas for the 18,000 miles he'd put on his Lincoln (twelve miles per gallon at thirty cents a gallon) in one year was okay with the government since the travel was business related. What the IRS had a problem with was the $566 he'd deducted over the two years for his room in Portland.

The IRS informed Ed by letter that his Portland living expenses were "not incurred in pursuit of your law practice and were not incurred for the benefit of your employer." The matter would drag all the way to the Tax Court of the United States in Washington in 1958—Ed's last year as governor—before he finally settled the matter for a negotiated payment of $285. (On September 8, 1953, Ed would receive approval to practice before the Tax Court of the United States.)

A Broken Back

At the time of his resignation from the OPS, Ed declined to comment on whether or not he was about to become a candidate for Democratic National Committeeman from Maine, but his quitting was a strong sign that he was, since the Hatch Act barred him from political activity while serving as Maine's OPS chief. Indeed, just a few days later at the Democratic National Convention in Chicago, Tom Delahanty, who'd succeeded Ed as minority floor leader in the Maine House, nominated him to succeed F. Davis Clark of Milo, citing Ed's political record and noting that he could do more for the Democratic Party in Maine than any other individual.

Since he was neither a delegate nor an alternate, Ed was absent when selected by the group over Gerald Keenan of Mars Hill, 6½ votes to 3½ votes. As Maine's newest Democratic National Committeeman, he joined National Committeewoman Lucia Cormier, also a Rumford native. In an early August interview, Ed echoed what he'd told Dr. Donovan's class at Bates a year and a half earlier, that the Democrats need to offer qualified candidates and a constructive program and that they couldn't expect to receive public support based solely on Republican weaknesses.

Whatever weaknesses the GOP had, it kept them well hidden during the following month's election for governor, with early results showing the expected big win for GOP candidate Burt Cross, who defeated Democrat Jim Oliver 128,374 to 82,026, with independent Republican Neil Bishop collecting 35,711 votes. Even in the dark cloud of yet another defeat, Ed was able to find a silver lining, noting that forty-eight percent of the voters had wanted someone other than Burt Cross.

Maine's early election was over and done with, but that didn't mean that Ed could take a break. As a National Committeeman he became a defender of the Democratic Party, a role for which the editorial writer at the *Portland Press Herald* should have been prepared when he wrote that, had President Truman stayed overnight in Maine, it would have been "a dubious distinction" and that Maine could "breathe easier" because he hadn't.

In a typically well-reasoned response, Ed wrote to the editor that even though he hadn't expected "kindly" treatment of a Democrat in the paper's editorial columns, the writers at the *Press Herald* still needed to understand that "the President of the United States [is] an exalted office to which Harry Truman had been elected by the people of this country. In that capacity alone, I am sure that the citizens of this state, including the many, many fair-minded Republicans, would have been proud to have Harry Truman as a guest."

He concluded his rebuttal by writing, "I could never support General Eisenhower for President, but would be proud to welcome him as a visitor." At the time Ed could have had no idea that in less than three years he'd be governor and would get the chance to personally welcome Ike to Maine.

Margaret Chase Smith had been mentioned as a possible Eisenhower running mate earlier in 1952 but quickly put that rumor to rest. A popular joke of the day said that when a reporter asked her what she'd do if she woke up one morning and found herself in the White House, she replied, "I'd go straight to Mrs. Truman and apologize. Then I'd go home." One reason Senator Smith was held in such high esteem—besides her record of integrity in the U.S. House and Senate since 1940—was because of the "Declaration of Conscience" speech she had given on the Senate floor on June 1, 1950. Without mentioning fellow Republican Senator Joseph McCarthy by name, Senator Smith called for an end of the use of smear tactics in the hunt for Communists in the Truman administration. (The term "McCarthyism" had been coined by *Washington Post* cartoonist Herb Block in 1950.) In so doing, of course, she was also chastising her fellow Maine senator Ralph Owen Brewster.

But "Tail Gunner Joe" persisted, even stepping up his attack to include members of the armed forces. These new accusations resulted in the 1954 Army-McCarthy hearings, which were broadcast live on the ABC and Dumont television networks and included the famous exchange between McCarthy and Army attorney Joseph Welch in which Welch asked the Wisconsin senator, "Have you no sense of decency?" McCarthy was censured by the Senate on December 2, 1954, and died in 1957 of hepatitis that was probably exacerbated by alcoholism.

Of course, Ed was fully committed to supporting Adlai Stevenson and John Sparkman in their November 1952 presidential contest against General Eisenhower and Richard Nixon. One of the requests to come into Maine's Stevenson for President headquarters (in Ed's Waterville law office) was from Don Nicoll, news director at WLAM radio in Lewiston, who was trying to get a seat on the train for the October 29 Worcester-Boston leg of Governor Stevenson's New England campaign swing. Nicoll and Ed would meet a year later in Augusta at a reverse press conference (in which the Democrats asked questions of the reporters), and although they didn't yet know it, they would soon become close political allies.

In the Muskie Archives at Bates College is an unused invitation for Mrs. Edmund S. Muskie to attend an event in Washington at the Mayflower Hotel Ballroom on the evening of November 4, 1952. It's a sure bet that Ed attended the gala event, which ended in defeat for the Stevenson-Sparkman ticket. Jane probably chose to stay home with the children.

With yet another Republican governor residing in the Blaine House, and with Stevenson's loss to Ike, Ed must have felt it was time to move on again—or maybe he just felt the need to better provide for his family. Whatever the reason, by early 1953 he had become involved with a group of lobbyists centered around the Maine State House. "He was helping Carroll Perkins, who was a very distinguished lawyer in Waterville, who represented various companies," recalled former chief justice of the Maine Supreme Judicial Court Vincent McKusick. [57]

According to the *Bangor Daily News*, Ed had been approached by the Associated Industries of Maine to represent the organization at committee hearings on proposed changes to the Taft-Hartley labor law in Washington. Ed would later remember that "1953 was the year I did some lobbying in the legislature for a couple of clients, the Maine Central Railroad among them. And also the electricians of Maine, practicing electricians . . . who put together a code for setting

standards for the practice of . . . those engaged in electrical work."[58]
(The article notes that Ed and Lucia Cormier were already working
with party leaders to ensure an active campaign in 1954 and that
Lucia was coordinating with the Maine Federation of Democratic
Women's Clubs to organize women voters in each of the state's 628
election precincts.)

Just as Ed appeared to be eschewing politics to become a member
of the "Third House" of lobbyists, Frank Coffin resurfaced, stepping
into the spotlight alongside his Waterville cohort as another potential
young leader of Maine's Democrats. The scene was the April 22, 1953
Jefferson-Jackson Dinner held by the Cumberland County Democratic
Committee in Westbrook. There, in his first major political speech in
three years, Coffin called for "the party to mount the ramparts," said
Don Nicoll, "and change the State of Maine."[59] After pointing out that
the Democratic party had consistently gotten forty percent of the vote
in spite of infighting, underfunding, and lack of viable candidates,
Coffin rallied the troops just as he had in March 1950:

> He urged a turnaround, calling for a "long-range
> view," attending "to the grass roots, recognizing that life
> seeps up, not down, perhaps hire a full-time staff, and
> hold meetings all through the state, a sort of an 'open
> cracker barrel.'" He ended with the clarion call that
> would be heard over and over again in the 1954 cam-
> paign, "It's time for a change."[60]

Like his speech three years earlier, this one received lavish praise
from the press, most notably the *Lewiston Evening Journal* and the
Lewiston Daily Sun, which two days later said that Coffin's address
was "the best Democratic Party speech made in this state in many,
many years. . . ." The paper went on to call him just the type of leader
the party needed if it hoped to escape "the 'Death Valley' of Maine
politics."

With the help of big business, the Republicans ran the show.
The power companies were interested in keeping their rates from

being cut, while the mills and factories—the ones that turned out shoes, textiles, paper, and even sardines—were interested in maintaining a large pool of ready labor, which was all the better to keep wages low. Copies of the speech were sent to Ed and State Committee Chairman James Sawyer, but only Sawyer would be able to help in the short term, because a couple days after Frank Coffin gave his rousing speech, Ed would be in the hospital, teetering on the brink of death.

His troubles began while he was in the middle of a renovation project at his Waterville home. In recent years Ed had become quite a handyman, learning much of what he knew of projects such as laying floors and building cabinets from books he'd borrowed from the library. "I finished two rooms on the second floor and completed the stairs."[61] Once the stairs were complete, Ed built a temporary railing for the safety of his son, Steve. His next project was the hall closet. "Is this how you want the linen closet?"[62] he asked Jane, as he leaned back on the temporary railing. She had just started to tell him it was fine when the railing gave way and Ed fell into the stairwell, landing on his back on the bottom step.

"Since then," he would write in his autobiography, "I have been reluctant to step back and appraise my work, literally or figuratively."[63]

Seeing how seriously Ed was injured, Jane called Dr. Richard Chasse, who advised her to give him a shot of whisky while he was on the way. Soon the ambulance arrived and took Ed to Sisters' Hospital (which would move out of Waterville's downtown in the mid 1960s and become Seaton Hospital), where he was still a member of the Junior Advisory Board—and where Jane's sister, Virginia, had attended nursing school.

Ed was unconscious for two days, and it would be another two weeks before the doctors were sure he'd pull through. His recovery was long and rocky. Once he was given the wrong medicine, which must have caused him to hallucinate, because he tried to jump out the window and was prevented at the last second when a staff member entered his room.

Even when Ed had been healthy, his family had just been scraping by, and his accident put a huge financial strain on them. An
adding-machine tape in the Muskie Archives at Bates College shows
the amount paid just to nurses between April 24 and June 16—the
approximate dates of Ed's hospitalization—to be $1,364. When he
was finally discharged from Sisters' Hospital, it was with a large back
brace and a pair of crutches. He was still unable to return to work,
although a late-July photo of the Waterville-area Chamber of Commerce's Fund-Raising Committee shows him in attendance. During
Ed's absence from his practice, his loyal and capable secretary, Marjorie Hutchinson, kept the office running as best she could with the
help of her father. The family's other saving grace was Jane's brother
Howard, who pretty much supported them during that period.

Though he was behind the eight ball financially, Ed still had
too much Muskie pride to accept a handout, remembered Lewiston
attorney Jere Clifford:

> And a number of the lawyers in, around the state,
> particularly a fellow named Al Lessard, who was here in
> Lewiston, was Democratic, later became a judge. Any-
> way . . . he had been active in politics and he contacted a
> number of lawyers and they took up a collection to help
> him financially, and Muskie wouldn't take the money,
> he returned it, which is, I don't think [you'll] find too
> many guys doing that today.[64]

After about a month recuperating at home, Ed was "dying of
boredom," remembered Jane, so the family moved out to China Lake
for the rest of the summer. Though the Muskies' cottage a mile south
of China Village was peaceful and scenic, it was far from a vacation
for the couple. The tiny camp did have an electric water heater, so
Jane could wash diapers, but it also had a labor-intensive ice box that
needed to be resupplied with blocks of ice from a local farmer.

Ed devoted himself to his rehabilitation, which consisted mainly
of shedding his large back brace and crawling down the embankment

to go swimming. A far cry from the invigorating boyhood swims he'd enjoyed with his father in Worthley and Roxbury ponds, these swims were painful, laborious sessions targeted at restoring strength and flexibility to his injured back. At first he could swim only a few strokes, but each day he forced himself to do a little more, and by the end of the summer he no longer needed his crutches. Jane, meanwhile, had to deal with the stress of standing on the shore, a baby on each hip, watching him to make sure he didn't drown.

Ed had plenty of time to think during his recovery. His thoughts naturally turned at times from family, finances, and his law practice to politics, "and that's when I began to have different ideas," he said, "about what I ought to be involved in in politics."[65] Though details of the exact date remain foggy, all accounts concur that it was "late summer" when he called the state's other rising Democratic star. "It started the end of summer in 1953 when Frank Coffin's phone rang. Edmund Muskie was calling to invite Coffin and his wife, Ruth, to a cookout at his China Lake summer home."[66]

"[H]e was the national committeeman and I was nothing," said Coffin, adding, "I had been a keynote speaker in 1950 . . . at our . . . Democratic convention, but that was a one-shot appearance, and nothing followed after that."[67] (He was overlooking his highly acclaimed speech at the Jefferson-Jackson Dinner just a few months earlier.) Over the course of the evening, Ed and Frank discussed ways of injecting new life into the party. "What they talked about that evening over grilled steaks would change the course of history for Democrats in the state,"[68] a commentator wrote recently, but the two ended the evening simply by agreeing to stay in touch. "Ed and Frank saw themselves as working to build the party—not necessarily as candidates," Don Nicoll later remembered. Neither one could have foreseen what their collaboration would accomplish.

Change didn't come right away; an October meeting of state Democratic leaders in Augusta, which Coffin didn't attend, "produced expressions of continued commitment to rebuilding the party, and a few organization and communication ideas, but no action."[69] Specifics of the meeting included a decision to hold the Democrats' late-March convention in Lewiston and the naming of Lewiston Representative Louis Jalbert as general chairman of the convention committee. In addition, the party members decided to set up a permanent headquarters (which not surprisingly, would be in Lewiston) complete with an executive secretary. They also selected "It's time for a change in Maine" as their 1954 campaign slogan.

> The committee ended two days' sessions with adoption of these planks recommended by Democratic members of the Legislature:
> Call a special legislative session to re-apportion House seats, a project bypassed by the last legislature.
> Obtain aid for Maine potato growers who Democrats claim are victims of an "apathetic" Republican national administration.
> Prevent the "quiet death" of the liquor-corruption probe while Maine citizens remain "bothered and confused."[70]

As Ed was returning to a more or less normal life, the hospital in which he'd been nursed back to health found itself in need of emergency care. In a situation that can only be described as ironic, he found himself accepting the position of chairman of the Citizens Fund for Sisters' Hospital. Originally scheduled to run through the last half of November, the goal of the fundraising drive was $127,000 to cover the hospital's $24,000 deficit and pay for such desperately needed improvements as electrical work, a water main, two new boilers, a laundry facility, a freight elevator, a deepfreeze, an oven, and painting.

The $50,000 contributed by the hospital's medical staff still left a lofty goal of $77,000—a lot to be raised in just two weeks' time. Ed asked every working man and woman in the area served by the hospital to "contribute at least a day's pay" to the campaign. While the committee would eventually reach its goal, it would take a lot longer than two weeks, with many accounts of the campaign having it go well into the following February.

Ed was still thousands of dollars in debt to the hospital while he was leading the fight to save it. He never asked the facility to forgive what he owed, probably for the same reason he'd returned the money his fellow lawyers had collected for him—pride. He would support his family, pay his secretary, pay back his brother-in-law, and pay off his bills on his terms, no matter how long it took—and it would take a long while. He'd still owe Sisters' Hospital $5,000 when he was elected governor a year later, and was saved only by the fees he received for speeches he gave around the country between the election and his inauguration. "I was in the red at the time, all right," he would later remember, "but I don't think my debts were overwhelming. But if I'd lost that election, I would have been in sad shape."[71]

Chapter Four

Improbable Victory

A Reluctant Candidate

On January 6, 1954, Maine's fifty-one-year-old Republican governor Burton M. Cross, who'd been sworn in just a year earlier, kicked off a new political season by announcing that he was seeking a second two-year term. "Prefacing his announcement, the governor grinned at the reporters attending his weekly news conference, then without a word drew a grey felt hat from a desk drawer and tossed it over his desk into the circle formed by the newsmen's chairs and remarked: 'This is the day, boys, I thought you might be interested.'"[1]

Cross had been elected governor in September 1952 but began serving in an acting capacity on December 24, 1952, rather than January 6, 1953, because outgoing Governor Frederick Payne had resigned to begin his term in the U.S. Senate. As senate president, Cross had been next in line to the governorship under Maine's succession rules (Maine being one of seven states to have no lieutenant governor). Cross was in turn replaced as Maine's acting governor for twenty-five hours on January 6–7 by Nathaniel M. Haskell before being sworn in to his two-year term of office, making him Maine's sixty-first and sixty-third governor.

Maine's Democratic Party was more determined than ever to change the state's politics into a two-party affair. On January 9,

Democratic State Committee Chairman James Sawyer and convention committee chairman Louis Jalbert appointed Judge Alton Lessard, a former Lewiston mayor, to serve as the permanent chair of the State Democratic Convention to be held in Lewiston at the end of March. Lessard was a good choice, but Sawyer's next move was a major misstep.

Three days later, Frank Coffin found a black-and-white photo of himself on the front page of the *Lewiston Daily Sun* accompanied by a headline announcing that Sawyer had appointed him chairman of the Interim Platform Committee, whose duty it was to draft a platform for the convention. This announcement was news not only to Maine, but to Coffin as well.

"[A]t first I was infuriated," said Coffin. "Jimmy Sawyer had announced it. I don't know why he announced it, or . . . who put him up to it."[2] Coffin called his friend Don Nicoll, the WLAM radio newsman. As Nicoll later recalled that conversation:

> [He] was absolutely furious, and he . . . was so offended that he was ready to tell Jimmy to take it and go stuff it, and he called me at the radio station and told me about his reaction and what he intended to do and we spent a fair amount of time on the phone, and I said to him, "you know, yes, it's rude, it's thoughtless, and you have every right to be offended. But it also gives you an opportunity to shape things here, so just ignore it and go ahead, and nobody will remember it, and he finally cooled down and said 'okay.'"[4]

As for who had put Sawyer up to appointing him, Coffin needed to look no further than his friend Ed Muskie. "Ed," said Nicoll, "working through Dick [Kennebec County State Committeeman Richard McMahon], got Jim Sawyer to appoint Frank to head the preconvention platform committee."[5] Years later Ed would admit that he had indeed been behind the plan, saying that he thought it was important for the Democrats to get a person like Frank Coffin "up front." "His name was also known—and although his name was Coffin—it really had nothing to do with the death of a party, but with the expected life of a party,"[6] Ed punned.

Ed had been staying busy in other ways, too. He had recently taken on the duties of Waterville's city solicitor—which added an extra $2,200 to his annual income—and was still giving occasional talks around the state on subjects such as "What the Democratic Party in Maine offers young people" and "The role of the press in public affairs," during which he managed to praise the objectivity of Waterville's *Sentinel* newspaper several times even though the paper would never endorse any of his candidacies because it was one of several owned by Guy P. Gannett (1881–1954), a staunch Republican.

In early February Ed received a letter from Guy Gannett political writer Peter Damborg. It suggests that Governor Cross may have missed a chance to appoint Ed to a judgeship, thus removing the young lawyer from politics. "Dear Ed," it began:

> I read with interest Lal Lemieux's speculation that you may be considered by Governor Cross for a Superior Court nomination—to provide representation for your party.
>
> Between the two of us, may I ask if there is any basis in fact to such a story and, if not, can you tell me whether or not Governor Cross has indicated that he will (1) elevate Judge Beliveau, and (2) replace Beliveau with another Democrat.
>
> Still no word on top ballot candidates. Anything new from your corner?

This possible missed opportunity on Cross's part would soon come back to haunt him.

In the meantime, one of Damborg's hunches played out when Governor Cross named Rumford Judge Albert Beliveau to the Maine Supreme Judicial Court, swearing him in on March 3. In a development that had to be related, Ed turned down an offer to work at "a prestigious law firm" in his hometown of Rumford (most probably Beliveau & Beliveau on Congress Street) after reportedly giving much thought to the matter.

Once he'd decided to accept the platform committee appointment, Frank Coffin got to work developing a platform with the help of fellow committee members Jim Oliver, a former Republican from Cape Elizabeth who made no secret of his plan to run for Congress in Maine's First District, and tax consultant and Hancock County State Committeeman Roland Guite of Ellsworth. The committee's goal was to come up with a platform that would be built on consensus, accepted by almost everyone, and praised by the press. The group's first order of business in February was to develop a questionnaire so they could find out which issues the people of Maine found most pressing.

Coffin based the survey on one developed by Kansas politician Mike Harder. The questionnaire, said Ed, was "about issues such as needs of sea and shore fisheries programs. What do we need in conservation or transportation? Industrial development?"[7] Questions included:

Is there any justifiable reason for not combining state and national elections in November?

Does the Executive Council serve any useful governmental function?

Is there any justification for the failure of the Republican leadership since 1950 to bring about a reapportionment of the legislative districts in accordance with the Constitution . . . as recently interpreted by the Supreme Court?[8]

"I helped with it. Oliver and Guite played a passive role," said Don Nicoll, who added that Jean Sampson of the League of Women Voters was another key participant. "Frank, his kids, and several of the rest of us volunteers"[9] composed the questions, prepared the list, and stuffed, addressed, and stamped the envelopes. Years later, when

Coffin remarked that his role had included "the important function of licking envelopes," Ed responded with, "It's the only way you
can lick your enemies."[10] (Ed's predilection for puns has a name,
Witzelsucht, which means "a peculiar addiction to trivial joking."
Once, when asked what he thought a wealthy man who owned a large
boat should do about something, Ed replied, "I think he yacht to do it."
A reporter who covered the State House when Ed was governor said,
"He may have been a great governor, but all I can remember are those
awful puns. They were terrible.")[11]

At the end of February, 800 to 2,000 six-page questionnaires
(estimates vary) were sent out to teachers, college professors, sea and
shore fisheries experts, politicians on both sides of the aisle, and,
of course, the press across the state. Though not directly involved,
Ed thought the questionnaire was a great idea, saying, "First of all
it gave us a helluva lot of coverage in the press. The press thought
it was quite unique, that here the Democrats didn't have a candidate for a goddamned thing at that point, and they had appointed
a non-French person from Lewiston to chair the platform committee."[12] During an interview decades later, Ed, Frank Coffin, and Don
Nicoll would all agree that Peter Damborg of the Portland newspapers, Lionel A. "Lal" Lemieux of the *Lewiston Evening Journal,*
and Edward Penley of the *Lewiston Daily Sun* had all been "paying attention to the Democrats," but Lorin "Doc" Arnold of the
Bangor Daily News was a different story. "Bangor, I guess," said
Coffin, "was always a tougher nut."[13]

Years later, while running for president, Ed would recall the
importance of ideas that are responsive to the needs of the people
and how his run for governor had benefited from their input: "Even
before we Democrats had candidates in 1954, we solicited ideas and
produced a platform that was regarded as an outstanding example
of its kind at the time. My preoccupation with ideas as the center of
the political process is as old as my involvement in the politics of one
state, and I shall continue to be preoccupied with it."[14]

GOP recipients of the questionnaire hadn't been expected to
respond favorably, and they didn't. In mid March, when Gover-

nor Cross and his interim commissioner of health and welfare, Dr. Dean H. Fisher of Wayne, traveled to Lewiston to be interviewed by Don Nicoll at WLAM, they brought a copy with them. "As they walked in the door, Doc Fisher was waving this questionnaire that he had received, and making very loud and scatological jokes about the Democrats, and what did they think they were doing, and this showed how silly they were. And I smiled quietly," said Nicoll, "and said nothing."[15]

In the end about one hundred people thought well enough of the questionnaire to fill it out and return it, whereupon the committee compiled and tabulated the responses. The results were then discussed at party meetings around the state, and a platform for the upcoming convention was built. "This was a novel approach to the platform," said Coffin, "which otherwise would have been thrown together in a smoke-filled room during a night of convention."[16]

In early March things were looking no more promising than usual for the Democrats, with Lewiston newsman Lal Lemieux leading the here-we-go-again chorus:

> The Democratic State Convention, to be held in Lewiston, is only three weeks away but interest is at a low ebb.
>
> The official convention call has been issued and some of the caucuses already have been held, but enthusiasm has been lacking. It adds up to another bad year in prospect for the Democrats, who have been out of power so long on the State level that they just about have lost their courage. (Can't blame them too much, either.)
>
> As of today, there is only one top-level candidate for office, Edmund S. Hiscock, Damariscotta grocer who is settling his grudge against the sales tax by running for governor. His candidacy has proved unattractive to his own party members, even though there is none other in the field.[17]

Lemieux noted that Jim Oliver was "acting like a candidate" but probably wouldn't enter the fray unless the rest of his party's top candidates were equally as strong. Oliver probably wasn't encouraged by the fact that, by the time the convention got underway, the only other potential candidate besides Hiscock was Rumford's Eli A. Gaudet, a twenty-eight-year-old freelance reporter who'd decided to run for Congress in the First District. (A week after missing the April 19 filing deadline for the June primary, Hiscock would request 500 petition forms so he could run on the "Independent ticket for governor" in the September election. Gaudet would lose to Jim Oliver in the June primary.)

Ed and Frank Coffin "scoured the state looking for candidates," Don Nicoll later recalled. Ed himself did not wish to be a candidate for office, in no small part because he wasn't sure he was physically up to it. He would continue to suffer pain from his injured back for the rest of his life. Ed would write in his autobiography that Coffin "was determined to build a team of candidates in that election, and although I had doubts about my own physical capacity for campaigning so soon after a back injury, I shared his conviction and determination."

On March 24, just two days before the convention kicked off in Lewiston, the efforts of a group of Bangor Democrats to draft former Bowdoin College president Dr. Kenneth C. M. "Casey" Sills to run for governor hit an unexpected roadblock. It turned out that Dr. Sills had been born in Nova Scotia and was therefore ineligible to run for the state's highest office. Even if he had been qualified to run, he probably wouldn't have. After first citing the commitments he'd already made for the next couple years, the seventy-four-year-old added that "he felt younger men should be the candidates for office. 'Old men for council, young men for action,' Dr. Sills declared."[18] He would soon offer his counsel to the Democrats—and would be taken up on his offer.

Ed arrived in Lewiston the day before the start of the convention so he could attend the weekly noontime meeting of the Lewiston-Auburn Rotary Club at the DeWitt Hotel at 40 Pine Street, where he was one of the guests who heard Harold Meyer, manager of WPOR radio, talk about the upcoming launch of television station WMTW. "Mount Washington TV will cover a larger area than any other TV station in the world," Meyer said, adding, "The target date for our operation is the Fourth of July."[19] With a coverage area of 25,000 square miles, the new station would reach 1.5 million viewers in the United States and 350,000 people in Canada. This meeting could have prompted Ed to consider the potential of television to help the Democrats in their campaign.

Ed's early arrival also allowed him to address the Bates College Citizenship Laboratory of Professor John C. Donovan that afternoon. As expected, Ed spoke on the benefits that a strong two-party system would have for Maine. "An active two-party system," he told the students, "has the same effect as the system of checks and balances in the Constitution in preventing control of the government by a single power-hungry group or man." He went on to note, "The two-party system is the very incarnation of the right to express the opposition point of view. Monopoly promotes inefficiency, waste, and corruption, whether it is in the marketplace or in government."[20]

The purpose of the convention was to come up with a platform, not candidates, and the discussion of that platform was done in public. One reporter wrote:

> [W]hen the three-man pre-convention platform committee met to discuss their work with the full committee of 30 or 40 in "executive session" Friday night, the doors were open to the press. (At least they were not closed.) Newsmen were allowed to listen and take notes without let or hindrance.
>
> Why is this considered so extraordinary? It is extraordinary because it has never happened before.[21]

The scribe concluded that the Democrats' open session had "proved that a lot of today's secrecy is unjustified. It proved the folly of the hush-hush policy imagined by so many politicians to be the only 'protection' against a snooping public."

There was one other thing that Ed made sure was included in his party's platform that year. "No one was for pollution, but the citizens of Maine were not aroused against it. The Maine Democratic Party platforms of 1954 and 1956 are instructive. In 1954 we called for enactment of an 'anti-pollution law, tested by experience elsewhere, together with necessary positive legislation to combat problems of industrial and sewage pollution.'"[22]

The program of the 1954 Democratic Convention got underway in the early afternoon of Friday, March 26, all sessions being held in downtown Lewiston. Taking the stage in the City Building following the keynote address of Richard Dubord of Waterville and the remarks of National Committeewoman Lucia Cormier of Rumford, Ed started his speech by taking Republican Senator Joseph McCarthy to task for calling the terms of FDR and Harry Truman "twenty years of treason" (because, McCarthy claimed, they had been soft on Communism) and said the members of the GOP "seek to remain in power—not by virtue of their own constructive accomplishments—but by forever blackening the name of the Democratic Party." In the last five paragraphs of his address, which was published in the *Lewiston Evening Journal*, Ed called for all good Democrats to spring to action, even if those efforts might not bear fruit for another two years:

> For too long we of the Democratic Party in Maine have permitted ourselves the luxury of apathy and discouragement. We have found it easier to say, "what's the use!," and then sit back while a mere handful has sought to retain at least a shadow of an organization.
>
> It is time for us to get up and go, and there will never be a better time than right now. The means and methods of organization are not nearly as important as the will to organize.
>
> Opinions differ as to whether we should first have finances, or legislative and county tickets, or candidates for major office, or an organization. We need them all—

now, and at the same time. We need workers at every level—workers who will come forward without waiting to be invited. We need candidates on the local level— candidates who will come forward freely and eagerly to organize and give assurance to prospective candidates for higher office.

We need candidates for major office who are willing to gamble, who place the cause of good government above their own chances for victory, who see a clean, aggressive campaign as a means of building for the future—for themselves and the party—whatever the results of this state election. We need—if we are to produce these people—a great resurgence of the boldness and daring, the vision and enthusiasm which made our party and our country great this past twenty years.

To do it is our responsibility. The success of a political party is not an end in itself. It is merely a means of service to our state and our country. In these days of suspicion and distrust, doubts of the past and fear of the future, it is our responsibility to meet the challenge and the opportunity which are ours today.

Ed's speech seemed to get more coverage in the local papers than that of the speaker who followed him, former ambassador to Russia and Great Britain W. Averill Harriman. (Just as Ed would enjoy success in his Maine campaign, Harriman would be elected governor of New York in the fall.)

On Saturday the Democrats had their say about Wisconsin Senator Joseph McCarthy. Although it wasn't a part of the official party platform, which was limited to Maine issues, an anti-McCarthy resolution by Biddeford attorney Simon Spill got everyone's attention. While not mentioning Senator McCarthy by name, Spill's resolution "attacks the 'leadership' of the investigating committees . . . and declares that 'the methods used' are breeding 'suspicion, hatred, and disrespect' for American Democracy while lending comfort to our enemies (and) demoralizing our leadership to the point where association with governmental service is considered undesirable, and where patriotic and honorable men hesitate to assume responsibility for fear of individual humiliation and degradation."[23]

The Democrats wrapped up their business by early afternoon, the Androscoggin County delegation having elected Frank Coffin to the state committee, a move widely seen as a step toward making him state chairman. The Young Democrats Club met following the convention, and there was a "tea and style show for women at the Elm Hotel" in Auburn. Entitled "Bandbox Delight Fashions," the show was sponsored by the Bates Manufacturing Company and featured "Bates Disciplined Fabric in fashions to cover all occasions. It [included] frocks and sportswear that can be fashioned at home as well as those representing the leading dress manufacturers of the country."[24] An early evening banquet was held at the DeWitt Hotel with Lucia Cormier serving as toastmaster.

While Ed's speech resonated with the party faithful, the members of the press were harder to convince. It wasn't long after the convention that one of those newspapermen who'd been paying attention to the Democrats noticed that they didn't have any officially declared candidates for the major offices and wrote that the party had gotten into first gear and then second, but was now back in reverse.

The following Monday, March 29—the day after Ed's fortieth birthday—Ed, Dick McMahon, Colby professor Paul Fullam, and convention chair Alton Lessard met in room 211 of the Augusta House hotel to try to put together a slate of candidates for the June primary before the filing deadline just three weeks away. The Democrats didn't expect to win any of the major contests in September, but it was important to put together a ticket of capable candidates in order to shore up the party's credibility in anticipation of a Frank Coffin gubernatorial run two years later.

The meeting was discouraging. During the weeks surrounding their convention, Ed, Frank Coffin, and other leading Democrats had approached a laundry list of potential candidates for governor and come up dry. In a recent interview Don Nicoll confirmed that the list of those asked to run for Maine's top office had included Henry Benoit, Harold Dubord, Carl Moran, Jr., Paul Thurston, Dr. Clinton Clauson, Edgar Corliss, and Perry Furbush. And the Augusta House meeting appears to have been just as fruitless.

The Republicans held their convention in Bangor in early April. While they remained confident of staying in power, some chinks were beginning to appear in their armor. First, they were trying to distance themselves from the increasingly bitter primary contest between Senator Margaret Chase Smith and former Owen Brewster secretary Robert L. Jones of Biddeford. "Jones [is] an avid admirer of Senator McCarthy," reported the Associated Press. "Mrs. Smith and McCarthy are not friendly."[25] (Senator Smith would defeat Mr. Jones by a five-to-one margin in the June primary.)

The issue of McCarthyism posed an even bigger threat to party unity than did the dust-up between Mrs. Smith and Mr. Jones. "Leaders were worried," wrote Lewiston reporter Lal Lemieux, "about the possibilities of a serious party split if the issue is fought on the convention floor tomorrow [April 2]. There were rising hopes that a watered-down version of McCarthyism, possibly reducing the Communism threat to its effect on Maine, could be sold to the violent anti-McCarthyites."[26]

As for the top tier of the GOP ticket, only Senator Smith and Representative Robert Hale faced any opposition in the June primary, with Ray W. Stetson of Portland and J. Horace McClure of Bath both challenging Hale in the First District. (Hale would go on to win his seventh term in Congress in September.) Governor Cross and Second and Third District incumbents Charles Nelson and Clifford McIntire were running without primary opposition.

A few days after their Augusta meeting, the Democrats held their state committee meeting, where they elected Frank Coffin to replace Jim Sawyer as Democratic State Committee chairman. (Two months later a Lewiston newspaper would note, "Here is an unusual coincidence which has escaped attention: Lewiston had not had a state committee chairman for some fifteen years when attorney

Frank Morey Coffin was elected a few weeks ago. Oddly, he occupies the same law offices as the last chairman, the late Fred Lancaster!")[27]

Although the quickly ascending Coffin had already demonstrated outstanding leadership abilities, he couldn't pull his party out of the doldrums alone. He needed troops to lead, including candidates. Jim Oliver, who'd announced his interest in the First District seat before the convention, was still the Democrats' only likely candidate for a major office—and now only two weeks remained until the filing deadline for the June primary elections. The party still needed four more candidates to fill out the top of the ticket. Besides a gubernatorial candidate and someone to challenge Senator Margaret Chase Smith, the Democrats needed people to run in the state's other two congressional districts (Maine having three representatives in Congress at the time).

In mid March, two weeks before the Democratic convention in Lewiston, Ed had obtained 500 nomination petition forms from the State Election Division in Augusta, but he remained tightlipped about whom they were for, telling the Associated Press that he was "not at liberty to say at this time" for whom or which office the papers would be circulated. "The number of petitions asked," speculated the reporter, "would be sufficient for a congressional nomination, or possibly statewide office."[28] (Just a week earlier, Ed had told the *Waterville Sentinel* that he was not interested in running for governor or for the Second District Congressional seat.)

A week after he'd procured the forms, the *Portland Sunday Telegram* ran an article under the headline "Muskie may run yet," which read, in part, "It is a fairly certain conclusion now that the 500 nomination papers which Muskie requested from the State House over a week ago are for Perry Furbush, Palmyra attorney and farmer." (Furbush would end up not running for any office that year, reportedly because of "business problems.") The article also said that Ed was probably going to run for Congress in the Second District.

The incumbent in the Second District "was an alcoholic," said Don Nicoll. "And in those days you didn't report those things in the newspapers or on radio, but reporters talked about it constantly and we were pretty sure that Charlie Nelson, who was the congressman, sooner or later was going to stub his toe publicly and be ready to be knocked off."[29] But when Nicoll years later referred to Nelson as "incompetent," Frank Coffin came to the representative's defense. "He himself was a brilliant man in his prime," said Coffin. "[I]t's just, it was sort of a tragedy that he ended up that way, but he was just a bright rising star for many years."[30]

Until the moment he announced that he was running for governor, Ed's intentions remained the subject of intense speculation. The day before his announcement, Ed told *Portland Press Herald* reporter Peter Damborg, "The situation is still fluid. There are still some things to be worked out." He then added, "I hope that something will break within twenty-four hours."[31]

Damborg went on to report that he'd been told by a Democratic insider that First District candidate Jim Oliver was going to be joined by either Thomas Delahanty of Lewiston or Perry Furbush of Palmyra in the Second District and John V. Keenan of Mars Hill in the Third District. The insider also told Damborg, "I know that they have a candidate in line for the U.S. Senate [to challenge Margaret Chase Smith], but I understand they have to clear it with his employer. I'm told this should be done within the next two or three days."

On April 8, Ed finally put an end to all the speculation and made it official—he was running for governor. The points he made in his announcement sounded familiar to anyone who'd been paying attention:

> Maine desperately needs two-party competition at the polls and in the development of sound programs for the benefit of our people. We of the Democratic Party believe this. Independent, thinking people in increasing numbers share that belief.
>
> We need it if we are to have a government actively and intelligently working for the best interests of all of us all of the time. We need it if we are to insure integrity and high moral purpose in public office.

I believe that Maine people are asking for young, progressive, constructive leadership—men who place the cause of good government above partisan politics, who see a clean, aggressive campaign as a means of building a better future for Maine. They want a forward-looking program for the betterment of our state. I believe they are asking us to make it possible for them to enjoy the benefits of two-party government.

I believe that we of the Democratic Party have a responsibility in that connection. The success of a political party is not an end in itself. It is merely a means of service to our state and our country. In that spirit, I have decided to seek my party's nomination for governor in the June primary elections. In this campaign, I will try to measure up to the standard of leadership which I have described. I will do my best to discuss the issues and conduct my campaign in such a way as to contribute something substantial to the cause of better government, whatever the results of the election.

I am willing to do my part in bringing two-party government to Maine. The rest will be up to the voters at the polls.

There are as many stories about why Ed finally decided to run for governor as there are people to tell them, and almost all of them include some version of Ed saying, "Oh, what the hell. I'll run." Jane Muskie recalled that it wasn't fellow Waterville politician Richard Dubord who talked her husband into the race; he was "more of a speech writer," she said. "[O]f course it was his father [F. Harold Dubord], bless his soul, who convinced Ed finally to run."[32] Don Nicoll's memory was that "Ed ran for governor because no one else would do it." Ed recalled in his autobiography that his first instinct was to run for Congress so that he would have to campaign only in the Second District and not throughout the entire state, "but after a number of fruitless calls to other prospects, I agreed to take on the incumbent governor."

Battle Joined

Governor Cross immediately said that Ed was less than the best candidate the Democrats could have offered for the race, and perhaps he was right. "This was going to be a building year," said Don Nicoll, "no expectation of winning any of the top races, but to establish the Democratic Party as a credible alternative with a program that would appeal to voters and begin to bring voters into the fold for the next round. And part of the objective was to put together a ticket of candidates that could campaign as a team and would coordinate their campaigns and collectively appeal to the voters. I don't think that either he or the other candidates looked upon Ed as the star at the top, at least starting the campaign."[33] The whole idea of the 1954 gubernatorial campaign was to lay the groundwork for a Frank Coffin run in 1956.

Once Ed's intentions had been made public, the candidates for Maine's three congressional districts all announced in short order. The next day "Big Jim" Oliver, a former Republican legislator, made official what everyone had known for weeks; he was running in the First Congressional District. "Jim Oliver," said Don Nicoll, "was the one candidate who declared on his own, the others had to be recruited."[34] Also announcing that day was Third District candidate Ken Colbath, a political newcomer who owned a small music store in Presque Isle. Though he was not as interested in politics as the other top candidates, Colbath was a respected businessman in Northern Maine and believed strongly enough in the two-party ideal that he was willing to help the Democrats however he could.

The next day young Lewiston attorney Tom Delahanty let it be known that he intended to run for the Second District seat held by Charlie Nelson. "The needs of the Second District," said Delahanty, "require a fresh approach in an effort to bring about a 'New Look.' I shall work with the other candidates for public office in an effort to fulfill the requirements of the people of this state, and shall campaign at all times with a deep sense of honor and decency, having in mind the tremendous responsibility of the position to which I aspire."[35]

Though his statement hit the right note, Tom Delahanty didn't really aspire to the position—at least not at first. "Tom didn't want to run," said Don Nicoll. "[H]e was very comfortable practicing law in Lewiston, and his wife, who had observed the political world in her father's family, did not want him to run."[36] (Delahanty's wife, Jeanne, was the daughter of U.S. District Court Judge John D. Clifford.) And the family's opposition to Delahanty's candidacy didn't stop with Jeanne. She remembered their kids going to school and telling everyone, "Don't vote for my father, we don't want to leave here, don't vote for my father."[37]

"And Tom figured he had nothing to lose, he could run and make his contribution to the party, and be safe and continue his law practice after it was over," said Nicoll. "[But] about two or three weeks before the election, he got interested in winning, but by then it was too late."[38]

On April 16, Colby Professor Paul Fullam finally made it official, announcing that he was indeed going to oppose Senator Margaret Chase Smith for her seat in the U.S. Senate. A week earlier, Lal Lemieux had reported that Fullam was nearly ready to give "a 'go' signal" for his candidacy, but then had second thoughts about running, and for good reason. "The principal reason he didn't want to run," said Don Nicoll, "was a cardiac problem, and he pretty much decided that, no, it didn't make sense."[39]

Fullam's decision to drop out sent the Democrats on a frantic weeklong search for his replacement, who, it appeared, would be Edgar Corliss, a Bridgton attorney, who was serving on the Public Utilities Commission. After having thought it over for a while, Corliss was about to commit to running when Fullam called party leaders and announced that he was back in the race. He had changed his mind after a simple walk with his son, Conway, said Don Nicoll. "One night he was outside with his young son Con, and Con looked up and saw a plane in the sky and said, 'Daddy, is that the plane with the bomb?' And that just hit Paul, and he felt passionately about the question of war, and he decided he would run . . . and proceeded to elevate the discussion."[40]

"For the past twenty years, I have been teaching that active participation in politics is the life blood of the democratic system," said Fullam. "I cannot refuse the call to be a candidate for the United States Senate in the Democratic Party without repudiating everything I have taught over those years."[41] And once he decided to run, said Frank Coffin, "he got more signatures than he needed in a couple of days."[42] The fact that the Democratic candidates had been able to gather so many signatures in so short a time gave the group their "first indication that we might have some sort of an organization after all," said Dick McMahon. "And from then on the campaign was under way and we were traveling by the seat of our pants."[43]

Most of the Democratic candidates made the April 19 filing deadline at the Secretary of State's office in Augusta (the lone exception being Edmund S. Hiscock, who failed to gather enough signatures and would run as a write-in candidate in September). Just after 2 P.M. that day, "Muskie filed 4,933 signatures, or thirty-six less than the maximum allowed by law. Fullam's petitions contained 4,698 names. The papers for both of these men were circulated within the past week and the number of names is an impressive testimonial to their popularity."[44]

Although the collection of signatures for some of the Democratic candidates had been very last-minute, they had fielded a roster of candidates committed to the cause *before* they collected signatures on their petitions—which hadn't always been the case, according to Paul MacDonald, the Assistant Secretary of State at the time:

> Well it used to be a joke. The Democrats on the day, the last day for filing nomination papers, would all gather out in the Hall of Flags, and they'd spread their papers out on those [three-foot-wide] window sills and try to match up. They'd have a lot of signatures from Biddeford, and from Lewiston, and Sanford, and Waterville, and up in the [St. John] Valley, but they had

trouble getting candidates. And they would finally get somebody to agree, so they'd put the name on the petition after the signatures were there. I knew what was going on, but I wasn't going to try to police the thing; I really felt sorry for them.[45]

Some of Ed's nomination papers almost hadn't made it to Augusta—at least not unscathed. Future Lewiston mayor John Orestis remembered nearly ruining some of Ed's nomination papers during the return trip from collecting them in Rumford. "I was in the back seat and I was eleven and it was my job to go over the nomination petitions and make sure that the names were legible, and the towns that they lived in . . . corresponded to the towns the petition was certified in, and on and on. And I was getting carsick reading them, I remember, and saying to my father, 'I'm going to throw up right on these things if I can't take a break here.'"[46]

Once the Democrats' top candidates had filed, they wasted no time in downplaying their chances for victory in September. This was to be a dry run in preparation for a real attempt at victory in two years, nothing more. "When they worked up their slate of candidates for this year," wrote Lal Lemieux, ". . . it was admitted privately by leaders that the 'play' was to offer some top-notch candidates and build an organization this year, then enter those same candidates, in as far as possible, for a victory run in 1956."[47]

And there remained an urgent need for candidates down the ticket. "Ed and Frank were heavily involved in recruiting candidates," said Don Nicoll. "First for those major offices and then for the House and Senate seats, and county seats at the state level."[48] The significance of the party's organizing efforts in rural areas could not be underestimated. While support in some larger communities was to be expected, they were also gaining footholds in small towns that hadn't seen any Democratic activity in years. Thanks to Coffin's efforts, 123 new town and city organizations would be created during the campaign.

For example, at a meeting of the Androscoggin County Democrats in Lewiston, Coffin stressed "the importance of offering a full slate of Democratic primary candidates, [saying], 'We've got quite a job ahead of us,' adding that he will soon have compiled a list of open Democratic positions on which the group could take action."[49] He then explained that he would give the list to the county committee chairman, whose job it would be to fill the vacant positions with write-in candidates. "It's not a one-man job," he said, pointing out that the chairman would need the group's help.

A week after the filing deadline Ed officially kicked off his candidacy "by speaking at a Gray meeting," remembered Frank Coffin, "and labeled himself a young, middle-aged man. That was a pretty good meeting, as I remember."[50]

Portland newspaperman Peter Damborg agreed. "The Democratic candidate for governor," he wrote, "opened his campaign here tonight with this promise: 'I will hit and hit hard at the administration's mistakes and omissions wherever I may find them.'" Ed seemed to be warning Burt Cross that it would not be smart to underestimate him as an opponent. "There can be no real doubt," he continued, "that two-party government is the overriding issue of this campaign. This fact does not comfort those who have been paying lip service to the principle for years, but whose personal ambition caused them to fear the emergence of a strong Democratic Party."[51]

The day after Damborg's piece ran, his editors at the Guy Gannett Publishing Company were less enthusiastic about Ed's kickoff appearance. Their editorial pointed out that while Ed said he wanted to bring the two-party system to Maine, it was because of the Democrats' previous weak candidates that there wasn't one. The writers also called Ed weak for criticizing the governor's long-range plan to close the tuberculosis sanatoria in Hebron and Presque Isle and consolidate treatment at the Fairfield facility. The piece did allow, however, that "he is a top-flight candidate, and can be counted on to wage his campaign with decency and intelligence," before concluding that "the race for governor could develop into an old-fashioned two-party scrap, of benefit to the entire state."[52]

(It's not surprising that the editorial found fault with Ed's stands on the issues while also praising his "decency and intelligence." Written four days after the passing in New York of the paper's

The Democrats' slogan for the 1954 campaign meant what it said, and members of the underfunded party worked hard to try to make it happen.

founder, Guy P. Gannett, the piece was no doubt scrutinized by the *Press Herald*'s publisher, Jean Gannett Williams, who, like her late father, was a strong supporter of the GOP. Once, when several of her reporters asked her at a staff meeting, "Jean, why won't you endorse Ed Muskie?" she said, "Because he's a goddamn Democrat, that's why,"[53] in spite of the fact that she claimed to admire him and enjoy his company.)

That same day Governor Cross launched his own offensive, saying that the Democrats, instead of fielding candidates for the top five spots on the ballot, should concentrate first on building the party's base by getting qualified people to run for local offices and the state legislature. He was telling them, in effect, "that they're trying to put the roof on their house before they build the foundation."[54]

First District candidate Jim Oliver "called the governor's remarks an example of 'his cute technique of divisionary tactics.' It was designed, said Oliver, to stimulate a 'defeatist complex' among the Democratic faithful. 'The fallacy of his comment becomes clearly apparent,' Oliver continued, 'when we look back to the original election—in 1932—of Louis J. Brann as Democratic governor of Maine at which time there was a similar dearth of Democratic candidates.'"[55] Ed noted that, at the time, the Democrats unofficially had 108 candidates for 151 House seats and 27 candidates for 33 places in the Senate.

But Burton Cross was hardly one to be throwing stones. Everything he said and did was closely scrutinized and often criticized—frequently by members of his own party. Early in the year, for example, Cross had engaged in a back-and-forth with Eastport newspaper editor Gerald White about whether or not the economic situation in Washington County qualified as a depression. Cross allowed that things were bad but said they were no worse than usual in the area. After studying the situation in January, Sea and Shore Fisheries Commissioner Stanley Tupper had submitted a report to the governor but told reporters that, "for their own salvation, [the area people have] got to show more initiative." Tupper elaborated that "They'll have to get out and scratch. They'll have to borrow money from their friends and go lobstering, they'll have to dig clams in less accessible areas. . . ."[56]

Burt Cross said that his man had written a "wonderfully fine report," and he'd need to study it further before commenting. In an interview decades later, Tupper (who would serve in the U.S. House of Representatives from 1961–67) would basically chide the governor for agreeing with it. "Burt analyzed it," Tupper said, "and the press asked him what he thought, and he said, well, he says, 'Those people there have got to pull themselves up by their own bootstraps.' Wrong answer. Wrong answer."[57]

"Burt Cross was a very hated man," said Presque Isle attorney Floyd Harding. "I mean he went out of his way to irritate people.[58]

In early May Ed was booked into a "single room with bath" at the Mayflower Hotel in Washington, D.C., for three days. His last day there, Ed had breakfast in the hotel's Chinese Room with Democratic National Committee Chairman Stephen Mitchell, who'd taken a great interest in Maine politics in general and Ed's fortunes in particular. During the meeting Mitchell told Ed that the national committee would do its best to provide the Maine Democrats with funds and nationally recognized speakers to support the campaign, but in the end the state's Democrats would be pretty much on their own.

Building an Organization

After returning from Washington, Ed made campaign appearances in Westbrook, Sanford, and Kenduskeag (where two hundred people turned out to hear him) over the next week before the Democratic State Committee's mid-May meeting in Waterville. There the party leaders discussed fundraising and the need to obtain write-in candidates for all counties.

They also previewed some of the issues on which they'd be concentrating during the upcoming campaign. U.S. Senate candidate Paul Fullam "suggested that 'blueprints' for programs in education, housing, highway matters, etc., be made ready for a possible depression, adding that such preparation would be 'national life insurance of major importance.'"[59] Second District candidate Tom Delahanty said he would be taking a close look at the voting record of Republican Congressman Charles Nelson.

Ed added that no real steps had been taken to address the problems exposed by the recent liquor scandal. He also took the opportunity to issue a challenge to the incumbent, saying that he would be "willing to debate GOP Governor Burton M. Cross 'anytime after the campaign starts on any subject.'"[60] Cross would spend the remainder of the campaign trying to avoid debating Ed.

Frank Coffin had recently decided that, in addition to organization at the county level, the Democratic Party needed to have a centralized location at the state level—starting with an executive secretary. In a letter to party members, he announced the beginning of a campaign to raise funds to hire "a full-time executive secretary and furnish an office. Without a full-time executive, the needed work will be done only after hours."[61]

A goal of $10,000 was set, and fundraising efforts commenced. Once about $2,000 had come in, including $100 from each of the state's sixteen county committees, Coffin hired an executive director, who would be in charge of "party press-radio-TV relations, will assist in fundraising activities, and set up a permanent headquarters at Lewiston, with files and mailing lists."[62]

"And this man," said Coffin, gesturing toward Don Nicoll, "was foolish enough to accept [the position]."[63] Nicoll worked at the job part-time until officially finishing his work at WLAM on June 7.

Twenty-seven-year-old Donald E. Nicoll had been born in Boston on August 4, 1927, and attended Boston English High School. He majored in history and government under Paul Fullam at Colby College and in 1952 received his master's degree in the same subjects from Penn State. The married father of two then moved his family to Buckfield and worked as a substitute teacher at Stephens High School in Rumford before joining WLAM as a copywriter and weekend announcer. He had been promoted to news editor and reporter in 1953. Frank Coffin thought so highly of the talented young newsman with a reputation for asking sensible, thoughtful questions that he had sought out Nicoll even though Nicoll hadn't been among the three people who applied for the job.

Ironically, in early July, Republican State Committee Chairman John F. Weston of Fryeburg would appoint station owner Frank Hoy's son, F. Parker, to be the party's publicity director during the campaign. Nicoll described Parker, who'd promoted him to news editor when WLAM added UHF television, as "a gentle soul," while remembering his father as "old-school, very gruff, and conservative." Born in Lewiston, the younger Hoy graduated from Bates College and Columbia University and, like Nicoll, was a married twenty-seven-year-old father of two.

Unlike Nicoll, whose position with the Democrats was permanent, Hoy's assignment would be a summer job for which he'd take a leave of absence from WLAM. Nicoll remembered that he and Parker "stayed good friends even though we were on opposite

An older Don Nicoll as he looked while working as Senator Muskie's administrative assistant in Washington in the 1960s.

sides of the fence, and Parker eventually became a Democrat and was elected to the legislature as a member of the House."[64]

By May 18, the Democrats had secured an office at 110 Lisbon Street in the heart of downtown Lewiston (although it wouldn't officially open until the middle of July). The party's new digs were hardly palatial, outfitted with a typewriter, a mimeograph machine, and little more. Remembered Nicoll:

> [I]t was a single room lent to us by Henry Ben-
> oit, who was the owner of Benoit's store. . . . [T]here

was a branch in Lewiston [at the corner of Lisbon and Ash Streets] and he owned the building and a couple of doors down Lisbon Street from the store there was a small office at the end of the hall. . . .

. . . [A]nd it was lent to us, we didn't have to pay rent. We had a small desk that had been in a storage space in Henry's store that was probably at that point about sixty or seventy years old and breaking down and the top was worn, and one chair. And a local union painter had come in and painted the office and painted the name . . . the Maine Democratic Party, on the door.

And I remember during that campaign Ed Muskie and Dick McMahon, who was his campaign manager, coming to do some work on the campaign with me. Ed got the chair and Dick and I sat on newspaper piles because that's all we had for furniture.[65]

Coffin called the office's humble furnishings appropriate, "because, after all, the Democrats do represent the party of the common man." He also stressed that the office was being opened "on a permanent basis" so that "all correspondence is coordinated and literature is disseminated without any delay."[66]

Around this time the Democrats announced that they'd be running a "sticker campaign" to fill in remaining slots on the June primary ballots, especially in Brunswick and in several towns in Aroostook County. The stickers could be applied to ballots in order to "write in" a candidate who hadn't filed by the April deadline. "Write-in candidates need only as many votes to qualify for the ballot as they would have needed signatures for primary qualification, [Nicoll] pointed out."[67] Frank Coffin cautioned those who'd be passing out stickers not to be "undignified" by standing too close to the polls on election day. (At about this same time, twenty-four Democratic senators in Washington voted against a bill giving eighteen-year-olds the right to vote, preventing the bill from getting the two-thirds majority it needed for passage.)

Sun rises 5:07 sets 8:22.
Length of day 15 hrs.. 15 mins.
Day's decrease 18 mins.
Moon 14 days old.
High Tides Portland 10:53 a.m.
DST.   JULY 13, 1954

LEWISTO

VOLUME XCIV   Lewiston Weekly Journal Established 1847
Lewiston Evening Journal Established 1861   **14 PAGES**

"ORGANIZING FOR VICTORY"

MAINE STATE DEMOCRATIC COMMITTEE

DEMOCRATIC HEADQUARTERS OPENED this morning at 118 Lisbon St., Lewiston, and on hand to outline the first day's plans were Executive Secretary Don Nicoll and State Party Chairman Frank Morey Coffin. The office was opened on a permanent basis to coordinate all Democratic activity throughout the State.

Democratic State Committee Opens Headquarters Here

Portland Man Goes To Jail for Smokes

PORTLAND /P—Charles I. Coffin of Portland is willing to go to jail for his smokes.

Official headquarters of the Democratic State Committee were opened this morning at 10 a.m. at 118 Lisbon St. with State Chairman Frank Morey Coffin and Executive Secretary Don Nicoll outlining the first day's program.

Boy! Is This F

ERDING, Germany
U. S. Army helicopter p
ing in flood rescue work
varia, told this one toda
He plucked sever
rooned people from
house. Later he took
from a housetop who
vaguely familiar.
"Didn't I bring you
few hours ago?" th
asked.
"Yes," replied the m
enjoy riding in a helicop
so I went back by row

Denies Rele Of Two Fro State Prison

PORTLAND /P - Feder
John D. Clifford Jr. refus
to release two convic
Maine's penitentiary at
ton.
Vernon S. Brown of Ca
Harry E. Turner of Hart
filed petitions for writs o
corpus in the federal cour
pers, claiming that statu
them from further relie
state courts.
Brown was sent to priso
for attempted murder o
vorced wife. His sentence
to 5 years. Turner was s
in 1950 to serve 5-10 yea
sex offense. Both have
gain release through par
petitions for habeas corp
addressed to state courts.
Judge Clifford said it a
on the face of Turner's p
he hasn't exhausted rem
the state courts. He turn
Brown's petition because
State Supreme Court Justi
A. Tirrell Jr. had dismisse
tion based on the sa
legations—that Brown isn'

To say that Frank Coffin and Don Nicoll operated the Democratic Party's state headquarters in Lewiston on a shoestring is to overstate their budget.

A late-May telegram to Ed from Dr. Kenneth C. M. Sills exemplifies what would become the campaign's collaborative tone. In Western Union capitals, it read in part: "WILLING TO SERVE HONORARY CHAIRMAN WITH NOMINAL DUTIES OF COMMITTEE IN YOUR INTEREST TO BE NAMED BY OTHERS THAN ME." The missive of the Canadian-born Sills produced the desired result. "It was a campaign infused with idealism," wrote Don Nicoll, "symbolized by the creation of the Democratic Maine Advisory Council chaired by former Bowdoin College president Kenneth Sills and including representatives from business, professional, and labor leaders."[68] Dr. Sills would die suddenly in November, a month before his seventy-fifth birthday.

The pace picked up for Ed and his fellow campaigners in the week before Memorial Day. Ed's week started with a speech before 160 supporters in Millbridge (where he talked about the plight of the Maine dairy farmer) and a letter to his high-school friend Charlie Taylor, now living in Chappaqua, New York, in which Ed gave an honest assessment of his campaign. "At this point," Ed wrote to his old pal, "I wouldn't presume to state it any more strongly than to say that there is a real fighting chance this year."[69]

The rest of the week included speeches in Machias, Manchester, and at Bowdoin College (many of Ed's speeches having been written by Frank Coffin based on information gleaned from reports of the Federal Reserve Bank in Boston). But the week's big event was the one-day visit to Maine of Democratic National Committee Chairman Stephen A. Mitchell—who, a week before his arrival, had notified party leaders that his visit would have to be cut from two days to one, thereby eliminating appearances in Lewiston and Aroostook County.

Mitchell received VIP treatment during his brief stay in the Pine Tree State. The national chairman and his assistant, C. Aubry Gasque, were met at Portland's Union Station by Ed, Frank Coffin, Henry Benoit, and Dr. Sills before a breakfast meeting with party members in his suite at the Lafayette Hotel. Around noon Mitchell was joined by a hundred southern Maine Democrats for a luncheon in the hotel's Mayfair Room, where he "attacked what he called the

'nonsense and misconception' contained in the label 'liberal Republican.'" He went on to say that Senator Margaret Chase Smith "gets
the advantage of this nonsense," and pointed out "that liberal Republicans yield to Republican discipline and vote as Republicans."[70] The
party leaders then traveled to the Queen City for another meet-and-
greet session at the Bangor House.

Mitchell's stop in Maine proved to be a shot-in-the-arm for the
state's Democrats but little else. "Steve came in and was very sup-
portive and encouraging," remembered Don Nicoll, "but about all
he could offer was moral support at that time. They [the Democratic National Committee] didn't have any money."[71] (Mitchell did
promise to return the $5,000 that the state had raised for the national
campaign, but pointed out that that money had come from Maine's
Democrats themselves.) In the end a couple of "go get 'ems" and a few
"attaboys" from the DNC chairman had cost the party—especially
its leader—several thousand dollars, Frank Coffin later recalled.
"Yeah, my money," said Coffin. "And Don said, 'Oh, well, you can
advance it and we can pass the hat later on.' Well we did pass the hat,
but we didn't get much."[72]

Years later Ed would explain the behind-the-scenes agreement
that got the Maine Democrats their money back from the DNC.
"One way we raised money," he said, "was we contributed money to
the national campaign on the condition they return the money to us.
I mean, we wanted to have a credit with the national campaign, but
we didn't have any money to waste or to spend on it."[73]

Though it may not have been raking in the money, the party's
work ethic was netting them favorable reviews. By the end of May,
Portland newspaper editorial writers were expressing much more
favorable opinions of the Democrats than just a month earlier. A
piece entitled "The Busy Democrats" had this to say:

> It may be that the Republican Party in Maine is
> working as enthusiastically and as vigorously for success
> at the polls as the Democratic Party in Maine is work-
> ing.

We say this may be the case.

But we cannot say that we have seen much evidence of such git-up-and-git spirit among Maine Republicans thus far in the current campaign.

There's such a thing as being too sure of yourself, too confident in the inevitability of your victory.

For their own good, we urge organization Republicans in Maine to avoid over-confidence, to rub the sleep out of their eyes and take notice of the new zip and dash animating their wide-awake opponents, the Democrats of Maine.

The visit of Democratic National Chairman Stephen A. Mitchell and leading Democratic Party workers and candidates for office to this city Tuesday [May 25] ought to have stirred a tremor or two along Republican spines, it seems to us.[74]

Two days later the Lewiston newspapers concurred, saying that while the GOP had adopted a "wait-and-see attitude," it was the Democrats "who are making the headlines as they show the most activity since the days preceding the famous 1932 victory of the late Governor Louis Brann of Lewiston. In fact, some of the older party leaders see in today's conditions and enthusiasm a repetition of the pre-Brann days and read into it signs of possible victory ahead."[75]

Twenty Thousand Miles on a Shoestring

As May turned to June, Ed crisscrossed the state, making campaign stops in Orono, Brewer, Newport, and Brunswick. Though things seemed to be going fairly well, the miles beneath his wheels far outnumbered the faces in the crowds. He was already beginning to become discouraged—and the June primary was still more than a week away. It was clear that he would need help, not only with the all the driving to far-flung campaign appearances, but also with keeping up his spirits along the way. That help would arrive in the person of short, heavyset, cigar-smoking Richard J. "Dick" McMahon. McMahon would turn out to be Ed's right-hand man. "He had been instrumental in the development of winning campaigns in Waterville for the city council and the mayor's office. . . ," recalled Don Nicoll.[76]

Ed called him "my man Friday. . . . [H]e drove my car, he traveled with me everywhere, he was a combination politician, [and] public relations [man]. . . ." McMahon took care of everything, remembered Ed, no matter how big or small. "He handled the nitty gritty details of campaigning; trying to find a meal for us, a place to stay overnight, driving the car, taking care of all that housekeeping."[77]

"[Dick McMahon] was really a great resource for the whole effort," said Frank Coffin. "He was perhaps the savviest political mind that we had."[78] "[H]e was very smart and very shrewd," agreed Ed's friend Shep Lee.[79]

"[Dick] was a wonderful driver," said Jane Muskie. "I didn't have to worry about them crashing or getting into any kind of an accident because he really took his job seriously. He thought he was driving the President of the United States or someone. He was so thrilled to be driving a car and campaigning."[80]

Most adamant of all about his importance to the campaign is Don Nicoll, who said that McMahon . . .

. . . was probably one of the most important people of the campaign. He was a very able, shrewd politician. He was an accountant by trade and had been treasurer of the City of Waterville and had gotten to know Ed [there]. Friar Tuck was a good description of him, and he was very good for Ed on the campaign trail as his driver, and he jollied him a lot. He was resourceful because they had to figure out where they were going to stay because there was never any money, and they had to get along with less-than-optimal planning at the local level.

And Dick had not only a good sense of politics on the retail level, one-to-one, he had a good strategic sense. He's one of the individuals not often noted in references to that campaign, but I think he was absolutely vital.[81]

McMahon's first outing with Ed—a three-day Aroostook County swing—would turn out to be a trial by fire. (While some accounts of the campaign say that McMahon didn't start traveling with Ed until after this trip north, the following two stories about the pair's adventures suggest otherwise.) The 600-mile trip would have been bad enough on its own, but the decision to take Ed's well-worn 1949 Lincoln only made things worse. As Ed sped north through the treacherous Haynesville Woods in a dense fog, his car's bald tires and erratic steering were enough to make McMahon—an ex Marine— crawl into the back seat and lie on the floor. From that point on, the two used McMahon's new Ford for their road trips—and ended up putting an additional 20,000 miles on the odometer in the process. (In 1965, Maine country singer Dick Curless [1932–95] would have a top-5 Billboard hit with the Dan Fulkerson–written "A Tombstone Every Mile" about the road through the Haynesville Woods. "There's a stretch of lonely road way up in northern Maine / that's never, ever, ever seen a smile. / If they buried all the truckers lost in them woods / there'd be a tombstone every mile.")

The second story involves the two campaigners attending church on June 13 in Presque Isle. Ed and Dick were almost always broke, so when it came time to put money in the collection plate, Ed had to borrow a dollar from Dick, leaving his friend with just fifty cents to contribute. When Dick asked Ed afterward why he'd borrowed the dollar, leaving him with just change, Ed replied, "Because I'm the candidate."

An important stop in Presque Isle the next day was a two-hour tour of the tuberculosis sanatorium with a few members of the press in tow. After walking around the facility, which Governor Cross wanted to close along with the one in Hebron, Ed pronounced that, although it needed a few repairs, he found it to be in generally good condition and far from being the dilapidated fire trap Cross made it out to be. Ed went on to note that proximity to the patients' loved ones was an important factor in their recoveries.

"[T]hat served a very useful purpose in raising questions about Governor Cross' priorities when it came to people, their needs, and so on," Ed remembered later. "Some of those issues," he said, "[were] a substitute for the research which we didn't have."[82]

A few days after returning from The County, Ed addressed the Congress of Industrial Organizations convention in Belgrade Lakes. Two days earlier Governor Cross had spoken to a meeting of the American Federation of Labor at the Augusta House. The following year the two organizations would finally end their longstanding estrangement and merge to form the AFL-CIO.

That afternoon he drove to the next gathering on his agenda, the annual Jefferson-Jackson Day fundraiser, a formal $20-a-plate event at the Poland Spring House that would last until almost midnight. The evening's first speakers were "the four Congressional aspirants, all of whom stressed the need of hard work on the precinct and ward levels in enrolling Democrats and getting them to the polls in September,"[83] echoing the sentiment expressed a few weeks earlier by DNC Chairman Stephen Mitchell. Many Democrats, Mitchell had noted, "deserted their party to vote for Eisenhower," and he advised that they be "welcomed back into the fold. 'Of course,' he commented, 'we won't make them deacons right away, but we should keep the church door open.'"[84]

After listening to the Maine candidates speak, the nearly 200 guests heard from U.S. Senator Warren G. Magnuson of Washington State, who "declared that although 'the people voted for Eisenhower in 1952, they got the same old Republican Party and the GOP's same old reactionary policies of deferring to the special few.'" Magnuson went on to charge that "the Republican mentality 'had not changed one iota.' He dissected Republican policy on agriculture, McCarthyism, the Federal budget, the National economy, and foreign affairs to prove it."[85]

Prior to the fundraiser, Ed received a note from State Senate candidate Alton Lessard, who'd chaired the Democratic State Convention in March, alerting him that he would be expected to speak for about ten minutes at the dinner and that he needed to type his speech so it could be distributed to members of the press immediately afterward. Lessard's note also informed Ed, "We are expecting you and Mrs. Muskie to be at the head table and have decided that at least the head table should be in formal attire. That doesn't mean silk hat and tails, but tuxedo and evening gown, the evening gown to be on your wife, preferably, not you."[86]

The following Monday an article about the dinner by *Lewiston Daily Sun* reporter Edward Penley included a sidebar about how quick thinking on the part of Frank Coffin had averted a fashion *faux pas* at that evening's gala:

> Democratic diners at Poland Spring were enlivened Saturday night, not by "who stole de ding-dong," but by which coat Toastmaster Coffin was wearing. The state chairman, in introducing Edmund Muskie, said he had originally agreed that if Muskie wore black formal attire, Coffin would also, despite the rather depressing implications his name brought to mind. But later it was agreed among the others to dress in white, so the toastmaster showed up in a white coat also.
>
> However, he felt he should carry out his promise to Muskie, so in full view of the delighted audience, Coffin stripped off the white coat and donned a black one prior to Muskie's speech.
>
> But that was not the end of it. After the gubernatorial candidate concluded, the toastmaster read a message from the movie cameramen. It said: "Please take off black coat and put on white one. We have half a roll of film showing you in white coat. People will think we

are making magic."[87] [A newspaper photo of the head table shows Coffin wearing the white coat.]

Not only was June 21 the first day of summer, it was also Primary Day in Maine, and enough voters trudged to the polls in ninety-degree heat to give the unopposed Burt Cross 97,052 votes, a figure he called "a whale of a vote of confidence" in his chances for reelection. (He had gotten 54,865 votes in 1952's three-way primary.) He had done so well, in fact, that there was even a rumor circulating at the time that supporters of Senators Smith and Payne were reluctant to endorse him, fearing that he'd do too well and decide to run for one of their seats in the future. Ed received 17,221 votes.

While Frank Coffin continued to address the party's other needs, such as finances and organization, Ed was more than satisfied by the list of candidates who were joining him for a run at the major offices. "[T]he most important ingredient," he would write later, "may well have been that team of candidates who had nothing to gain from the campaign, but who believed in their cause, took the party's platform seriously, and were able to offer Maine voters a genuine alternative to one-party domination of the state."[88]

Paul A. Fullam was a forty-seven-year-old college professor from Sidney whose first attempt at politics would be to challenge Margaret Chase Smith for her seat in the United States Senate. A native of Portsmouth, New Hampshire, he had graduated from Portsmouth High School and Harvard University and had joined the Colby faculty in 1941. He became chairman of the college's History and Government Department in 1949 and had been granted a leave of absence from the school so he could campaign without losing his status as a professor.

"Paul at Colby had been my advisor when I was an undergraduate there," said Don Nicoll, "and I used to [say]. . . Paul didn't have students, he had disciples—he inspired students. His Democratic sentiment was well known though he had been a Republican because, in his view, the only place to influence the final choices in September was to participate in the Republican primaries."

Fullam's earlier support of his opponent Margaret Chase Smith, when she had run against Owen Brewster, would cause him problems when, two days before the election, she'd come out and say that Fullam was a registered Republican and had supported her. With no time to respond before the election, Fullam would take the unusual step of finding the money to go on television two days *after* the election to defend himself.

James C. Oliver of Cape Elizabeth, running in the First District against Robert Hale, was a fifty-nine-year-old real estate salesman who had graduated from Bowdoin College. He was married with one son. He had served as a Republican state legislator from 1937 to 1943, but had become a Democrat in 1949 and had run unsuccessfully for governor against Burton Cross in 1952. He had served as an army officer in World War I and as a Coast Guard officer in World War II.

Thomas E. Delahanty, opposing Charles Nelson in the Second District, was a forty-one-year-old Lewiston attorney who was married to the daughter of U.S. District Judge John D. Clifford, Jr. A former minority leader of the 95th legislature, Delahanty had graduated from Lewiston High School and Columbia University School of Law, and had been a lawyer since 1938. His first public office was as corporation council of the City of Lewiston, following which he spent three years as an FBI agent during World War II. In 1945 he was named assistant county attorney of Androscoggin County. He was elected alderman in 1949 and served as president of the Lewiston city council in 1951 and 1952. His civic affiliations included memberships in the Elks Club, the Rotary Club, and the Knights of Columbus. He and law partner Alton A. Lessard maintained an office in the Knights of Columbus building at 103 Park Street, the next street over from the tiny Lisbon Street office of the Democratic State Headquarters.

Kenneth B. Colbath, running in the Third District against Clifford McIntire, was a fifty-six-year-old Presque Isle music store owner. A University of Maine graduate and World War I navy veteran, he was married with two daughters. According to Don Nicoll, Colbath "was probably the most apolitical of all the candidates, but well respected—a thoroughly decent guy, and willing to do anything to help the party."[89]

The campaign now intensified, and Ed began making an increasing number of appearances throughout the state. He and the other top-of-the-ticket Democrats traveled to Portland the Sunday after the primary to appear live in a spot they'd purchased on WCSH television. The objective of the half-hour spot, said Ed, "was to introduce the issues of the campaign and also let the voters know that . . . Democratic candidates did not have horns."[90] Paul Fullam spoke first, followed by the three congressional candidates. Ed closed out the program, which ended with a wide shot of the candidates and their spouses.

The 7 P.M. airing went well in spite of the fact that Frank Coffin, the program's moderator, was probably a bit tipsy by the time the group arrived at the studio. They'd rehearsed their appearance at the Cape Elizabeth home of Democratic Party elder Henry Benoit, who turned out to be an overly attentive host. Unbeknown to Coffin, who was concentrating on the task at hand, Benoit kept refilling the drink glass sitting next to him, and Coffin's "one drink" turned into several. But he handled himself well, and the members of the group assured him that only his close friends could have detected any change in his demeanor.

Television coverage had swept the state just in time to help the Democratic Party promote its gubernatorial candidate, who seemed tailor made for the new medium. The first station to go on the air (in early 1953) had been WABI in Bangor, which was owned by former GOP governor Horace Hildreth. By Thanksgiving, Lewiston's WLAM launched its own short-range UHF station, which broadcast on channel 17, and quickly partnered with another UHF station, WPMT in Portland, to form the Maine Television Network.

While the state's two UHF stations would be short lived (WPMT would close in December 1954), more of the powerful VHF stations were about to hit the airwaves. Just before Christmas 1953, NBC affiliate WCSH began sending its 100,000-watt signal from its studio at Portland's Congress Square Hotel, and in May 1954 Guy Gannet's CBS-associated WGAN (now WGME) also began broadcasting from Portland. And, as mentioned earlier, plans were underway for WMTW television, which would have studios in Poland Spring and a broadcast tower atop Mt. Washington.

"We devised a plan," said Don Nicoll, "to use television at the beginning of the campaign to introduce the major candidates, and then at the end of the campaign to reinforce it."[91] While television did play a role in the campaign, its status as a game changer has been exaggerated by many of the pundits, said Don Nicoll. "Television was important only, I think, because it introduced to key audiences in the metropolitan areas the Democrats for the first time so the voters could relate to them as individuals, and not as labels. And the whole effort of our television advertising," noted Nicoll, "was to present the candidates as individuals, as reasonable [people] who could identify with the voters, and with whom the voters could identify."[92]

Ed himself had a higher opinion about the value of television, maybe because he was out there in front of the cameras and could see for himself how well they were doing in their efforts to appeal to the people of Maine. "[T]elevision, in my judgment," he would later say, "was a much bigger factor in the results in 1954 than the media had ever credited."[93] Ed figured out early on how to appeal to almost every television viewer, something Burt Cross never learned to do. (Some people never would figure out how to come across well on TV. Ed said of his friend and 1968 running mate, Hubert Humphrey, "He was too 'big,' too 'hot' for television, and there was in his style a strong strain of the evangelist, almost a shouter—effective in some crowds, and all wrong for the medium of television.")[94]

Governor Cross's appearances in front of the camera were almost universally panned. Maybe he had no sense of how to campaign in a general election; for years the big action had come as the Republicans fought it out in the June primaries, and a GOP landslide in September was a foregone conclusion. He was "a no-nonsense small businessman," said Don Nicoll, "who felt that you did your job—and if you did your job, you would succeed."[95]

Former UPI reporter Jeb Byrne recalled that, on television, Ed "came across as very articulate and with his progressive program as compared to his incumbent opponent, Burt Cross, who came across as sort of self-satisfied and arrogant."[96] Others noted that the Republican candidates in general came across as shopworn reruns on TV. "The Democrats offered the new show, the new faces, on television."[97]

Cross's bigger problem, according to just about everyone who knew him, was his personality. He was "very staid, longwinded, slow, pleasant," said WABI newsman Phil Johnson, "your father-type image person. Nice guy, tried very hard to provide what the newspaper people wanted, and tried to adjust to these new guys with their cameras and microphones, which seemingly by contrast, came like second nature to Ed Muskie, thanks to Don Nicoll."[98]

"It was a lot easier," said Johnson, "to anticipate a couple of good questions and quick and brief answers from Ed Muskie than it was with the typical political figure of the day, who usually, once he saw the lights on and the microphone in his face, started making a stump speech." Ed thought about what he was going to say, a trait that led not only to well-reasoned responses but to a conciseness that television reporters loved. He was "very sensitive to the idea that long-windedness led to an awful lot of editing at the studio, and he learned to use the thirty-second sound bite very readily."[99] Without realizing it, Ed may have uttered the very first political sound bite when he said, "Maine desperately needs two-party competition at the polls and in the development of sound programs for the benefit of our people."[100]

With television his Achilles' heel, it's no wonder Burt Cross was reluctant to debate Ed on TV—or anywhere else for that matter—even though Ed had been challenging him to do just that since May. It's also accepted political wisdom that the frontrunner has little to gain and much to lose by sharing a stage with his challenger. There is only one mention of a debate in the campaign. Former *Press Herald* reporter Roger Snow, who had recently become the publisher of the *Westbrook American*, remembered moderating a debate between the two on short-range UHF-TV, probably WPMT in Portland. "I don't think many people watched it," said Snow. "But both Muskie and Cross accepted the invitation. And it was a walk-away for Muskie. Cross, I think, didn't think he had to do too much homework for it. He expressed his opinions without documenting them. Muskie would express an opinion and document it."[101] That one debate probably decided Cross against accepting any others, and he probably considered himself lucky that not many people saw it.

June 29, 1954, was a pivotal day in Ed Muskie's campaign—and his life. By all accounts that was the day he stopped being a competent public speaker and became an eloquent, charismatic orator. Everyone involved, including Ed himself, credited his Rumford roots and his father for the change. On their way to Rangeley, Ed and Dick stopped in Rumford, where the candidate spent time in quiet conversation with his father, who was seventy-two and not in the best of health. The rest of the way to Rangeley, where Ed was scheduled to address a sportsmen's group, he thought about his happy childhood and the times he'd camped and fished with his father at nearby Four Ponds. Just before they reached their destination, the pair stopped to take in the majestic view from the Height of the Land scenic turnout, and the memories of his boyhood days became even more vivid.

That evening "he just got carried away by the memories and he carried everyone there away with him," said McMahon, who was sitting in the back with *Press Herald* reporter Peter Damborg. "[A]nd you could hear a pin drop, the guy was so sincere. They came there expecting to hear him tell them about why he ought to be governor and instead he's telling them about fishing with his father. It was wonderful."[102]

"And he talked about what a great country it was, his father, a tailor, coming over to this country and how he had been able to get an education and was able to really join the mainstream of American life. And Damborg wrote that as he carried on this theme, everybody in the room just became riveted to him."[103]

Years later Ed still remembered that talk vividly:

[A]ll I know is that I caught fire for some goddamned reason. And you know, I forgot about rigid
speeches and all that. I had something I wanted to talk
about, and it just flowed. And it had apparently an ignit-
ing effect, you know. The crowd got very enthusiastic,
and I began to like it and enjoy it. And so I acquired,
I think, the beginnings of a campaign style that night
and that I embellished as the campaign went along.
And it was amazing, the crowds that we drew from
then on. The spark began to spread, and the people got
excited, and we got these editorials in these small-town
papers."[104]

"[Ed's] own magnetism as he developed into a campaigner,"
agreed Frank Coffin, "certainly played a very large part [in his
success]."[105]

As June turned to July, while the Republicans were meeting in
Rockland, Ed was addressing a church group at a chicken-pie sup-
per in Castine, where he once again captivated his audience, talking
about how young Mainers were leaving the state to find good jobs.
"Night after night he soared on that point, as mothers wept in the
front rows of little Grange halls. Watching those tears one night,
McMahon found himself thinking perhaps they did have a chance.
'And in a minute, Jesus, I was crying myself. Of course, I'm a senti-
mental bastard, but still. . . .'"[106] In September Ed would carry heavily
Republican Castine with 125 votes to 108 for Burt Cross.

Ed spent the nation's 178th birthday in Portland, where he made
the most of his recent Office of Price Stabilization contacts, not to
mention his and Dick's connections with AMVETS and the VFW.
And he once again chided the governor for his callous comments
about the state of the economy in Washington County. "That they
have accomplished so much," he remarked, "is to their everlasting
credit."

A week after the Fourth, when Ed was appearing at the Belfast
Broiler Day festivities, Augusta hardware dealer Leroy Hussey grudg-

Looking very much the candidate, Ed enjoys the chicken at the Belfast Broiler Festival in July 1954. The shoestring campaigner and his "Man Friday," Dick McMahon, never passed up free food.

ingly agreed to give his endorsement to "the GOP ticket for this year, if leaders ask for it."[107] A former chairman of the governor's advisory council, Hussey had engaged in a bitter primary battle with Burt Cross two years earlier, and Republican leaders were afraid he might join a new statewide movement called Republicans for Muskie.

The ringleader of the anti-Cross movement was Neil S. Bishop, who had been the third member of that contentious 1952 GOP primary battle along with Hussey and Cross. A mustachioed fifty-year-old farmer from Stockton Springs, Bishop "was a quixotic character," said Frank Coffin, "a little rougher version of Ross Perot in some respects." One writer described the rogue Republican as "a morose political maverick."[108] Having been defeated in the 1952 primary, Bishop had run as an independent candidate and managed a respectable 36,000 votes in the general election, becoming a one-man political party in the process, since he'd received more than one percent of the ballots cast in a gubernatorial election. Now he decided to support Ed and founded the Waldo County Republicans for Muskie.

He urged those who'd supported him in the past to get behind Ed, and a lot did. Just how many converts he made is unclear, but they included such prominent Republicans as Mort Harris of the Harris Oil Company in Portland, car dealers Ike and Norris Friend of Newport (who erected a huge billboard in support of Ed), and Palmyra dairy farmer Obed F. Millett, whose support of the Democrat would end up costing him a government appointment the following year.

After the election, Bishop would claim that he and his followers had spent $654 in support of the young Democrat. Bishop's support would evaporate, however, once Ed declined to give him a seat at the table in the new administration. Eventually Bishop would revert to his Republican roots, running against Frank Coffin in the 1958 Congressional race.

By mid July the *Lewiston Evening Journal*'s Lionel Lemieux (the "dean of Maine political writers," according to an unattributed piece in his own paper) was predicting a GOP landslide in the general election. "The vote in the primary," Lemieux told the Lewiston Kiwanis Club, "shows that the much-heralded Democratic resurgence is only a ripple on the political lake."[109] It was hard to argue with him at the time, Governor Cross having outpolled Ed by nearly six to one in their respective primaries. If Ed "really had captured the imagination and hearts of the Democrats of Maine," Lemieux continued, "his vote would have been nearer 30,000 [than the 17,000 he actually received]."

"Frank [Coffin] was very upset about that story," Lemieux recalled decades later. "As a matter of fact . . . for a while there he was kind of offish. But we became friends again as the years went by."[110] Following Ed's victory in September, the Democrats called Lemieux "Ripples."

Two days after his Belfast stop, Ed made a trip to Portland for an appearance on WCSH. This latest television appearance was probably on Channel 6's *Community in Focus* program, which ran from 6:00 to 6:15 P.M., right after *The Betty White Show, Pinky Lee*, and *Howdy Doody*. Of the spot's fifteen-minute running time, Ed had to fill thirteen-and-a-half, which he probably did with an off-the-cuff talk based on a few mental notes.

Around the middle of July, the Democratic candidate made a stop in Ellsworth where he likely was the guest of honor at one of the many bean suppers he attended that summer. "Muskie had been holding these bean suppers all over the state," said former Deputy Secretary of State Paul MacDonald, "which was something unique so far as political campaigning was concerned. But it was just right for Maine people; they love bean suppers."[111] And bean suppers were okay with Ed and Dick too; not only did they attract a good crowd, they also meant the two would be able to eat—something they couldn't usually afford on their long road trips. Over the course of the campaign, Ed would lose twenty pounds.

Passing through Newport one night, they had enough money between them for only a pack of cigarettes, two coffees, and a donut—which they split. The nights on which they were able to return home to Waterville, they usually arrived long after dark and always hungry, "and we would sit around and they would tell me everything that had happened all day along the route," said Jane. "The worst part of it was that they never had any money left. . . . I kept saying, 'Now do you remember I gave you so much money this morning?'"[112] But she knew what was coming. "[T]hey always talked me into giving them a very late dinner every night."[113] (Contrary to what most people believe, Jane frequently traveled with her husband, once saying that she had campaigned in every county except Aroostook.)

"They started broke," wrote Muskie biographer David Nevin, "and things didn't get any better."[114] On the rare occasions when

Ed could afford to eat at a restaurant, he'd take the opportunity to engage in what he called "sabotage," although it was hardly the stuff of spy novels. On a microfilmed roll of Ed Muskie newspaper clippings in the lower level of Ladd Library at Bates College are two items. The first is an undated United Press newspaper clipping with the headline, "Democrat knows sabotage methods," below which is the following brief article:

> A Democratic candidate for governor in the dominantly Republican State of Maine had told party workers how he acts when he goes into a town where he is not known.
> "No matter how good the food is at the restaurant where I eat, I complain about it," explained Attorney Edmund S. Muskie.
> "No matter how good the service is, I find fault with it. And as I depart without leaving a tip, I tell the waitress, 'Don't forget, vote Republican.'"

Below that is a typed response from a "Nebraska Republican," who says that Ed really isn't as clever as he thinks he is:

> We aren't worrying. These Republican waiters and/ or waitresses aren't so dumb—they more than likely spit in his soup or victuals long before he departs without leaving a tip.

Ed and the rest of the Democratic Party were attempting to engage in retail politics on a shoestring budget. "A hundred dollars would be a big contribution here," said Frank Coffin. "Several people would give $500, but mostly it was nickel and dime."[115] By the time the Maine Democrats had raised $14,000 of the $18,000 they'd eventually accumulate (which included the $5,000 the DNC had returned), Tom Delahanty told a Massachusetts politician how much they had. "Jesus Christ," retorted the southern New Englander, "in Boston we spend that much for beer alone!"[116] And that $18,000 would be for all five of the top races! By comparison, the Maine GOP had set its fundraising goal at $41,000 by early August—$29,000 of which had been earmarked for the Republican National Committee.

The Democrats' total television budget for the campaign was $2,000—although some people recall it being twice that amount. Fifteen minutes of prime time TV cost $100, and a front-page newspaper ad was fifteen dollars. Besides investing in electronic and print media, the Democrats also had to buy bumper stickers, of which they could afford only 1,000 at a time. Since the bumper stickers represented a considerable investment, party leaders tried to make sure they'd be put on cars that would be on the road a lot during the campaign—and that they'd stay on them until the election was over.

"There was only one candidate who did better than us in bumper stickers," joked Frank Coffin, "and his name was Ausable Chasm"[117] (a tourist attraction in New York State). On at least one occasion Ed had to write back to a supporter who'd asked for a few bumper stickers and tell him they were temporarily out, but he'd send some along as soon as the next shipment arrived.

Another big investment was a bullhorn that Ed and Dick put to good use during their travels. Though it had cost twenty-eight dollars, nearly a week's wages for many workers at the time, the bullhorn more than paid for itself by helping the two assemble small crowds in the town squares of the countless rural communities through which they passed. Once a few people had gathered, Ed managed to impress most of them with his well-reasoned argument about why Maine needed two-party government and why he was the one to bring it to them.

It was this one-on-one interaction with people that Ed valued most, and he couldn't get it from TV. "You get that important response directly from audiences, if you are sensitive at all to them. I am sensitive not just to applause, but to the feel of an audience, whether it's good, whether it's bad, whether it's thoughtful, or whether it isn't. You get comments afterward; they aren't exhaustive, but they are representative, and you get the evaluation of the local press."[118]

He didn't just talk to people, he listened to them—which was something the Republicans had not been doing enough of recently. Thanks partly to their sure-of-themselves attitude and partly to the backlash caused by President Eisenhower's landslide win, Ed found his door-to-door canvassing—even in staunchly Republican Bangor—to be "reassuring."

Between visits to the coastal communities of Portland and the Boothbay region, Ed stopped in the Central Highlands town of Winn, where he took issue with yet another of the administration's projects, the state's roads. Ed told the rally that the highway reclassification plan Governor Cross had proposed was a "weak-kneed approach" to the matter of maintaining Maine's deteriorating roads and would not provide a solution. Indeed, he argued, it would only intensify the problem by shifting more of the burden onto the state's cities and towns.

He closed out his July travels with a southern swing through the Augusta area, to Democrat-friendly Androscoggin County, and finally to Springvale. Upon his return home, Ed composed a letter to an old friend that sounded a lot more optimistic than his late-May note to old friend Charlie Taylor. In this letter Ed told his former AMVETS acquaintance Elliot Newcomb in Paris, France, that the "heavy shooting" would commence in a few days and continue for the next six weeks.

The GOP, he told Newcomb, already had a lot of television and radio time bought and paid for, as well as money for newspaper publicity and campaign literature to use in the sprint to the finish. "The talk now, which is gaining momentum," he wrote, "is that I am going to win. This kind of talk can be drowned out by a deluge of propaganda from the other side. Somehow we have got to match their television and radio time, at least."[119] Soon he would have another reason to be optimistic.

By early August the issues of the campaign were well established and becoming contentious. Ed said in Sanford that, while Maine's paper industry continued to thrive, he was concerned about the future of the state's textile industry, particularly that of

Goodall-Sanford, which had just been acquired by Burlington Mills Corporation.

Burlington "should lay its cards on the table," said Ed, "to facilitate ironing out any disadvantages the firm may feel about continuing operations here."[120] He also urged the Cross administration to become more actively concerned about the state's economic well-being, and he called for a comprehensive study as part of a plan to get Maine out of the economic doldrums.

Appearing with Ed that evening was U.S. Senate candidate Paul Fullam, who "said the United States didn't spend enough money to help Afghanistan. He said the Russians have reportedly offered $250 million in technical aid for the strategic hill country." Fullam also told the group that he'd recently been endorsed by Eleanor Roosevelt, who "telegraphed her 'wholehearted' support and told him she was misunderstood in a news conference that quoted her as backing his opponent, Republican Senator Margaret Chase Smith."[121]

This wasn't the first time the former first lady had gotten into a touchy situation involving the senator and her rival. Back in April, while driving through Maine on her way to Campobello, Mrs. Roosevelt had spent a night in Bangor, where she was planning to give her support to Senator Smith. But a funny thing happened on her way to the Bangor House—that was when Paul Fullam decided that he would run for the Senate after all. A quick call was made to Madelin Kiah, one of the few Democrats in the Bangor area, who was hastily dispatched to the Bangor House's Presidential Suite to ask Mrs. Roosevelt to throw her support behind her fellow Democrat instead.

Mrs. Kiah's daughter, Mary Ellen Johnson, remembers her mother coming to school to pick her up in a taxi. Mrs. Kiah was wearing only a slip beneath her coat, expecting to pick up her good dress at the dry cleaners on the way to Mrs. Roosevelt's suite. Much to her dismay, however, the dress wasn't ready, and she had to go to the meeting as she was. Leaving Mary Ellen in the hall, she explained the political situation to Mrs. Roosevelt, who invited her to stay for tea. Mrs. Kiah tried to make a clean getaway by saying, "'[T]hank

you, but my little girl is outside the door, and we need to go back
. . . .' And [Mrs. Roosevelt] said, of course, that she would endorse
the Democratic candidate. Well she invited me in, too, and we had
tea with Eleanor Roosevelt, and finally my mother told Eleanor
Roosevelt why she couldn't take her coat off, and she thought it was
quite funny."[122]

In Chisholm (between Livermore Falls and Jay), Ed continued
his assault on the Cross administration by pointing out that the state
had suffered a population loss of 16,000 in the previous four years
and ranked forty-sixth in industrial employment growth over the
past fifteen years. "If this is the record that Governor Cross proposes
to campaign on this year, we are happy to debate it with him," he
said. "They forget about you after election. I think it's time you ask
them before you give them your vote, 'What have you got to offer?'
Let's bring competition to politics."[123]

Governor Cross wasted no time returning fire. The next day he
told the press that Muskie showed "a deplorable lack of precise knowledge on what state government is doing and has been doing."[124] The
governor said that surveys on matters such as industry and human
resources were ongoing projects at the state level, and he was "aston-
ished" that his opponent wasn't aware of that.

> [Cross] said that he would be glad to talk the matter
> over with Muskie at any time.
> "Did you say talk or debate?" the governor was
> asked.
> "Talk," the governor replied quickly.
> Earlier in the campaign candidate Muskie issued a
> public challenge to debate with the governor but it has
> never been picked up.[125]

During an overnight trip to Portland the same day, Ed told more
than 200 supporters at the Falmouth Hotel that the administration
needed to do more to support and promote Maine's seaports, and
repeated "that a full-dress, comprehensive 1954 survey by skilled personnel is needed to put the economic picture in proper focus."

After the rally, Ed and Dick probably saved money by staying at the home of a supporter, since no one who recalls the campaign could remember the pair ever paying for a hotel room during their travels. Ed sometimes "packed" for a trip by dropping his razor and toothbrush into his coat pocket, and on at least one trip to Portland he forgot to tell Dick that they were staying overnight.

Following a meal at the Pagoda Restaurant on Congress Street (which was probably on the house), Ed collected a $100 donation from proprietor Henry Wong, and the two went off to sleep at the Longfellow Square apartment of local attorney Jack Agger. Agger claimed the couch, which left Ed and Dick to sleep in the same bed, with Dick squeezed between Ed and the wall—which made things difficult for Ed's stocky friend each time nature called during the night.

> In the morning, McMahon who is five foot seven and weighs over two-hundred pounds told Muskie, "Never again. The next time we travel together we're going to have to make better arrangements than this." Later he commented, "I made up my mind it was the last time I was going to have to crawl over that lanky, bony son of a gun every time I had to go to the bathroom. And he hadn't even told me to bring my toothbrush."[126]

Ed would end up having the last word with Governor Cross on the survey issue—even if it wasn't face-to-face. In Ed's words:

> I think the turning point in the campaign came in early August. I had called for an economic study as part of a program to get Maine out of the doldrums. My opponent ridiculed the proposal. And then a young college professor, who had been combing newspaper accounts of my opponent's career, discovered that the incumbent Republican governor had made a similar proposal during the 1952 Republican primary and had

never followed up on it. That broke open the state's economic problems and Republican indifference as the central issue of the campaign. We pounded the theme home in town after town in the final weeks of the summer, trying without success to get the governor to debate me.[127]

A couple days later Ed was in Bangor telling the viewers of WABI that Governor Cross needed to "'get off his cloud, put his ear to the ground, and listen to what people are saying' about state government these days."[128] Burt Cross was also in Bangor that day, making his Governor's Day visit to the Bangor State Fair. He "stopped by the Democratic Party's booth and said he picked up campaign literature. He also chatted there with Fullam's daughter, Mary Ellen, whom he inaugurated as 'Girls State' Governor in 1951 when he was president of the Maine Senate."[129] The election was five weeks away.

"As of today, both political parties have launched their election ships," wrote Lal Lemieux. "The ripples and waves will be watched closely from here on in." Noting that Governor Cross had eschewed the "no recognition" technique used by Senator Smith in the primary and was choosing instead to respond to the issues Ed was bringing up, Lemieux called the governor "a hard-hitting campaigner who doesn't believe in running away from a fight."[130]

Cross next appeared at a GOP celebration in Strong for the founding of the national Republican Party there 100 years earlier. (Vice President Richard Nixon was to have been the special guest, but ended up sending his regrets.) At a reenactment of the party's founding, John Willard Bolte of Wilton played the part of his great-grandfather, Major J. H. Willard, who had given the Republican Party its name. Cross used the occasion at the American Legion Field to assure the faithful:

> The Republican administration in Maine has shown its ability to keep our State of Maine solvent in a time of Democratic free spending, and to keep our credit sound in a period of wild speculation by New

Deal idealists. We can now work closely with a Republican administration in Washington, giving honest value for every tax dollar, and we will continue to do so for many years to come.[131]

Meanwhile Ed was about as far north as he could get and still be in Maine, addressing a rally in Eagle Lake. It was a perfect opportunity for him to again take the governor to task for his plan to consolidate the state's TB sanatoria, which he labeled "irresponsible thinking." It was irresponsible, Ed said, "because it was made without adequate knowledge of the facts in terms of the humane conditions involved," calling such a plan "penny wise and pound foolish."[132]

After his stop way up north, Ed headed to Down East Maine to spend a couple days in Calais, where he addressed the Rotary Club, and then Lubec. Ed was joined that evening in the Lubec Theater by fellow candidates Paul Fullam and Ken Colbath. The trio was the second part of that evening's double feature. "Come early," the ad proclaimed, "see the show first." (The movie for Tuesday, August 10 was *Untamed Heroes*, starring Judy Canova, Don Barry, and Taylor Holmes.) No doubt the theater's enterprising owner was just trying to pull himself up by his bootstraps.

Back in the heart of Maine, Ed preceded a return trip to Rangeley with a stop in Milo, where he blasted the governor for "reaching into the bag of political tricks to come up with glowing promises for the future to obscure the lack of progress in the past."[133] He predicted that Republicans would employ more of this tactic as the election neared, and cautioned, "What height they will reach we can only guess, but I wouldn't be surprised to read an announcement that Maine will be the site of a launching platform for the first rocket to the moon."[134]

Two days later, at a Democratic State Committee meeting at the home of Mr. and Mrs. Charles Mills in Belgrade, Frank Coffin amplified Ed's point, remarking that Governor Cross, by "'reaching' for campaign promises, appears to be 'our best campaigner.'"[135]

Ed takes a break from his travels during the 1954 campaign to try to figure out where he is.

By this point in the campaign, the days must have been running together for Ed. On Tuesday he was in Bucksport and Castine before addressing most of the hundred members of the Deer Isle Grange. (The Deer Isle Grange would close its doors in July 2013 "because it couldn't attract even seven members to its meetings, the number required to keep its state charter.")[136] Wednesday's trip included campaign stops in Auburn and Rockland. Ed's talk in Auburn was to the noontime meeting of the city's Exchange Club, where he hit a familiar note:

ISTON EVENING

16 PAGES   LEWISTON, AUBURN, MAINE   WEDNESDAY, AUG

Staff Photo by Philbrick

DEMOCRATIC CANDIDATE VISITS AUBURN—Edmund S. Muskie, Waterville attorney and Democratic nominee for Governor, was presented to the Auburn Exchange Club today by Attorney L. Damon Scales of Auburn. The candidate was the speaker at the weekly meeting at the Hotel Elm. Left to right at the head table: Richard Davis, club president; Muskie; Scales; Herbert E. Callahan, vice president.

Mt. Cardigan Fire Warden's Body Found

CANAAN, N.H. (P)—The body of Wyman M. Larrabee, 66-year-old fire lookout, who had been missing for more than 24 hours, was found today near his cabin on 3,121-foot Mt. Cardigan just off the main trail.

First reports did not indicate the cause of death.

The state Forestry Department employe had a record of never missing a "report check" in his 12 years service.

He failed to make the usual report to District Fire Chief James Q. Ricard at 9 a.m. yesterday.

The forestry agency said 75 to 100 are taking part in the search.

Muskie Proposes Experimental Textile Plant to Prove Industry Can Run Profitably in Maine

By L. A. LEMIEUX

Construction of a modern, one story textile plant in Maine, to serve as an experimental unit and demonstrate to the industry that textiles can operate profitably in this State was proposed here today.

his speech to the industrial picture in this State, contending that Maine must "establish a strong working partnership between the State and the communities in order to realize industrial development." The Maine Development Commission, he argued, has "too

Candidate Muskie in Auburn.

He again called for a full-scale survey of present industries, those which have not survived in the past few years, and of the labor force requirements of possible new industries as the preliminary steps which would provide the "working tools" for the job of industrial redevelopment.

The survey should be "town by town, area by area"
so that the state could find out "where the resources are"
then make them available to new industry.[137]

After touching on his idea for establishing a department that
would be dedicated solely to the development of industry and commerce in the state, Ed floated the idea of building an experimental
one-story textile plant to prove that the industry could operate profitably in the state were it freed from "discriminative federal laws" that
tended to favor the South. The operations in a single-story plant, said
Ed, would be much more efficient than those "in multi-floor buildings where everything must be handled many times."[138]

While Ed may not have captivated the largely Republican group,
at least one of the meeting's attendees brought new meaning to the
term "captive audience." It seems that Harry Small, manager of the
George M. Roak Company, had been lax of late in his club attendance, so a few other members decided to do something about it.
They went to his Auburn home, handcuffed him, and brought him
to the meeting in an ambulance. A photo in the local paper showed
Small being carried into the meeting by half a dozen well-dressed
litter bearers. "The fact that Harry is a Republican and the guest
speaker was Democratic nominee for governor Edmund S. Muskie
of Waterville had nothing to do with it (they said)."[139]

Debate Me, Governor Cross

Following his appearance in Auburn, Ed went to that evening's
scheduled campaign stop on the town pier in Rockland only to learn
that the governor was appearing at a GOP rally a few blocks away.
There, Burt Cross was already busy tearing into Ed's experimental
textile plant idea. The Bates, Continental, and Pepperell firms, he
told his fellow Republicans, were world famous for their products and
modernization methods and did not need to be told by a political
candidate how to operate in Maine.

Ed and Frank Coffin, tired of the governor's business-as-usual approach, saw a golden opportunity and jumped on it. "Because the situation invited it," said Coffin, Ed—already knowing the reply he'd receive—dashed off the following note inviting the governor to debate the issues immediately following their appearances:

> Apparently by coincidence we are both appearing in Rockland tonight. A challenging issue which has developed out of the past two weeks of campaigning is the industrial situation in Maine. It strikes me that we have an opportunity to give the voters of Maine a comparison of our positions, fact for fact.
>
> I therefore am willing to debate this issue with you this evening, following the close of your regularly scheduled program. The messenger will be happy to carry your reply.[140]

Ed was the event's next scheduled speaker, so he stalled for time by repeatedly signaling congressional candidate Tom Delahanty to "keep talking" as he waited for Cross's reply, which was:

> It was a pleasure to hear from you directly this evening. It is my thought that the campaign will bring out this industrial picture as well as other issues clearly.
>
> I appreciate your willingness to discuss this issue with me, but see no useful purpose to be served at this time. You have your views and I have mine. I shall present the facts to the people of Maine and they shall make the eventual decision.[141]

By drawing a crowd of about seventy-five people—the same number Cross had attracted—in a town where Republicans outnumbered Democrats three to one, Ed had already achieved a small victory that evening. But once he had the governor's reply in his hand, Ed took to the stump and let loose, increasing the size of his victory even more. "'When we're talking about what will benefit the people of Maine and the governor says it will serve no useful purpose to debate, who is he representing?' he asked, waving the slip of paper, and down he went through his litany of issues, summing up each with the cry, 'Would no useful purpose be served by discussion of that?'"[142]

Once the press started writing about what had happened there, the size of Ed's win that day increased even more. Coverage of Cross dodging the debate prompted people to think that perhaps his opponent was making legitimate points that the governor was ducking. Ed's credibility increased.

Before stopping in Waldoboro, Ed appeared on WABI television in Bangor. While the use of television was undoubtedly a big part of the Democrats' election-year strategy, Don Nicoll would later suggest that radio played a much bigger role. "There were two major new public relation techniques applied in [the 1954] campaign," he said. "[T]elevision was one, radio was the other. Radio is generally ignored in accounts of the campaign. . . . [T]he television stations covered a fairly narrow part of the population," he pointed out. "[R]adio, on the other hand, was ubiquitous and cheap."[143] Ed agreed that it was important. "[R]adio, too, local radio, which people hear in their cars, and housewives listen to in the kitchen. This coverage is important."[144]

While both sides purchased television time toward the end of the campaign, the Democrats took to the radio waves in what could only be described as a blitz. Each of the top five hopefuls recorded fifteen five-minute messages (five of which were played in the morning, five at noontime, and five in the evening) to be broadcast on a rotating basis around the state five days a week for the final three weeks of the campaign. These messages ran on "probably at least twenty to twenty-five stations—statewide coverage," said Don Nicoll, who thought that "radio was more influential in building a sense of comfort and identification."[145]

Ed made an appearance in Brunswick before heading inland to kick off the last week of August in West Minot, where forty-two people turned out to hear him talk about the governor's plan to close the tuberculosis sanatorium in nearby Hebron. Ed told the group, which was often forced to crowd under the roof of the old Maine Central Railroad station in intermittent rain, that "the basic cure for tuberculosis, even today, is rest. For rest to be effective it must be without anxiety and care and that can best be accomplished if the patients are close to their homes."[146] (If you drive up the Greenwood Mountain Road from Route 124 in Hebron, you can still see the overgrown foundation of that sanatorium at the top of the hill on your left.) Among those in the group who thought the young Democrat made a lot of sense was an eighty-three-year-old "lifelong Republican who made no bones of the fact that he plans to split his ticket this year for the first time for Muskie."[147]

That evening Ed and Jane continued on to Rumford, where he was feted at a testimonial dinner at St. Rocco Hall. The driving force behind the dinner was Elizabeth (Spinney) Campbell, who'd been president of Ed's Stephens High School class. Two years earlier, at their twenty-year reunion, there had been some talk about Ed running for governor. Campbell had decided back then to honor him, she said, if he ever did run—and now was the time. She had hoped to get all the members of the 1932 debating team to attend, but one was missing; Dorothy Poulin, the redhead who'd been Ed's first girlfriend, had moved away.

The dinner ended up turning into an impromptu Stephens High reunion, remembered former classmate Larry Harpe:

> But, so we went to that supper, and there was so many of us from the class of '32 that someone [shouted], "Hey, there's so many of us here, why don't we have a little class reunion?" So a few of the fellows went around and took up a little collection, [and] they went out and got a little bit of liquor. . . . But anyway, they come back with it and we had a little party. I do remember dancing with Muskie's wife.[148]

Covering his geographic bases, Ed next spent a couple days in the midcoast area, first speaking to the Rotary Club in Belfast before appearing at a rally in Unity that evening. The next day he made stops at the Union Fair and the Boothbay Rotary Club before going to Portland to address the viewers of WGAN. That same evening, Paul Fullam appeared on WCSH TV.

A little over a week after the governor had refused to debate him there, Ed returned to Rockland, where he took a different tack in his assault on Burt Cross's fitness for office. In what could have been the beginning of his reputation as "Mr. Clean," Ed said that Maine's Republican leadership "sticks its head in the sand and refuses to admit that there is a problem of pollution. It is either unwilling or afraid to face the problem squarely and do something about it. The only action the state has taken has been to classify streams on the degree of their pollution and dump chemicals into the rivers to try and reduce the smell."[149]

Governor Cross appeared to be paying attention to what his opponent and probably much of his constituency was saying about the tuberculosis sanitoria. During speeches in Jackman and Madison, Ed mentioned to his supporters that Burt Cross had "reversed himself" on the matter of closing the Presque Isle sanatorium. While this was certainly a noteworthy development, the gubernatorial campaign was about to get a lot more interesting.

On the last Sunday in August, the race for the Blaine House heated up when the GOP got Vice President Richard Nixon to break into "the tag end of a vacation at Ogunquit for a half-hour TV-radio program starting at 10:30 P.M."[150] on four television and five radio stations. Nixon's address came four and a half hours after Paul Fullam appeared on WCSH TV with a young Massachusetts Democrat, Senator John F. Kennedy, who happened to be vacationing in Northeast Harbor at the time.

If Burt Cross was the Democrats' "best campaigner" with his political gaffes, his GOP cohort Richard Nixon was probably number two. "[T]he appearance of them was very stiff and accusatory," said Don Nicoll.[151] Ed went on the air five minutes after the Republicans finished their program. "I answered [Nixon], and I said, 'This is our election.' It had nothing to do with him. We don't need him to come in here. And I don't know what words I used, but he . . . I said to him, 'Maine people, we're our own thinkers.'"

This political ad touting Ed for governor, Paul Fullam for U.S. Senate, and Jim Oliver and Tom Delahanty for Congress ran in southern and central Maine newspapers just before the election.

At the end of August, Hurricane Carol—the first hurricane to hit Maine in sixteen years—made landfall. Governor Cross suspended his political appearances to return to Augusta, from where he monitored the situation on a Civil Defense radio receiver at the Blaine House. The next day, after accompanying his Civil Defense director Colonel Harry A. Mapes on a 200-mile tour of the devastation, Cross announced that the damage caused by Carol would total "at least 10 million dollars." Other GOP candidates continued to campaign in Penobscot County.

The approach of Carol kept Ed close to home the last two days of the month, with appearances in the Waterville area, Bath, and throughout Sagadahoc County. As Labor Day approached, with the election two weeks away, Ed's campaigning took him back to the familiar territory of his boyhood. After a stop in Canton, he and Jane continued on to Rumford, where they visited his family before heading out to shake hands with old friends and acquaintances.

Many of Ed's campaign stops during the first week of September saw him either shaking hands at one of Maine's many fairs or appearing on television. After a stop at the Gardiner Shoe factory, he went to the Windsor Fair before traveling the following day to Bangor, where he could be seen by viewers of WABI. Over the next two days he returned to Washington County and shook more hands at the Springfield Fair, then finished the week with television spots on WGAN and WCSH in Portland.

With five days to go before the Monday election, Ed maximized his remaining campaign time by flying up to Houlton, from where he traveled to Dyer Brook prior to a 6:00 P.M. rally at the Patten Opera House. On Thursday, Ed, Paul Fullam, and Ken Colbath campaigned in Old Town and appeared on WABI TV before Ed, Paul, and Tom Delahanty breakfasted with Democratic Party workers at the DeWitt Hotel in Lewiston on Friday. Later that day in Bangor, Ed challenged the governor one last time to debate him, probably more for the publicity he'd get from the challenge than from any real belief that Cross would take him up on it. Ed took the opportunity to assure his audience that, if he were elected, he would gladly debate his opponent "on any issue at any time." And then Maine's weather turned unusually foul.

Two days before the September 13 election (and just twelve days after Hurricane Carol had caused widespread damage), Hurricane Edna blew into Maine, her high winds and heavy rain causing considerable damage, especially along the coast. Once again Burt Cross found a way to do Ed's campaigning for him. In the beginning of the year he'd suggested that Washington County needed to pull itself up by its bootstraps, and in the wake of Edna he concluded, after flying over Portland, that the damage there was "not half as bad as Stan [Tupper, his Sea and Shore Fisheries Commissioner] said." When people have just lost everything in a hurricane, "you don't tell them there's no problem," said Tupper decades later.[152] Having now shot himself in the other foot, Governor Cross limped back to the Blaine House, where he'd announce that federal aid was on its way to Maine and await the election results. He still predicted that he'd win reelection by 45,000 votes.

That Saturday evening, Lewiston political writer Lal Lemieux wrote that the Democrats had peaked about three weeks too early, and the only thing he wondered about was how much the Republicans would win by:

> Republicans and Democrats alike were wearing confident smiles today as they predicted victory for their candidates in Monday's State election.
>
> But the Republican candidates were the ones who were the "favorites" to win despite the most active and successful Democratic campaign in 20 years.
>
> As this was written, the big question was just how badly the Democrats could slash the winning majority of Governor Burton M. Cross. Observers appeared in agreement that attorney Edmund S. Muskie of Waterville, the Democratic nominee for governor, was going to make a good showing but that his chances of taking a second term away from Cross were remote.[153]

(Shortly after the election, Lemieux's byline would virtually disappear from the *Lewiston Evening Journal* because he'd been promoted to the position of the paper's city editor.)

Edna was bad news for a lot of people, but it may have been a good omen for Ed. Pundits were predicting that a light turnout (of around 225,000 voters) would have the young challenger breathing down Cross's neck because the Democrats were much more motivated. Even with a heavy voter turnout (of around 250,000 voters), the incumbent's projected margin of victory had been cut from 50,000 votes to as few as 20,000.

Ed would later recall that "on election day [Captain Frederick "Boyd" Guild] was adrift in a hurricane . . . off the coast of New Jersey in the *Victory Chimes*. And we wondered about the symbolism. Victory chimes in all night."[154] (Launched in Delaware in 1900 as the *Edwin & Maude*, the three-masted schooner had been converted from a freighter to a "dude cruiser" in 1946 and renamed the *Victory Chimes* by Captain Guild when she came to Maine in 1954. The *Victory Chimes* survived Edna and would be named an American National Historic Landmark under the Maritime Heritage Program of the National Park Service in 1997. She is shown sailing past the Pemaquid Lighthouse on the reverse of Maine's 2003 state quarter, and today sails out of Rockland, Maine.)

We Know How the Story Ends

As Edna passed, travel around the state once again became possible, but less than 24 hours remained for campaigning. To get their message out, the Democrats again relied on statewide television, which meant that they had to be in Portland at 6:00 P.M. and in Bangor by 11:00. (Remember that there was no Interstate 95 then, "and it was a stormy night," said Don Nicoll.) After his last public appearance of the contest, Ed and Dick McMahon retired to a local restaurant. "As he sat in the Pilot's Grille in Bangor on Sunday night after giving his final speech, with the flame from a candle on the table playing over his face, he reviewed the campaign. 'At least,' he concluded, 'they can't say we haven't worked at it. We've given it everything we've got.'"[155]

Election Day dawned gray and blustery as the remnants of Edna pulled away—and Ed's confidence in his chances of victory were every bit as unsettled as the Waterville weather. He'd later admit to thinking to himself, "Well, this has been a pleasant interlude; now I can stop this foolishness about wanting to be governor and get down to earning a living."[156] At other times during the day, he'd tell people

Ed and Jane always voted at their local polling place in Waterville. This photo was taken on Election Day 1956.

he could feel that he was going to win, but mostly he seemed resigned to losing. (Years later, when he was running for president, he'd say, "I've always been fatalistic about politics. A Democrat in Maine can't be otherwise.")[157]

After voting in the morning at their usual Ward Seven school-house, the Muskies readied themselves for election night at the Elmwood Hotel, where two six-dollar suites had been rented for the occasion. Ed handled the stress of the day much better than Jane, who had been feeling under the weather to begin with. Things got

worse at her mother's home, where she was helping with preparations for that evening. "And I'd make a batch of sandwiches," she
said, "and then I'd go in the bathroom and throw up. Yeah, I was
that nervous."[158] Eventually she felt well enough to leave her children,
five-year-old Stephen and three-year-old Ellen, with her mother and
join the festivities.

Sure of his son's victory, Stephen Muskie spent much of the
evening pacing back and forth in the Elmwood suite and smoking,
which he was doing just for this occasion after having kicked the
habit on the advice of his doctor. Ed's mother got tired and went
to bed. Early signs were promising, with Ed winning 3,000 votes in
rural Hancock County instead of the usual 1,000. Everyone's spirits
improved when one of Jane's brothers showed up with a case of whis-
key, and the other with a case of beer.

Spirits soared even higher around 10:30 that night when it was
becoming clearer that Ed was gradually pulling away from Governor Cross and would win the election. As word of his impending
victory got out, friends and supporters flooded in, forcing the hotel
to open additional rooms to accommodate them all. Even with the
handwriting clearly on the wall, Burt Cross, evidently hoping for a
miracle, waited until 1:45 in the morning to call Ed and concede. "It
was an overwhelming moment," said Jane. "Unless one has had the
experience of having an opponent call and admit defeat, it is difficult to understand how one feels. Ed and I just sat there with tears
streaming down our faces."[159] When the counting was done, Ed had
collected 135,673 votes to Cross's 113,298, and had lost Cumberland
County to the incumbent by just 346 votes (21,810 to 21,464).

Even fourteen years later, when he was running for vice president, Ed would still be in awe of what he and his overmatched team
had managed to accomplish in 1954:

> We won against hopeless odds. We won with almost
> no resources. We had had to literally walk that state
> from one end to the other. We had to talk to Republi-
> cans who had never even seen a live Democrat in their

The front page of the Lewiston Evening Journal *mirrors almost everyone's surprise at Ed's upset victory.*

entire lives. We had to learn the political skills that none of us had ever developed. We had to do it against an establishment, against a machine, against a political organization which had had a century to entrench itself, and we did it.[160]

The other top Democrats running for office—Paul Fullam, Jim Oliver, Tom Delahanty, and Ken Colbath—were all defeated by the Republican incumbents. Burt Cross would return to the family flower business after leaving office the following January.

With Ed's victory came a long list of firsts. In addition to making Jane the nation's youngest first lady at twenty-seven, his win also made him the state's first Polish-American governor and its first Democratic governor in two decades. He also became Maine's first Catholic governor since 1843, when Edward Kavanagh had been appointed governor by John Fairfield, who was leaving office to become a senator. "[T]he question of religion never came up," said former *Press Herald* reporter Edgar Comee. "And here's a guy whose middle name is the name of half a dozen popes, Sixtus. The question never came up, which is a credit to the State of Maine."[161]

Maine's next governor even had a kitten named after him by Mr. and Mrs. Edwin H. P. Lowell of Bath, who'd gotten little Muskie on Election Day. Ed heard about the kitten after it was mentioned in the *Central Maine Cat Club Bulletin* and sent the couple a nice letter thanking them for naming their pet after him. The only problem was that the Lowells were Republicans and had voted for Governor Cross.

When he was asked how he felt about his son's unexpected triumph, Ed's father simply said, "I hope he can stay honest." At 6:30 the next morning, after Ed and Jane had gotten ninety minutes of sleep, their doorbell started ringing, remembered Jane:

> First there were three reporters. They had made the trip all the way from Boston to get the story. They were followed by more reporters and then photographers and radio and television people. The phone rang constantly. As a result of one call, Ed and I agreed to go to New York City to appear on a television network. I tried to get dressed and make coffee at the same time. I hadn't quite finished either when the children . . . came home [from Jane's mother's house]. Steve was shouting to everybody, "My father's the boss of the whole state!"[162]

Thanks to Maine's September election, Ed's win became the first major Democratic victory in the nation since the Eisenhower landslide nearly two years before and was featured in several national publications, including *Time*, *Newsweek*, and the *New York Times*, which summed up Ed's triumph in the article's first two paragraphs:

> Edmund S. Muskie was elected Maine's first Democratic governor in twenty years largely because he made

up his mind long ago that he was not going to be afraid of the Republicans.

He went about defying Maine's traditional rock-ribbed Republicanism in a way that was methodical and scientific, but it also had a touch of the colorful and the human."[163]

Literally overnight, Ed had gone from being unknown outside Maine to being the DNC's most sought-after speaker. DNC Chairman Stephen Mitchell, who had been able to do little more during the campaign than offer Maine Democrats moral support and return the $5,000 they'd raised, took just three days to return to the state. The day after that, Ed and Jane were off to the first two of the seventeen states he would eventually visit in an effort to help the Democrats retake Congress. Maine's first couple-elect stopped in New York City to be interviewed by Dave Garroway on *Today* and spent a half hour with Mayor Wagner in City Hall before Jane returned to Maine and Ed continued on to Indianapolis.

In Indiana he attended a meeting of the convention committee of the Democratic National Committee, where the party faithful were read a letter from former president Harry Truman (who'd recently undergone gall bladder surgery and was unable to travel) about the need to give President Eisenhower a Democratic Congress in the hope "we can save him from the misdeeds of his own party," before adding, "The Republicans have not learned a thing since 1896."[164]

The letter was read to party leaders who had "gathered in a highly confident mood following the upset victory of their gubernatorial candidate in traditionally Republican Maine. 'A Democratic tide is running and gaining in momentum,' Mr. Mitchell told reporters. 'I believe that we have in the making the greatest Democratic sweep since 1936.'"[165] The following evening Ed addressed several hundred people attending a $100-a-plate fundraiser.

Besides helping out fellow Democrats, Ed's speaking tour worked out well for him. He would take in roughly $5,000 in speaking fees between the election and his swearing-in, using most of that money to pay past-due bills. He had stopped paying everything except his mortgage and electric bill so he could afford to crisscross the state several times during the campaign—and he still had a stack of outstanding medical bills to take care of.

The Muskies also needed to rejuvenate themselves after the election, and spent the first few days of fall fishing with Ernie Ronco, caretaker of the Guy Gannett Publishing Company camp on Ross Lake. Except the one he kept for the photographers, Ed released all the fish he caught (mostly lake trout and togue, using streamer flies and a light leader) after they'd been netted into the boat by Jane, whose fishing license he'd forgotten to bring. She hated missing the birthday of her daughter, Ellen, she said—the children were staying in Palmyra with Mr. and Mrs. Perry Furbush—but it was the only time Ed had to get "such a wonderful rest." He finished up the whirlwind month of September by returning to New York on September 26 to appear on NBC's *American Forum*, where he discussed the topic, "What does the Maine election mean?"

As September turned to October, Ed and his team of friends must have felt like the dog that finally catches the car he's been chasing. When they weren't addressing budget and staffing issues there were myriad other matters to attend—when Ed wasn't flying around the country, that is. The many stops he made in October included Worcester, Massachusetts; Baltimore; Connecticut; Wheeling, West Virginia; Kansas City, Kansas; Chicago; Burlington, Vermont; New Hampshire; and Boston. During his stop in Chicago he caught up with Bates classmate Betty (Winston) Levinson for her husband's fortieth birthday. While there, Ed had the pleasure of explaining the meaning of the Maine election to the Executives' Club of Chicago at a luncheon in the Grand Ballroom of the Hotel Sherman. One commitment he couldn't keep that month was an October 12 lobster dinner in Washington, D.C., that was held in his honor.

When he wasn't on the road trying to help other Democrats win in November (Maine would not begin holding its elections in November until 1960), Ed spent most of his time in Augusta, enveloped in budget hearings, which is where he was on October 12. "I soon found out that the state's needs far exceeded our tax revenues," said Ed. "I also found out that the governor had very limited control over departmental budgets and expenditures. The legislature appropriated what amounted to lump sums for the departments to spend in the biennium."[166] That day he learned he would need to cut $11 million from departmental budget requests for the next two years.

All of this work on the budget was done with Ed paying his expenses out of his own pocket. Even if the move then afoot to increase the governor's salary from $10,000 to $16,000 had succeeded, it wouldn't have helped Ed, who would have been ineligible for a pay raise passed during his term in office. For this reason, Frank Coffin advocated for an appropriation of a few thousand dollars for the governor-elect so he could cover the expenses related to preparing the budget and his inaugural address—and maybe even hire a secretary. Speaking at the Waterville Rotary Club, "Coffin expressed belief that the three months before a governor takes office are more important than the three immediately afterwards, when the Legislature is acting on the program prepared by the governor."[167]

Ed was still on the national campaign trail on Halloween, making a last-minute push in support of other Democrats. He finished the month in Boston, where he appeared at a rally in Symphony Hall in support of Massachusetts State Treasurer Foster Furcole and State Representative Robert F. Murphy, who were running for U.S. Senator and Governor, respectively. In Portland two days later, Ed told reporters that the close contests in the just-completed election "suggests that both parties will have to be on their best behavior if they hope to win the country as a whole in 1956." He went on to note that, "The results of elections nationwide make it plain that the Maine election was decided on local issues. If you had projected the result of the Maine election nationwide, it would have meant an overwhelming Democratic victory. The actual results indicate that the Maine election was a local proposition decided on state issues."[168]

While President Eisenhower wasn't up for reelection in 1954, the Democrats did well nationally, taking control of both the House of Representatives and the U.S. Senate, where they had 48 of the chamber's 96 seats plus the vote of Independent Senator Morse of Oregon. The November elections also saw a record number of women serving in Washington, with one senator (who happened to be from Maine), and sixteen women in the House of Representatives, including a nonvoting member from Hawaii.

A week after the national election, Ed hired thirty-five-year-old Floyd "Tom" Nute of Augusta to start as his press secretary in January. Nute, a United Press stringer who wrote the weekly "State House Report" column for several newspapers, "had a very acerbic way of looking at things sometimes," Jeb Byrne, another former reporter, recalled of his colleague, "and very colorful language about describing things that were going on, particularly to his friends and associates."[170]

Another decision Ed made around that time was to bring Marjorie Hutchinson from his law office to work for him in the State House. "Everybody loved her," said Joan Arnold, the governor's appointment secretary. "She was very attractive, had a lot of style, smiled easily, and very efficient. She was just a very, very bright woman."[171] She was a good choice for the job all the way around; not only did she know all of Ed's friends from Waterville, she also had what was referred to as the "motherly touch," often brushing her boss's unruly hair before the photographers came in.

Maury Williams, a Republican in the state budget office with whom Frank Coffin had become friends while defending Governor Payne during the liquor scandal, became Ed's administrative assistant for $145 a week, and Ed's trusted friends Frank Coffin, Dick McMahon, Don Nicoll, Tom Delahanty, and Dick Dubord became his closest advisors. During November and December the governor-elect and his team (relying heavily on Williams's expertise in the area) came up with a budget that covered "current services," but then he unveiled a second budget, the "supplemental budget." "And so the result," said Ed, "was that the deficit wasn't made to look like a deficit. It was made to look like an opportunity to provide more services."[172]

Two days before Christmas, while Ed was busy preparing his budget message in Waterville, his lame-duck predecessor took part in the laying of the cornerstone of the new office building being built next to the State Capitol. For many years the building would be known as the State Office Building, or SOB, before eventually being named the Burton M. Cross Office Building. (If the naming of Augusta government buildings were a competition, Ed would probably have won this one too, with the Federal Building just up the street on Western Avenue being named in his honor.) And just in case he needed one more opportunity to tweak Burt Cross's nose, the Associated Press named Ed's victory Maine's biggest news story of 1954, ahead of "the smashing visits of Hurricanes Carol and Edna."[173]

Chapter Five

Governor Muskie

Welcome to the Blaine House

Ed's unexpected win was a victory for his finances as well as the two-party system in Maine. The governor's salary was $10,000 a year with a $15,000 expense account, and the twenty-seven-room Blaine House was rent free and came with a staff of seven, including upstairs and downstairs maids, a cook, a laundress, and a houseman. (Jane kept reminding herself that the family's stay in the Blaine House was temporary and that soon she'd once again have to run the household and raise her growing children without the help of staff.) The couple hired as their social secretary Mrs. Catherine Rines of Gardiner, who had served as a state vice-president of the Maine Federation of Music Clubs. The Muskies were able to rent their Waterville home for another $85 a month.

With her husband at work on his inaugural address, most decisions about what to bring with them to the family's new home fell to Jane. Among the most precious of those items was a Greydon Piper painting of the couple's two children, which would be hung over the marble mantelpiece in the Blaine House, and the newest member of their family, a four-month-old collie named Sir Winston Churchill and answering to Winnie.

Governor and Mrs. Cross graciously offered to move back to their Riverside Drive home on December 31, a week before Ed's inauguration, "so that the children could get settled in their new home before the big events."[1] Joining the first family in the Blaine House was Jane's mother, who took the bedroom between Steve and Ellen to help keep an eye on them. The family would continue to spend summers at the China Lake camp, on which an addition would be built to accommodate a dining room and living room.

The family's religious needs in Augusta were met by an old friend from Rumford, remembers Ed's boyhood friend Cecil Burns:

> [M]y youngest brother became a Catholic priest, and after he was ordained the second place he went was Augusta. And Ed was the governor, and he was a Rumford boy, and he knew my brother Lee, and that was the church they went to anyway, and so they cordoned off a section just for the Muskie family. And Ed was awfully good to my brother, very good to him. He's been good to a lot of people around here.[2]

The major bottleneck of Inauguration Day had always been the luncheon at the Blaine House, into whose narrow corridors way too many people tried to squeeze. The Muskies decided to avoid this headache simply by doing away with the luncheon. "Anyone who wants to greet the Muskies and see the Blaine House will be welcome at an open house between 2 and 4 P.M.," announced the *Kennebec Journal* a week ahead of time.

On January 6, 1955, Ed walked out of the governor's office with Burt Cross. The pair paused beneath the capitol rotunda, shook hands, and went their separate ways. Maine's newest governor then proceeded to the House of Representatives, where he found himself momentarily upstaged as he readied himself to give his inaugural address to an overflow crowd:

Even while being sworn in as governor, Ed still looks like he can't believe he won.

As Governor-elect Muskie walked into the packed House the crowd broke into riotous applause that was a real ovation. But it was not Governor Muskie who stole the show. It was his young son, Stephen, five years old, who in the split second after the ringing applause stopped, piped out in a clear high voice, "Hi, Daddy," to the delight of the entire crowd.[3]

When it was Daddy's turn to speak, Ed delivered an 8,000-word address described as "a bold statement of policy" couched, as much as possible, in conciliatory language so as not to alienate the Republicans, whose support he would need. In his address, Ed touched on the myriad needs and problems facing Maine: highway improvements, industrial development, port improvements, pollution, an

Stephen and Josephine Muskie on the day of their son's inauguration in 1955. Stephen would die the following year.

aging hydroelectric power capacity, high power rates, insufficient opportunities for labor, and the need for more conservation, parks, education opportunities, more robust institutions, greater health and welfare, a survey of state government, and provisions for civil defense.[4]

That evening's inaugural ball, an invitation-only affair, began at 8 P.M. at the Augusta Armory. Ed didn't forget old friends from home, such as Kenneth Bosworth. "When they had the Governor's Ball," he said, "we all got invitations."[5] (More than forty years later, the names on the inaugural ball guest list would become the starting point for the more than four hundred interviews that make up the Muskie Oral History Project of the Muskie Archives at Bates College.) Jane would later recall that she wore out four pairs of gloves shaking 6,000 hands that evening.

"The cards were stacked against me,"[6] said Ed about the beginning of his first term, when he jumped from the frying pan of developing a budget into the fire of dealing with legislators, whose five-month biennial session had begun as soon as he'd taken the oath of office. The Republican Party still held overwhelming majorities in both chambers (117–34 in the House and 27–6 in the Senate). "It wasn't their inclination to roll over and play dead,"[7] said Ed of a legislature that viewed him as an interloper, though he would be able now and then to get some help from a group of rural Republicans who called themselves the Little Guys. He also had to deal with a seven-member Executive Council appointed by the legislature. The council oversaw the governor's decisions in the areas of appointments, pardons, and many financial transactions, and naturally, every member was a diehard GOP partisan.

A throwback to the days when Maine had been part of Massachusetts, the Executive Council had been perpetuated through the ensuing 134 years by a nearly unbroken string of Republican-controlled legislatures. In fact, very little about Maine's laws and ways of governing itself had changed since the Civil War, remembers former judge Vincent McKusick. "We had in Maine almost unadorned common law leading up to that time, and a lawyer from 1856 could have come into a courtroom in 1956 and felt completely at home. . . ."[8] Throughout his two terms, Ed would unsuccessfully attempt to abolish the Executive Council, have it elected by the people (as were the nation's only other executive councils, in New Hampshire and Massachusetts), or at least have its role reduced to an advisory one.

After four months in office, he'd confide to a reporter, "It is a handicap being of a different political party. I can't assume that things are being done as I want them done, or that, if they are not, I will be forewarned. It requires keeping a closer check."[9] Finally Ed "made up his mind," said Jane, "that he was not going to fight with [the Executive Council] the whole time he was governor, and he just decided there was no reason why they couldn't be friends, and that's exactly what happened."[10] But it wouldn't happen right away.

A week after delivering his inaugural address, Ed unveiled his proposed budget for the next two years. Since Maine law prohibited deficit spending, he presented the legislature with a two-part budget that he and his team had been working on since November:

> Part I related to current services and Part II included proposed new services. Part I was to be financed out of revenues and Part II would be financed out of new taxes. The Republicans had hoped that I would submit an unbalanced budget that would enable them to tag me with their traditional Democratic "tax and spend" label. I was determined that the voters should know what current services were costing them and understand clearly what unmet needs had to be financed out of higher taxes.[11]

The first part, Maine's traditional budget of $69.5 million ($34,780,100 for 1955–56 and $34,717,796 for 1956–57), sailed through the legislature. It would be Part II, the $10 million supplemental budget ($4,765,778 for 1955–56 and $4,926,062 for 1956–57) that would become a thorn in the side of everybody at the State House for the next four months. The legislature immediately said no to Ed's suggestions to fund the second budget—a one percent increase in the state's four-year-old sales tax or the establishment of a state income tax—and reduced it by half, with most of that cut being the $4 million surplus Ed had planned to use for a building fund reserve for new schools and institutions for the next two years.

The increase in Maine's sales tax would be defeated after a peremptory sixteen-minute public hearing before the Taxation Committee in March. (The sales tax increase would be passed two years later, but Maine wouldn't get an income tax until one was instituted by Democratic Governor Ken Curtis and a Republican legislature in 1969.) The legislature's plan for funding the truncated measure consisted of a few piecemeal taxes—on corporate franchises, cigarettes, wine and liquor, and a two percent sales tax on private automobile sales—that Ed said wouldn't generate enough revenue to fund even the smaller budget.[12] While the brouhaha over the supplemental budget dragged on, other issues and obligations occupied much of Ed's time during his first couple months in office.

Toward the end of his second week as governor, he welcomed to the capitol former Republican Governor Percival Baxter, who offered to give Maine an additional 2,000 acres of wild land to be added to its 166,000-acre Baxter State Park. This latest addition to the park would be around Second Grand Lake in Township 6, Range 9 in Piscataquis County. Baxter also offered to remove hunting restrictions on the park's 16,000 acres north of Trout Brook near Patten after sporting camp owners in the Shin Pond area expressed concern that access to their hunting grounds would be cut off. The very next day, both branches of the legislature suspended their rules so they could speed the acceptance of the gift and ratify the acceptance of another 14,000 acres the former governor had given to the state the previous year. Another bill would permit the state to build trails and access roads in the park.

At the end of the month, the Water Improvement Commission released "a report recommending classification of seven to eight thousand miles of Maine waters by degree of pollution—the first stage of the state's present plan of pollution control."[13] Class A included rivers and streams that were free of pollution (and found mostly in wilderness areas); Class B waterways were suitable for recreation and, when properly treated, for drinking; Class C waterways were somewhat polluted but capable of supporting aquatic life; and Class D rivers and streams were designated for industrial and sewage use. The commission also recommended honing the Class B category, which was thought to be too broad, by dividing it into B1 and B2 subcategories.

During the campaign, Ed had accused Republicans of refusing to admit that Maine had a pollution problem and doing nothing more to address the issue than adding more chemicals to rivers in an attempt to ameliorate the foul stench that arose from them. Now he pushed hard to get the legislature to adopt the new waterway classification scheme, but the legislature was packed with executives from some of Maine's largest manufacturers—paper mills, textile mills, tanneries, and food processors—who depended on rivers and streams to flush away their process waste. Ed would eventually succeed in getting a classification bill to sign based on the commission's report. Though he once referred to the compromise legislation as a mere "illusion of an anti-pollution effort," he eventually came to regard it as a small victory—at least a start. "Jobs were important and they came first," he wrote in his autobiography, *Journeys.* "The people in the towns that lined the rivers depended upon industries for jobs and a tax base and believed that you shouldn't rock the boat and impose impossible burdens upon their industrial resources."

Like everyone else in 1954, Ed saw pollution as a problem for waterways; air pollution was not yet something anyone even considered. He could not have predicted as governor that one day, as a U.S. senator, he would shape and sponsor the Clean Air Act. But his developing passion for environmental issues could no doubt trace its roots back to his childhood days in Rumford, days of having to take surreptitious dips in the already-polluted Androscoggin and seeing what the smokestacks of the Oxford Paper Company were spewing into the air.

In late February Ed was feted at a banquet at Lewiston City Hall, where the speakers included Mayor Ernest Malenfant and Denis Blais, area director of the Textile Workers Union of America, CIO, which had purchased and distributed some forty percent of the 350 tickets sold. All speakers were limited to five minutes except for Ed. Two months later he would be photographed standing between Blais and Bates Manufacturing executive Louis Laun while attempting to mediate a strike at the mill. A cropped portion of the photo and misleading caption would be used against Ed in the next election.

The supplemental budget wasn't the only battle between Ed and the Republicans during his first few months in office. A second front opened over the establishment of a department to help bring more industrial development to the state, and with it better-paying jobs than those offered by the summer tourist trade and other seasonal employment. The only state-level economic development effort at the time was the twelve-member Maine Development Commission, which was chaired by Harold Schnurle, a vice president at Central Maine Power. The commission operated independently of the governor and focused its efforts on tourism, Schnurle feeling strongly that business development was best left to business leaders and that government should stay out of such matters.

Ed wanted to dilute the influence of big businesses, mainly the power companies and paper mills, on Maine's economy, so he proposed the creation of a new department that would answer to him and "devote itself to real industrial and economic development."[14] When the Republicans disagreed in mid March, Ed took his case to Portland's Cumberland Club, where his talk was well received. The press started labeling the Republicans "obstructionist" since they wanted to derail the governor's plan yet had no alternative ideas to offer. As Don Nicoll remembered:

> CMP was not promoting the development of industry, which would have led to their selling more electricity. [Republican Senator] Jim Reid dug in his heels on economic development. [Senate President Robert] Haskell thought that the GOP was digging itself into a hole, and said to the Republican caucus, "If you SOBs don't work out an agreement with the governor, you'll be blamed for every f-ing chicken that dies in this state over the next fifty years." That was the end of the argument.
>
> And Jim Reid got the assignment of working with the governor's office on the new agency, which became the worst-named agency in the history of the state—the Department of Development of Industry and Commerce.[15]

By all accounts Robert N. Haskell, a tall, ruddy-faced VP at Bangor Hydro-Electric, was one of the most brilliant minds ever to serve in the Maine Senate. In the days before computers and even calculators, "[h]e was known as 'Slide-rule Haskell,' and was, as Don Nicoll once put it, 'totally impatient with everyone not as smart as he, which was nearly everyone.'"[16] He had at first agreed with Schnurle, but after seeing the handwriting on the wall and realizing that the GOP could be giving the next election to the Democrats "on a platter," he addressed the Cumberland Club a week after Ed and agreed with most of Ed's arguments for the new department.

By early April, the two had agreed that the creation of the new department should go forward, and Haskell promised to speak for the compromise measure when the controversy over the Maine Development Commission was aired at a hearing of the Appropriations Committee.[17] His influence in the legislature was nearly as formidable as his intellect, and the deal was as good as done. Haskell told reporters that he hoped this newfound spirit of cooperation would continue through the remainder of the 97th Legislature.

Ed realized early on that he'd need to do a lot of compromising to achieve any of his goals, and he wasted no time doing just that. During his first two or three months in office, Haskell construed Ed's conciliatory efforts as a sign of weakness, but by the time the two men finished their collaboration to establish the Department of Development of Industry and Commerce—in the process doing away with the Maine Development Commission and its autocratic leader Schnurle, whom Haskell despised—Haskell had come to respect Ed as a capable politician who held the state's best interests at heart.

Before long, Haskell began stopping by the governor's office most evenings for a drink, and some people even told the pair that they were becoming "pals," an accusation that always drew red-faced denials from both men. Whatever the true status of their friendship, one thing was clear from then on: Whenever "Muskie and Haskell would agree on what should be done, between the two it was done."[18]

The art of compromise would help Ed achieve a lot of goals over the next four years—even when he didn't get what he wanted.

"[E]very time I lost, I won; I lost but I shaped it so that there was a clear image in the public mind of what was at stake."[19] And he won a lot, too, by working with GOP lawmakers to adjust what was in their bills before they were passed so he wouldn't have to veto them. Later, looking back on his time as governor, Ed would recall, "[A] lot of times [the Republicans would] go back into conference and produce a bill that made more sense. I guess we saved maybe a hundred bills that way and we could have made each one a battleground."[20] (In four years, Haskell's desire to be governor would earn him and Ed one small victory each in Ed's last days in the Blaine House.)

Ed got his new department of development with just over a month remaining in the lawmakers' regular session, but the supplemental budget was another matter altogether. After having cut Ed's proposal in half, the Republicans added a million dollars (raising the total to $6 million) to cover the small pork-barrel measures they needed to help their reelection chances. Ed argued that the GOP's piecemeal taxes couldn't possibly generate enough revenue to cover the extra million they'd tacked on, even citing the pessimistic estimates of Finance Commissioner Raymond Mudge, a Republican appointee.

Using Mudge's figures was just a ploy by Ed. Everybody in Augusta knew that Mudge's revenue estimates were routinely low, but the Republicans couldn't dispute his calculations because he was one of their own. The matter was resolved at the eleventh hour when Ed said he would agree to let the budget become law without his signature if the Republicans would agree to take the blame for any shortfall in funding, to which they agreed. "All the legislature's resolution said was that it believed its own estimates to be accurate, which was obvious anyway,"[21] but it made the Republicans look like the spenders instead of the Democrats. The two budgets, which took effect on July 1, combined for a record $74,589,000 in spending over the next two years.

In a news conference at the end of the session, Ed talked about the failure of the GOP to pass so many of the things Maine needed. On the other hand, he had managed to get half of his supplemental budget passed by the other party. Deputy Secretary of State Paul McDonald, a Republican, pointed out that the compromise had come at a high price. "You call it a compromise, but you're giving me a rabbit and I'm giving you a horse," said McDonald. "And he had to give away a lot of horses, you know, to get a few rabbits."[22] (McDonald was serving under Secretary of State Harold Goss, also a Republican. The legislature would elect McDonald to succeed Goss as secretary of state in 1961.)

But Ed had never really expected to get another horse in exchange for his own, said Don Nicoll—that wasn't what he has after:

> Ed was never looking for the mythical middle, he was looking for the desired result. And the first step was to find a point on which everybody could agree—the desired result—and to identify those areas where there were strong disagreements. And he would continue to try to persuade people on disagreements, but be flexible on setting those aside if he couldn't persuade. And then the compromises took place, not in terms of what you were going to achieve, what your ultimate goals were, but the compromises came on the ways and means. And so you were always persuading, and you were looking for ways with which you could bring people on board.[23]

Between Sessions

Once the legislature adjourned its regular session and the political wrangling temporarily receded, Ed's days became a little more routine, a big part of that routine involving meetings with people from all walks of life. "I have to devote much more time than I expected," he told a reporter, "to people who want to come in and see me about almost any problem under the sun."[24] He'd hired as his new appointment secretary Joan Arnold, who said, "I just liked him right off, you know. He was very warm, he had a twinkle in his eye. And very upbeat, very easy."

But in the beginning, Arnold sometimes made the mistake of scheduling too many visitors to see the governor in too short a time, which brought to the surface another of Ed's well-known personality traits, his quick temper, which hadn't changed much since his Rumford childhood and the shouting matches with his father.

"How could you possibly have thought I was going to be able to see twenty different people today," he'd scold Arnold, "and give them any real decent quality time, and be able to think and sort out my thoughts and decide issues. This is impossible, this schedule is just impossible."[25] If he was having a bad day, remembered Arnold, "I would refer to him as 'Ugly Ed.'" But never to his face.

No one was more aware of this facet of his personality than Ed himself. He discussed it in his autobiography many years later. Remembering an interview in which he was asked if he had any weaknesses, he recalled saying:

> "Yes, I do, of course I do." When pressed further for an inventory, I said that, among other things, I do have a temper. I don't know of very many human beings who don't get angry. My father had a pretty good temper and I have one too. He always emphasized to me that the important thing was to learn how to discipline yourself, and with his sometimes physical assistance I gradually learned how to do it.[26]

Try as he might, Ed would never be able to keep his temper completely in check, even after becoming a senator. "It has become an old saw in Washington: 'I asked Muskie about his temper—and he lost his temper.'"[27]

Between Memorial Day and the middle of June, Ed was kept busy with official and honorary functions, beginning with the annual Jefferson-Jackson Day dinner at Poland Spring, where attendees heard Senator Estes Kefauver, a Tennessee Democrat, criticize President Eisenhower for delegating too many of his responsibilities and not spending enough time in the White House. Ed told the crowd that he had "received a substantial amount of cooperation from the overwhelmingly Republican 97th State Legislature, not because the GOP wanted to cooperate, 'but because it didn't dare not to.'"[28]

Soon after, Ed addressed the Bates class of 1955 at their mid-June commencement exercises in the nearby Memorial Armory. After receiving an honorary Doctor of Law degree from the college, he stressed to the graduates the importance of devoting part of their lives to "service to community, state, country, and fellowman." Ed then took a personal tack in his talk to the seniors and their guests, telling them that, when he'd received his Bates degree nineteen years before, he felt that he'd attained all knowledge, but that he'd since learned otherwise:

> "You have but scratched the surface of knowledge," he told the graduates, as he urged them to become informed, concerned, and active in everyday affairs about them, and to become leaders in their own community, state, and nation, even though [doing so would] entail personal sacrifice.[29]

On June 21, Ed nominated his old friend and mentor, five-time Waterville mayor F. Harold Dubord, who'd practiced law in the city since 1921, to a seven-year term as a Superior Court judge. Dubord replaced Justice Percy T. Clarke, who'd been promoted to a seat on the Maine Supreme Court. In Dubord's absence his son and law partner, Richard, took over the practice, which also included Democratic State Representative Albert Bernier of Waterville.

Then came one of those tragedies that make everyone reassess the things that really matter. In the late afternoon, just after he'd returned home from congratulating Harold Dubord on his nomination, Paul Fullam suffered a heart attack and died. Ed was informed of Fullam's passing just as he was about to address the Boys State assembly in Orono, and he used the occasion to pay tribute to his

friend instead of giving the speech he'd prepared. He talked about
Fullam's political and personal life, quoting the famous statement
that "[t]he politician works for the next election. The statesman
works for the next generation." (Attributed to James Freeman Clarke,
the quote is usually given as "A politician thinks of the next election, a statesman, of the next generation.") Muskie went on to say,
"'This statement exemplified Fullam's policy of giving his heart to
his work.'"[30] Ed then canceled his remaining public appearances
prior to Saturday, when he attended requiem mass at the Sacred
Heart Roman Catholic Church in Waterville at 9:30 A.M. Paul
Fullam left behind his wife and three children: Mary Ellen, twenty-two;
Richard, fifteen; and Paul, six.

Addresses to the Maine Lobstermen's Association and the Maine
Dental Society took Ed back to Rockland, scene of the previous year's
"non-debate victory" over Burt Cross. Ed had also been in Rockland
a week earlier to address an osteopaths' convention "and was forced
to eat lobster because a muskellunge, sort of an overgrown pickerel
[commonly known as a muskie], didn't arrive from Michigan in time
for the banquet."[31]

A Visit from the President

With the first week of summer in Maine came a visit by President
Dwight Eisenhower, who was wrapping up a weeklong northern
New England vacation with three days in the Pine Tree State. Two
weeks before his arrival, the president had been offered some advice
on picking a good guide from Maine humorist John Gould via the
New York Times. Gould also unwittingly foreshadowed the partisan
nature of the president's upcoming visit to Maine:

> Of course Maine has plenty of hardworking guides,
> skilled and capable, who could set anybody, even a pres-
> ident, over reluctant trout and salmon, but I think most

of them are too honest and respectable to have the connections that would lead to a political position at the
oars of a Presidential foray. Party allegiance, I suspect,
may dictate some of the arrangements, and it will be a
shame if Ike gets guided by somebody who passes nomination papers with zeal and always sits on the platform
at rallies, but doesn't know dri-ki from a bank beaver's
slide. This would leave Ike idly whipping a fly where it
wouldn't do anybody any good, and is one of the drawbacks of our two-party system.[33]

After visiting Vermont and stopping in New Hampshire, where
he helped commemorate the sesquicentennial of the discovery of
the Old Man of the Mountain rock formation in Franconia Notch,
Ike entered Maine in the early afternoon near Wilson's Mills. At
Parmachenee Lake he was met by Don Cameron, a veteran Maine
guide who was much more focused on fishing than filibustering.
Cameron took Ike first by motorboat to the island site of the Brown
Company's Parmachenee Club, and subsequently to Rump Pond,
where the First Fisherman came up dry, and to Little Boy Falls and
the Riffles on the Magalloway River, where he enjoyed better luck.
    President Eisenhower fished again the following day, but took
Monday off to relax on the porch of the Parmachenee Club. He
enjoyed fishing in Maine so much that over the next two months he
completed an oil painting of Don Cameron from photos of his trip
and sent it up to Brown Company chairman Laurence F. Whitte-
more to present to Cameron. (Local camp owner Bruce Verrill said,
"The portrait Ike painted of Don was burned up somewhere around
1974–76 when the Parmachenee Club Lodge burned—unless someone stole it beforehand."[34])
    In addition to his secret service detail, the president was accom-
panied on his trip by a telephone company trailer so he could remain
in touch with Washington. Also in attendance were about seventy reporters and photographers and "a dozen or more politicians
[including Senator Frederick Payne of Waldoboro], all Republicans,

and important industrialists. One of the industrialists, William F. Wyman, president of the Central Maine Power Company, is regarded as the political boss of this state."[35] But world-famous Maine outdoorsman L. L. Bean, still strong and straight as an arrow at eighty-three, was not invited and ended up sending the president a picnic set in a leather case by way of Senator Payne.

Although he'd been addressing the convention of the National Outdoor Writers Association on Saturday evening in Rangeley, less than forty miles away, Ed wasn't invited to join the Republican fishing party either, and wouldn't get to welcome President Eisenhower to Maine until the third day of Ike's visit, just a few hours before he was scheduled to head back to Washington from Bangor. The president's itinerary that day took him to Rangeley and then on to the Skowhegan Fair Grounds, where he became the first sitting president to give a speech in Maine.

There, 5,000 people saw Ed present the president with a two-foot wooden "Salem American Eagle" carved by fifty-seven-year-old John Upton of Bremen. Afterward Ed invited Ike, who'd recently been teasing the press with contradictory hints about whether or not he planned to run again, to return to Maine "annually hereafter, whatever your occupation."[36] The VIPs then adjourned to Senator Smith's home on the Kennebec River, where she hosted a private clambake on the west terrace of her lawn.

Dwight D. Eisenhower was then more than halfway through the first of his two terms as America's thirty-fourth president. The old general, D-Day mastermind, and first commander of NATO was smarter than many gave him credit for being, smart enough to have seen in 1952 that the Korean War could not be won by conventional means, pragmatic enough to believe that the use of nuclear weapons was unthinkable. An excellent poker player (he stopped playing at West Point when his fellow cadets got tired of losing to him), Eisenhower had maneuvered Communist China into a war-ending armistice by threatening the use of nuclear weapons. The July 1953 armistice came just six months into Eisenhower's term, fulfilling a major campaign promise to war-weary America. According to biog-

Maine's First Couple followed Maine Senator Margaret Chase Smith and President Dwight Eisenhower at the Skowhegan Fairgrounds during Ike's 1955 visit.

rapher Stephen Ambrose, Eisenhower had been unanimously urged by his State Department, joint chiefs of staff, and national security council no fewer than five times by the end of 1954 to launch an atomic attack on China, but had refused each time to do so.

Eisenhower had opposed President Truman's use of atomic bombs on Japan in 1945, believing that Japan had been poised to surrender and that America should not have been the first to use such weapons. In 1953 he had made nuclear-disarmament over-tures to the Soviet Union, but when those went nowhere, he sought instead to contain the nuclear arms race while at the same time see-ing in America's nuclear deterrent a chance to reduce conventional forces and thus the overall defense budget. The last seven years of his presidency would be marked by relative peace, yet he presided over an escalation of the Cold War. He became a strong advocate of

Putting a happy face on the worst-case scenario, Jane shows Stephen and Ellen the bomb shelter at the Blaine House.

air power, much to the disdain of army leaders. And Ike supported his secretary of state, John Foster Dulles, even though Dulles's talk of "going to the brink" of war made Americans cringe. Under the specter of mutually assured destruction, homeowners constructed fallout shelters and schoolchildren were taught to "duck and cover," as if hiding under their little wooden desks would protect them from the blast of an atomic bomb.

A moderate Republican who had claimed no party affiliation prior to 1951 (when Truman pressed him to run for president as a Democrat), Ike must have felt at ease with the politics of Margaret Chase Smith, his host that summer day in 1955. Like Smith, Ike had detested Joseph McCarthy's communist witch hunt, though he had avoided open opposition to McCarthy for fear of losing all support from conservative Republicans, with whom he had often been at odds. "If the right wing wants a fight they are going to get it," he had proclaimed in 1954. "[B]efore I end up, either this Republican Party will reflect progressivism or I won't be with them anymore." Democrats had gone on to win control of both houses of Congress the previous November, and the era of McCarthyism had ended with McCarthy's censure by Congress in December. Three months after the clambake on Senator Smith's lawn, President Eisenhower would suffer a heart attack, but he would recover to run for—and win— reelection in 1956.

While he would make cuts to some government activities, Eisenhower would also expand the Social Security program during his administration. He had begun championing a federal highway system in 1954 and would sign the bill authorizing the Interstate Highway System in 1956. He would send federal troops to Little Rock, Arkansas in 1957 to help enforce school integration there. He would preside over a period of economic prosperity. And during his farewell address to the nation in January 1961, he would express his concerns about the dangers of big government in general and the "military-industrial complex"—a term he coined—in particular. Ever averse to sweeping statements, more comfortable playing his cards close and keeping options open, he would finish his presidency proud of having held the specter of nuclear war at bay. The record was mixed. His administration planned the Bay of Pigs invasion of Cuba that would become President John F. Kennedy's disastrous failure. Nevertheless, history has judged Ike more kindly than contemporary critics did.

By the middle of July, Ed figured he was due for a vacation of his own and took a couple weeks off from work, which he and his family spent at China Lake. He swam, spent time with his family, and did odd jobs around the place. Though he was only fifteen miles from Augusta, Ed said not a single person approached him to discuss politics or government, although "[m]embers of his staff occasionally brought him papers to sign . . . and kept him posted on developments."[37] The governor returned to work looking "tanned and more rested" than when he'd left for vacation, one newspaper reported.

Fall 1955

Ed returned to politics as usual at the State House in early August, when the Executive Council refused to approve his nomination of their fellow Republican Obed F. Millett to the Maine Milk Commission. Democratic Committee Chairman Frank Coffin blasted the council, saying that their refusal to approve the Palmyra dairy farmer "was nothing more nor less than party politics, and a warning to Maine Republicans not to stray from the fold as Millett did."[38] A year earlier, Millett had joined the Republicans for Muskie movement even though he was chairman of Palmyra's Republican committee at the time. Some of the councilors explained that they had turned Millett down because he was a milk dealer in the Boston market and therefore not qualified for the Maine post.

While attending the national Governors' Conference in Chicago, Ed reaffirmed his longstanding commitment to America's vets when he previewed a speech that he planned to give at the thirty-fourth national convention of the Disabled American Veterans in Des Moines. The disabled veteran asked only a "helping hand in getting started back on the road to overcoming the disability," he said. "Beyond that he chooses, as far as is possible, to paddle his own canoe with deep gratitude to those who helped him. His pride asks for nothing more—our appreciation for his sacrifice permits us to give him nothing less."[39]

On August 20, ninety days after the legislature had adjourned, the new Department of Development of Industry and Commerce replaced the Maine Development Commission, which, ironically, had been established during the term of Louis Brann, the state's previous Democratic governor. Even though former MDC member Carl Broggi had initially opposed the idea of the DDIC, saying that the MDC only needed more funding to work well, he would nevertheless be confirmed as commissioner of the new department in early October, and his first step would be to appoint the department's heads of recreation, research and planning, and industrial development. Earle Doucette, who had served as publicity director of the old MDC, would continue in that capacity for the new DDIC.

Among the other eight hundred or so new laws taking effect on August 20 was one that repealed the 1909 Fernald Law, which prohibited the sale of Maine-produced electricity to other states, and one that called for a thorough professional survey of Maine's state government. (The legislature's "piecemeal taxes" on cigarettes, liquor, private car sales, and franchises had already taken effect on July 1, the start of the new fiscal year.)

With the Labor Day weekend just two weeks away, Ed announced a "declaration of war" on drunken driving, reckless driving, and excessive speed. In the previous thirty-five days there had been thirty-eight fatalities on Maine's roads. "Almost every accident involved a violation of the motor-vehicle laws," Ed said, and "[a]t least fifty percent involved an abuse of intoxicating liquor."[40]

Tapping on his desk for emphasis, Ed said that the new effort to cut down on accidents would begin on September 2 and would involve a thirty percent increase in patrols to about 150 men. Plain-clothes officers in unmarked cars would spot the scofflaws and radio ahead to patrol cars. "They will be directed to use all their ingenuity and all their skill in every possible way to apprehend violators," said Ed. "Days off will be cancelled and special non-highway activities reduced to a minimum during what I consider to be the period of emergency."[41]

In early October, *Harper's* magazine writer Bernard DeVoto "set forth that eyesores cluttered the Maine coast and U.S. Route 1 from Newburyport, Massachusetts, to Penobscot, Maine."[42] In response, Maine's recreation director, Everett F. Greaton of Auburn, contacted *Harper's* editor, John Fischer, and canceled all of Maine's promotional advertising in the magazine. Fischer complained to the governor's office that Greaton's actions amounted to an attempt to intimidate the press, a concern with which Ed agreed, and he soon had the state's advertising buy restored. Everett Greaton said that he shouldn't have done what he did, adding "Concerning the charges of intimidation, I never gave it a thought."[43] Three days after the matter

Governor Muskie with a brace of ring-neck pheasants in Richmond—reportedly after bagging each with one shot.

was settled, the Harvard-educated, Pulitzer-winning DeVoto died of a heart attack.

During October, Ed managed to do a little bird hunting in Richmond and spent some quality time with Jane at Camp Phoenix in Nesourdnahunk Township (Township 5, Range 10) on the western edge of Baxter State Park. The time away from Augusta allowed him to prepare for the long slog of the campaign trail ahead; even though he had yet to complete his first year in office, it would soon be 1956—

and time to start running for reelection. While the time wasted by Maine's two-year gubernatorial election cycle was lost on no one, it would take a couple more years to overcome the business-as-usual mentality in Augusta.

"Whether he spends a year or only a few months going after that second election," said the *Press Herald*, "he will be denying the state valuable hours of his administrative time, hours he could be devoting to more serious problems if Maine adopted a four-year term."[44] Ed lobbied for the change in the press, saying, "I was elected to a term of two years. I shouldn't spend more than one of those years as a candidate."[45]

By Halloween, State Chairman Frank Coffin announced that "Once more the Democratic Party is going to the people for the issues in its state campaign."[46] But the party's expectations had increased dramatically this time, and so too did its efforts. The three-man panel that had put together the pre-convention platform in early 1954 would be replaced this time by "a ten-member steering committee and fifteen three-member subcommittees."[47] Coffin added that each subcommittee would include a member from each of Maine's three congressional districts. In January the Democrats would send out a 130-question survey to a thousand Maine residents, building on the successful survey of 1954.

While Ed was off stumping for fellow Democrats in New York, New Jersey, and Pennsylvania, the state's political pundits predicted that his most likely challenger for the Blaine House in September would be Republican House Speaker Willis A. Trafton, Jr., of Auburn. For once they'd be right.

In late 1955, Ed nominated his former campaign manager, Richard McMahon, to a position on the Public Utilities Commission. McMahon was confirmed in December to replace fellow Democrat Edgar Corliss, whose seven-year term was ending. There he'd serve with Chairman Sumner Pike of Lubec and Frederick Allen of Portland, both Republicans. (The rules said that at least one member of the three-man PUC had to be a member of the minority party.) The thirty-three-year-old McMahon, an accountant and Waterville city treasurer, would be paid $8,500 a year. Born in Houlton in 1922, McMahon would serve as a PUC commissioner until 1962, and then would begin a ten-year stint as director of the Farm Home Administration of Housing and Urban Development. (Richard Joseph McMahon would die at age sixty-four in 1987 after losing both legs to diabetes, leaving behind his second wife, Marie, a daughter, two sons, and three stepdaughters.)

It was rumored in late 1955 that Democratic State Chairman Frank Coffin would challenge U.S. Representative Charles Nelson for his Second District seat. Again the pundits would turn out to be right (eventually) about Coffin tossing his hat into the ring, but they'd be wrong about his opponent. There had been recent rumblings among members of the GOP that Nelson's political strength had "dwindled," and there were "faint rumors about a bit of searching to find a strong Republican to challenge Nelson's bid for renomination in the primaries."[48] Three months later Nelson would announce that he would not be seeking another term.

Waterville chiropractor Clinton Clauson decided to once again become active in the Democratic Party after his long stint as the state's Internal Revenue Service collector. (Ed's longstanding dispute with the IRS over his Office of Price Stabilization deductions wouldn't be resolved for a couple more years.) Many party regulars faulted Dr. Clauson, who would campaign against Charles W. Naufel to replace retiring Waterville mayor Richard Dubord, for having been relatively inactive in Democratic issues while working for the IRS between 1933 and 1952. But Doc Clauson, who also operated C.K. Clauson, Inc., fuel dealers with his son, Cornelius, would eventually use his mayoral victory as a springboard to the Blaine House.

One of Ed's final public appearances of the year came in mid December, when he cut the ribbon to officially open the Maine Turnpike extension between Portland and Augusta, exactly eight years to the day after the opening of the highway's first section between Kittery and Portland. While the first section had been completed six years after the legislature had authorized the Maine

All lit up, the Blaine House was a beautiful sight at Christmastime, as seen from the steps of the Capitol.

Turnpike Authority in 1941, the current section had taken two years and $55 million to complete, extending the turnpike to a total length of 64 miles. Federal funding help for highway construction would be enhanced the following year with Eisenhower's signing of the bill creating the Interstate Highway System.

On December 13, the highway's first day of operation, Lewiston and state police officers armed with submachine guns escorted a shipment of bonds worth $11 million to Portland, where it was put on a train for Boston. During the turnpike's first full year of operation, it would be used by 5.4 million cars and trucks. In 2004, 75 million vehicles would travel the Maine Turnpike.

Another Campaign

The cold, gray days of 1956 began with Ed welcoming the new Bluenose ferry to Bar Harbor on its "maiden run" from Nova Scotia (even though the $4 million luxury ferry wouldn't begin carrying passengers until midsummer) and chatting with George Curtis on his WGAN television program "Let's Talk It Over." During a trip down east to Calais and Machias, the governor toured the Passamaquoddy reservation at Peter Dana Point on Big Lake in Indian Township and was shocked by the substandard conditions in which members of the tribe lived. The problem was not a new one, said the *Press Herald:*

> At least once every biennium some official makes a visit to one of the reservations and is righteously indignant over bad housing, bad plumbing, bad education, bad morals. With equal regularity a few half measures are taken. Housing and education needs get a bit of added attention but it all adds up to very little indeed in terms of a permanent solution to the "Indian problem."[49]

A week later, Ed turned his attention back to laying the groundwork for his reelection. In a letter published in the *Bangor Daily News*, he listed some of the state's accomplishments of the previous year, such as the turnpike extension and completion of the Bangor Auditorium. ("The Aud" would be torn down in 2013, replaced by the Cross Insurance Center.) He also noted the "industrial additions" to the Lewiston, Sanford, and Dover-Foxcroft areas. After touting increased aid to education at all levels, Ed finished up with an obligatory affirmation of his belief in continuing progress through the skills and "reawakened faith" of Maine's people.

That same day, he tendered his resignation as a Democratic national committeeman. "Because of the pressure of official duties to which I must devote my full attention, it has not been possible for me to attend national committee meetings for the past year,"[50] he wrote in a letter of resignation to Frank Coffin. There was also the fact that as a national committeeman, he'd have had to spend as much as a week in Chicago during August—just prior to Maine's September election—during which time he could have incurred real losses to the GOP gubernatorial candidate.

Even though it seemed obvious to most observers that he intended to run for reelection, not everyone was convinced that Ed wanted to serve Maine from within its borders. No less a political expert than U.S. Senator Margaret Chase Smith speculated that Ed would back state chairman Frank Coffin for the governorship in 1956 while he challenged U.S Representative Charlie Nelson for his Second District Congressional seat. She also speculated that President Eisenhower wouldn't seek another term due to his recent heart issues, and "that the most likely 1956 Republican ticket will be a [Vice President Richard M.] Nixon-[U.S. Ambassador Claire Booth] Luce combination"[51]—thus confirming that she was no better at prognostication than the press.

Ed took his show on the road during the second week of February, becoming "Maine's number-one salesman" during stops in Boston and New York City. In Boston, noted outdoor writer Bud Leavitt, "Muskie will speak to the Boston University Club at noon, [and] attend the 33rd annual New England Sportsmen's and Boat Show at 2 o'clock,"[52] in the Mechanics Building. It was there that L. L. Bean and what seemed like half the population of Freeport had once promoted Maine, and Bean's guaranteed outdoor gear, to the "sports" from away—until the shrewd merchant decided he was better off spending his money on mailing lists of Midwesterners, that is. Ed finished his day in Beantown by addressing the Advertising Club of Boston at the Harvard Club that evening.

In the Big Apple a few days later, Maine's chief executive and his wife attended the premiere of *Carousel* at the Roxy Theater and hosted a real Maine clambake that included four barrels of Camden seaweed, one and a half tons of rose granite from Southwest Harbor, 500 Penobscot Bay lobsters, fifteen bushels of Friendship clams, and 100 white-meat leghorn broilers from Belfast. (The $4,000,000 20th Century Fox movie starring Shirley Jones and Cameron Mitchell had been shot, in part, on Brewer's Wharf in Boothbay Harbor.) After the movie's premiere, they partook of the supper buffet at the city's famous 21 Club restaurant. While in New York, Ed made several other appearances and conducted at least half a dozen television interviews.

Being governor isn't all work and no play. Ed got to hobnob with actress Jayne Mansfield and The Lobster restaurant co-owner Mike Linz after the New York premier of the movie musical Carousel. *Preparations for an authentic Maine clambake had been underway for days at the 145 West 45th Street restaurant, and included a replica 60-foot-square pit, four barrels of Penobscot Bay seaweed gathered by Rockport schoolchildren, and a ton and a half of Maine granite from Southwest Harbor. Five hundred Penobscot Bay lobsters, fifteen bushels of clams from Friendship, and a hundred leghorn broiling chickens from Belfast were flown in for the occasion.*

About the only bump in the road during the Muskies' visit to New York came when the governor's two-year-old limousine broke down for the second time during the trip. Fortunately the First Couple was within walking distance of their hotel at the time. Unfortunately the limo, whose make was not disclosed, would quit twice more during the next three weeks, once on the Maine Turnpike and a final time while Ed was on his way to Fort Kent, turning that trip into a nine-hour ordeal with a flight back to Augusta. After the fourth breakdown, many local papers ran an Associated Press article under a headline alerting motorists, "Scrutinize hitchhikers, it might be Governor Muskie." Within two months there would be a new limousine carrying Maine registration number 1.

At the end of February, Ed's father died of a heart attack. He'd been in failing health for a number of years, and those close to him had known that it was just a matter of time. Shortly before his death, Stephen Muskie had made sure that all his affairs were in order so his wife, Josephine, would be taken care of. One day he headed down the hill into town for a drink with his friends at the Elks Club and maybe a game of cards. Afterward he took the bus back up Falls Hill, but it dropped him off a block from his home, and the walk into a cold headwind proved too much. His daughter found him on the lawn, holding his glasses in his hand.

Ed was well aware how much he owed his father: the joys of boyhood; the swimming and fishing trips they had gone on together; the discussions and arguments that shaped young Ed's beliefs and ideals. Yes, Stephen had once whipped his son with a belt, but Ed had inherited and occasionally struggled with that same temper. More enduring were the sacrifices Stephen had made to keep Ed in college and get him started in law school. As a payoff, Stephen Muskie got to see his boy get married, start a family, and become governor of Maine—the stuff of dreams for a young tailor who had left Poland alone at age sixteen and immigrated to America.

> [Stephen Muskie] had spoken in the past of a
> modest funeral, but Muskie was adamant. His sisters
> remember Muskie, face drawn, saying, "He didn't get
> much out of my success, but he'll have that, at least." . . . It
> was an elaborate funeral, at which Stephen Muskie's son
> arrived in the gubernatorial limousine, Maine One. But
> the actual service was small and private.[53]

Josephine Muskie was left temporarily alone in the house on Hemmingway Street. "We moved in with her because she didn't want to live alone," said her daughter Lucy.[54]

Just over a week after his father's passing, Ed announced to the surprise of no one (except perhaps Margaret Chase Smith) that he was running for reelection. He derived maximum benefit from his announcement by waiting until just a couple weeks before the party's Bangor convention, prompting some members of the press to speculate just prior to the announcement that the delay was "designed to get Democrats to stir their candidacy stumps in their communities and counties. Folks who see Muskie so purposing think he'll consent to head only a well-fleshed ticket."[55] Campaign slogans such as "Go ahead with Ed" and "One good term deserves another" soon followed the announcement.

Ed's early March announcement came on the same day that he and the state would suffer another tragic loss. Department of Development of Industry and Commerce Commissioner Carl Broggi died of a heart attack at the age of forty-seven. Shortly after hearing the news, Ed began experiencing chest pains of his own, and Marjorie had Joan call his physician, Richard Chasse, who examined the governor and said that the problem had probably been caused by indigestion.

Broggi, a Republican and former state senator, had been born in Sanford in 1909 and graduated from Sanford High School in 1926 and Bates College in 1930. He had served in the state legislature and helped to start the Sanford-Springvale Chamber of Commerce when the area's Goodall-Sanford mills closed in 1954. Broggi's position would be filled by Louis Shapel. A few weeks later, Shapel would fend off a recommendation that the name of the DDIC be changed to the Department of Economic Development (DED). After giving the matter some thought, he said that the new name wouldn't do, because whatever his department was, it wasn't "ded."

Later in 1956, Broggi was played by Darrin McGavin in the NBC program "The Town That Refused to Die," which was narrated by John Cameron Swayze. Broggi's efforts in the Sanford area had been a big reason why Ed selected him to head the DDIC. He was survived by his wife, Margaret, and daughters Joan and Judy. His son, Carl, Jr., had drowned in 1947. At the memorial service, Ed called Broggi "an inspiring and dedicated leader in our effort to build a common future."

In 1957 the legislature would vote to name parts of Routes 111 and 202 between Biddeford and East Rochester, New Hampshire, the

Carl J. Broggi Highway. (Unfortunately, the highway would become a dangerous one, with one section seeing 110 accidents between early 2011 and the middle of 2013, including several head-on collisions. The Department of Transportation has plans to install centerline rumble strips in Lebanon in 2014.)

The editorial writers at the *Portland Sunday Telegram* called 1956 "a do-or-die year" for the state's Democrats. Everyone in the party knew what was at stake: Either the Democratic Party would become a big dog in Maine affairs, or it would get whacked on the nose with a rolled-up Republican newspaper and be sent whimpering with its tail between its legs to hide under the front porch for another couple decades.

If Ed had been delaying his announcement to run for reelection in hopes that it would "stir" other viable candidates into action, it may have worked. Two weeks later, Frank Coffin announced that he would be seeking the U.S. House seat currently occupied by Charles Nelson. Or perhaps Coffin's decision had more to do with the fact that Representative Nelson had announced a month earlier that he wouldn't be seeking another term. Maybe Coffin was simply seeking the reward he felt he'd earned in 1954, when the long-range plan had been for the Democrats simply to lay the groundwork for a Coffin gubernatorial run in 1956. Or maybe the Lewiston lawyer just hoped to help his party solidify the gains made two years earlier.

Coffin's announcement came on the eve of his party's biennial convention, which was being held in the Brewer Auditorium and at the Bangor House and Penobscot Hotel in Bangor. As state party chair he presided over the affair, which enjoyed a record turnout despite being nearly snowbound. The convention's unusual schedule included contests for membership on the state committee and a debate session. Thanks to the absence of scheduled speaker Henry "Scoop" Jackson, a U.S. senator from the state of Washington, who'd been snowed out, "A home-grown collection of talks by the party's leaders was put together, mixing very little in political messages with a lot of humor, and all climaxed with remarks by Cape Elizabeth delegate and iconic actress Bette Davis."[56] This was the first convention for Miss Davis, who sported a green felt hat with long gray "donkey ears" and a bandage above one eye covering a cut she'd suffered in a fall at home earlier in the week.

The Democrats' platform for 1956 was constructed on a combination of new and recycled planks:

> Standbys include shifting the state election date from September to November, abolition of the Governor's Council, a four-year term for governor, and annual legislative sessions. The party also calls for revision of milk-control laws, more pay for teachers, an increase in old-age assistance, creation of a Department of Conservation, and stronger anti pollution laws.[57]

The party once again floated the idea of establishing a state income tax to help pay for new programs, but the more popular notion remained an increase in the sales tax, which could be tailored to have the smallest impact on the people who could least afford it.

Three weeks after the Democratic convention, Ed had the opportunity to again address the Bates College Citizenship Laboratory. The timing of his engagement there was not coincidental, coming right after the Republicans had held their convention in Portland and provided him with a big target at which to take potshots. Squarely in his crosshairs was the recent comment by presumptive GOP gubernatorial candidate Willis Trafton, Jr., that the Democratic platform was "politically immoral." "If we're immoral, then they are too,"[59] said Ed, pointing to recent newspaper reports showing that the GOP platform was "almost a copy" of the one the Democrats had recently unveiled. And he continued to blast the Republican-appointed Executive Council, saying that it should either be done away with or at least elected by the people.

By mid May, a month after the filing deadline, Frank Coffin was conducting his campaign with the skill of a seasoned political veteran, which, in a way, he was. Even though he was the clear favorite over fellow Lewiston resident Roger Dube in the upcoming June 18 primary, the wily Coffin was taking nothing for granted. "His

A young supporter and the Democratic mascot boost Governor Muskie for reelection and Frank Coffin for Congress in 1956.

main campaign 'gimmick' will be 'coffees for Coffin,' a clever way of appealing to women voters, used successfully in Massachusetts by Senator John F. Kennedy a few years ago,"[60] one source reported. While Dube chose to cover a lot of ground quickly, Coffin, by contrast, "moves at a much slower pace, mainly because he feels that it is not fair to smile, shake hands, and move on. . . . Most everyone that he meets gets this question: 'What should your Congressman do for you?'"[61] (Coffin had been reelected as the Democrats' committee chairman, so while he was busy campaigning, Don Nicoll was left in charge of day-to-day operations at campaign headquarters.)

Coffin had been nervous about running against fellow Lewiston businessman and "bon vivant" Roger Dube, and for good reason. Dube, who'd run for the U.S. Senate in 1952, called his opponent "'Little Lord Fauntleroy' and accused him of being part of 'that rare minority in our party with the soft hands and slick hair who had jumped on the bandwagon which we, the little fellows with dirty faces, have built through effort and heartaches in the lean years when the weak of heart dared not run for office.'"[62]

But Dube's plea for support from his fellow Franco-Americans fell on deaf ears. Clearly the better candidate, Coffin prevailed easily in the primary, winning seventy percent of the vote. He would be opposed by Senate Majority Leader James L. Reid in the general election. In the First District, Big Jim Oliver defeated Owen L. Hancock and would take on the GOP's Robert Hale of Portland in September, and Republican Clifford G. McIntire of Perham would be challenged by University of Maine professor Gerald Grady in the Third District.

Any early bravado from Republicans regarding their chances of regaining the Blaine House soon died away. Ed tallied 9,000 more votes than he had two years earlier in the Democratic primary, while Willis Trafton netted 13,000 fewer votes in the GOP primary. As he'd done two years earlier, Ed kicked off his campaign in Gray, this time just two days before the beginning of summer.

One of the highlights of his many campaign stops was an early one in Rockland when, after a speech, he was approached by the owner of a local radio station. The man told Ed that he had something the governor might be interested in hearing. It was a tape that contained the Republican campaign strategy for the entire summer, which the owner had listened to but refused to run. Ed asked him if he'd sent it back to the GOP yet, and when the man said that he hadn't, Ed asked if he could listen to it.

"So he played the whole goddamned outfit," he said, "you know, what they planned to run for the next several months. And it was all attacking me, tax and spend, and all that amateur stuff, you know. So after he got through with them, I said, 'Can I copy them?' And he said, 'Sure.'"[63] Ed then purchased fifteen minutes of television time and played the entire tape after making the following introduction: "Look, in every campaign there's a place to educate the public about the issues and talk about the politics, and all of that. But this is the

Besides making notoriously bad puns, Ed often entertained guests—especially those from out of state—by "hypnotizing" a live lobster.

sort of thing that the other side is going to do, and I thought you'd like to hear it."[64]

Ed campaigned almost as hard in the summer of 1956 as he had two years earlier. "And I think that's why Ed's second election was so easy," said Jane, "because by then he had met everyone in Maine."[65] "By then handshaking had become almost a reflex," according to one report. "One evening, returning home from the hustings, he was greeted at the door by his wife. Muskie automatically stuck out his hand and asked, 'How are all the folks up your way today?'"[66]

In early September, newspapers ran articles about an "artist in residence" who had been commissioned to paint Ed's portrait at the governor's mansion. Evidently capturing the likeness of Maine's chief executive on canvas was a lengthy job, since Ed's official gubernatorial

In 1961, after he had become a senator, Ed's mother got to unveil his por-
trait in the Hall of Flags at the Maine State House.

portrait wouldn't be unveiled until four and a half years later. He and
three of his sisters would attend the February 1961 ceremony, where
they watched their seventy-year-old mother pull away a white satin
cloth to reveal the Claude Montgomery painting.

On September 2, eight days before the general election, the
Boston Herald ran a photo purporting to show Ed in the act of strik-
ing some sort of nefarious deal with CIO area director Dennis Blais
in the governor's office. The caption read, "POWER IN MUSKIE
CAMPAIGN is Denis Blais, left, Lewiston CIO leader, shown here
with Governor Muskie. Blais' CIO-PAC wields the balance of power
with Democrats in the Second District of Central Maine. Blais runs
an around-the-calendar political campaign among CIO workers."[67]

If the photo had been genuine, it would indeed have constituted damning evidence against the governor. But it was neither current nor accurate. It had been taken eighteen months earlier when Ed had met with Blais and Louis F. Luan, assistant to the president of Bates Manufacturing, in an attempt to settle a strike at the Lewiston textile mill. The newspaper had cropped Luan, who was standing on the other side of the governor, out of the picture.

"Well, my answer to that," said Ed, "was to run the original picture in a similar fashion. I bought the time, ran the picture, described where it had taken place, and how they tried to portray it."[68] On television three days later, Ed said, "A Boston newspaper had cropped a photograph to indicate that a CIO official 'is directing my campaign and wielding power over the Democratic Party.'"[69]

Denis Blais did have a hand in Democratic policies of the time. "When [Ed] was elected for the second time, he asked me to write a labor program, or something," said Blais, "and I concentrated principally on unemployment compensation, and he used it in his inaugural address almost word for word."[70] But that hardly meant that Ed had been corrupted and was on the take. Denis Blais was an active member of the Democratic Party, having been a delegate to the National Democratic Committee, and had been recently named chairman of the Democrats for Labor political action committee.

In the closing days of the campaign, Ed's supporters rolled out Operation Speak Up For Muskie, in which citizens from both parties explained in one-minute radio spots why they supported the big Democrat for reelection. The ads, which ran on Portland radio stations WGAN and WPOR, featured a few unknown Republicans and several Democrats with familiar names, including: Adam Walsh, Arthur Benoit, Gary Merrill, and Bette Davis.

When election day rolled around, it became clear that Ed had never had much to worry about. His popularity was so great that he was a virtual shoe-in for a second term, and Willis Trafton, Jr., hadn't been a formidable opponent. "He was a very poor candidate for governor," said former Republican legislator Robert Wade. "He, well, he didn't have a common touch in a way, and he didn't work as hard as he should have."[71] Ed defeated Speaker Trafton by 177,344 votes to 122,494, giving the governor the highest vote tally in any Maine gubernatorial election to date.

As the size of the Democrats' political committees had increased dramatically since the previous election, so had the size of their war chest. On his reelection campaign alone, Ed had spent pent $29,370 of the $29,444 he'd raised. Other Democrats used another $16,000 to help their party bat .500 in the four top-of-the-ticket races, with Frank Coffin defeating James Reid to become "the only freshman Democrat elected to the house east of the Mississippi in 1956."[73] (After the [re]counting was finished in the First District, Jim Oliver ended up losing to GOP incumbent Robert Hale of Portland by just twenty-eight votes.) The Republicans claimed to have raised $60,000 for the primary election and $100,000 for the election campaign.

Second-Term Governor

On the first day of December, Ed finally closed the Waterville law practice he'd taken over on 1940 (although the firm's checking account would remain active until July 10, 1963). Ten days later Frank Coffin officially resigned as chairman of the state committee in order to assume his new position in Washington. He would be replaced by Dr. John C. Donovan, a thirty-seven-year-old Bates College government professor, who told the committee, "It is becoming increasingly clear to the people that they are seeing the image of a new kind of political party which stands for something."[74] Dr. Donovan would also publish a thirteen-page case study about Coffin's congressional run called *Congressional Campaign: Maine Elects a Democrat* (Henry Holt & Company, New York, 1958).

Less than a week after Coffin's departure, the resignation of Don Nicoll became effective, as Coffin's trusted right-hand man prepared to become the new congressman's administrative assistant in Washington. (In 1960 Nicoll would become Ed's administrative assistant

in the senate after Coffin finally got his chance to run for governor—
and lost.)

Melinda, the Muskies' third child, was born on December 28,
1956, making her only the second child to be born to a chief executive
while living in the Blaine House. (Republican Governor and Mrs.
Carl E. Milliken had welcomed Dorothy Blaine Milliken into the
world there on January 22, 1920.) Shortly after Ed was reelected, the
Muskies had set about remodeling the General Pershing Bedroom,
where "Black Jack" Pershing had once slept, into a nursery. To pull
off a budget makeover, the couple hung bright yellow curtains and
replaced the four-poster bed with a crib. The room's new bipartisan
wallpaper included both donkeys and elephants, among other ani-
mals.

When Catherine Rines, the couple's social secretary, arrived at
the hospital to visit Jane right after the birth, she walked into the
room to see Ed sitting on the edge of his seat, fidgeting. By then she
knew him well enough to realize that he wanted to get out of there,
and sure enough, he asked her if she could stay with his wife and new
daughter. "'Do you see this envelope?' he said. 'I have written, I have
started my inaugural address on this envelope,' and he said, 'I've got
to get home . . . because I haven't had a chance to sit down and get
the thing together.' He . . . did not particularly like people writing his
speeches at all."[75]

Ed's address to the 98th Maine Legislature was well received by
members of both parties. "His second inaugural address was smooth,
almost conversational, without the heavy tone of deference he had
assumed two years earlier,"[76] according to one report. He called again
for the date of the general election to be moved to November, and he
called again for a four-year term for the next governor, both of which
he'd get. He also lobbied (unsuccessfully) for annual legislative sessions and for changes to the Governor's Executive Council.

The idea of moving Maine's election date back to November to
coincide with the rest of the nation was far from new. According to
several newspaper accounts, this marked the thirty-sixth time that
the constitutional amendment had been submitted to the legislature

The Muskies and their growing children, perhaps late 1957 or early 1958. From left to right: Ellen, Melinda, and Stephen.

since Maine had become a state in 1820—and the sixth time that Lewiston Democrat Louis Jalbert had proposed the change. According to Jalbert, moving Maine's Election Day to November "would eliminate the September conflict with harvest time and remedy a situation which finds Maine Congressional candidates uninformed of what national issues will be paramount in November elections in the other 47 states."[77] The old slogan, "As Maine goes, so goes the nation," would have to be retired, but it had often proved unreliable anyway.

Ed had already gone on record saying that it was foolish for the state's chief executive to have to spend the second half of his two-year term campaigning for reelection. He felt at least as strongly about the matter after his reelection, saying that he favored "a four-year term for governor with no limit on the number of terms. 'The four-year term is so important that I would be willing to go along with a limit on the number of terms if it were necessary to get it passed,' he said."[78]

A few days after his inaugural address, the governor's 9,500-word budget address also went over well, due in large part to the fact that the Republicans had proposed many of the same programs. In his speech, Ed laid out his "program for progress" budget, which called for a highway bond issue, school consolidation, and the continuance of industrial development using state credit to attract risk capital for new buildings. In addition to his $82,250,000 general fund budget, Ed also proposed a supplemental budget of $15,800,000. To help raise money for new spending, he asked for an increase in the sales tax from two to three percent.

"I am confident," said Senate President Robert Haskell, "that both political parties in the Legislature will cooperate with the Governor in working out sound solutions to the General Fund and Highway Fund problems."[79]

This time the process of developing a budget had gone much more smoothly for the governor and his advisors. Ed had proved a quick study in late 1954, "But it was two years later, when we prepared the budget for the second term," said his assistant Maury Williams, "that I found out how well he had learned [the complex figures]. He gave another discussion comparing the new figures with the old, and now he had both sets in mind with a sort of built-in comparative analysis."[80]

Ed's political house may have been in good order, but the Blaine House was falling apart. As he had noted when the family moved into the 1852 mansion, "We enjoyed it, we loved it. But it hadn't been very well kept up."[81] And the way it was treated by the Muskies' own children certainly hadn't helped matters any, said Jane's sister Virginia Harvey. Steve and Ellen, she remembered, "were pretty undisciplined kids, pretty wild, and you know, they just ran that place, sliding down the banister, walking on the pool table."[82]

Once, when Jane had briefly lost track of Ellen in the big house, she found her in Governor Blaine's library, getting ready to color in a hand-illustrated biography of him. Jane recued the book from her daughter just in time, but her relief was short lived; Sissie, as she was called, had already added a black eye to the bust of James G. Blaine.

When Ed got home later that afternoon, he viewed his daughter's artwork with a laugh and said that, as a politician, this certainly wouldn't have been the first black eye Blaine had suffered. Hundreds of annual visitors and the nearly continual hosting of events only added to the wear and tear of the aging building.

Former governor Percival Baxter helped get the restoration ball rolling with the Executive Council after visiting the Muskies for lunch one day and seeing how much the Blaine House had deteriorated since his time there during the early 1920s. "[H]e asked me if everything was to my liking," said Jane, "and I said, 'Not really,' because there were a lot of things that should be taken care of. That since this house belonged to the people of the State of Maine, I certainly hoped that it would be in better shape when we left than it was when we arrived. And he said, 'Like what?' And I walked him around the house and showed him things."[83]

By February 1957, Ed and Niran C. Bates, a planning engineer of the Bureau of Public Improvements, had compiled a list of the building's needed repairs. The lengthy to-do list included repairs to the bulging plaster walls and their coverings, replacing tattered curtains and drapes, installation of wall-to-wall carpeting, painting, the addition of storm windows, and some new furniture. Even the old piano could no longer carry a tune. "Perhaps," said Bates, "an individual or civic organization may wish to make a gift of a new piano to the Blaine House."[84] It was the peoples' house, after all. The total cost of needed repairs and renovations was estimated at $24,300.

The Muskies would sell their own house on Silvermount Street in Waterville to N. Richard Hallee a couple months later. The selling price of $14,000 was $6,000 more than they had paid for the house less than a decade earlier. (During the same period the price of heating oil had increased from 9.4 cents a gallon to 16.1 cents.) On that same day in early April, Ed also sold his office furniture to real estate agent Joseph A. Roy, who would occupy the building at 131 Main Street for "many years," for $500. Rumford businessman J. Harold McQuade would eventually purchase the Waterville building and have the 5½-foot by 3-foot mahogany desk that Ed had used shipped back to

Rumford, where it is now used by the town manager. (McQuade was also chairman of the committee that raised $100,000 in 2000 for the construction of a large stone monument to Ed, which is located next to the town's information center at the famous Rumford Falls.)

To help foster cooperation across the aisle, Ed decided in early February to hold an informal weekly meeting with legislative leaders while they were in session. No attempt would be made to reach binding agreements during these discussions; rather, they would be "opportunities to explore our thinking and clarify the issues so there might be better understanding of the other fellow's position."[85] It wasn't long before those amicable meetings began to pay off.

Later in the month Ed made a plea for public support of an industrial building authority that would place the state's credit behind new factory buildings. "We have already wasted too much time in planning for our industrial future," he told an overflow crowd at Portland's Eastland Hotel. "It is time we struck out into the water and started swimming. Tomorrow may be too late. This is something we should have done yesterday."[86] The bill would have the state insure industrial building loans of as much as $500,000 for up to twenty-five years. But the measure, which would require approval of the voters, was in danger of not getting the two-thirds vote it needed to get out of the senate.

When Ed heard that Senator Harold Schnurle and Senate President Robert Haskell were likely behind the bill's holdup, he let it be known that he planned to go before both chambers in a joint session to stump for the bill. When Haskell got wind of the governor's plan, he sprang into action and called the Senate Republicans into caucus. "They met behind closed doors for about a half hour. Insiders report that Haskell 'really laid it on the line.' The Senate reconvened, reconsidered its previous vote, and only seven voted against it."[87] (Though many people at the capitol had recently accused Haskell and Ed of becoming "pals," no one would ever accuse Haskell and Schnurle of being friends even for a little while.)

Most of Maine's politicians were in favor of helping new businesses and industries establish themselves in the state, but not at the expense of families. That appears to have been the reasoning behind the governor's signing of a bill that tightened the nine-hour work-day law for women. "Now employers are forbidden to work women more than nine hours. As amended by the new legislative act, the law would forbid women to accept employment under such conditions."[88] At the same time, the legislature was arguing over whether or not to raise the state's minimum wage to seventy-five cents an hour. (The federal minimum wage was then a dollar per hour.)

As summer 1957 drew closer, the legislature enacted Ed's $85 million general services budget without debate and sent it to him for signature. He also received approval for a $68 million highway pro-gram, which included a $24 million bond issue that would need to be approved by the voters. Since approval of the highway bond question was a prerequisite for Maine's participation in the interstate highway system (signed into law by President Eisenhower the year before), the governor said he planned to "take to the stump" in August to drum up support for that measure and four other bond issues that were up for approval in September. The $17 million portion of the bond ear-marked for Interstate 95 would trigger an additional $152 million in federal funds for use on interstate roads between 1957 and 1968. The remaining $7 million was earmarked for the improvement of Maine's secondary roads—for everything from reducing steep grades to fix-ing blind corners—since Ed saw roads as an economic lifeline for the state.

In early June the movie *Peyton Place* was filming in Camden—and Ed was invited to appear as an extra on the reviewing stand during a parade sequence. "I'm looking forward to it," he said, "and I hope that my weekend schedule allows me the time."[89] His pay would be $10 a day, the same as for other extras with no lines. The 20th Cen-tury Fox movie would make $12,000,000 at the box office and earn Lana Turner an Academy Award nomination for best actress.

The Democrats held their annual Jefferson-Jackson Dinner at the Samoset Resort in Rockport on June 21, 1957. The 550 enthusias-tic Democrats (and a few Republicans) who attended the $15-a-plate event were treated to "vigorous, down-to-earth" speeches by the governor and Senator John F. Kennedy of Massachusetts. According to a *Bangor Daily News* editorial, the crowd also "heard Frank Coffin, who wrested the Second District Congressional seat from the Republicans, discuss the 'supreme' party opportunities in Washington. They also heard Muskie hint that Coffin might be Democratic gubernatorial nominee next year."[90] The editorial also noted that the GOP now "lacks issues. It lacks candidates. It lacks inspiring leadership."[91] Things had changed in three short years.

Though Ed was popular with the majority of Maine voters, there were still a few people who wished the worst for him. One "crackpot" went so far as to threaten to kill him. (The "crackpot" correspondence file kept by Ed's staff would grow to three folders.) "There was some hate mail from somebody signing, calling themselves 'German Ike,' threatening to kill him," said former *Press Herald* reporter Jeb Byrne. "I don't know whether it was religious or what kind of reasons [the writer said he didn't like Catholics and foreigners], and they had to put a state trooper outside . . . the governor's suite. And the Governor wanted the press not to mention this at all. And to my recollection, we went along with him. I don't think that would happen today."[92] The press withheld stories about the threat until around Labor Day, two months after the letter had been received, the writer having said he would kill the governor in August. Police theorized that the letter's Baltimore postmark could have been a red herring. The incident led to tighter protection for Ed and his family from the state police, which in itself made some people uneasy, remembers Jane's niece Judy Harvey, who was ten at the time. "This one time when we were going for dinner," she said, "and we drove up to the Blaine House, every window had a State Police officer with a gun in it. . . . And I remember going in there and being really scared, and everybody was talking about it."[93]

In a light turnout for September's off-year balloting, Maine's voters apparently heeded Ed's August appeal for support and approved all five referendum questions, including the moving of future elections from September to November; a four-year term for future governors; a state guarantee of industrial construction

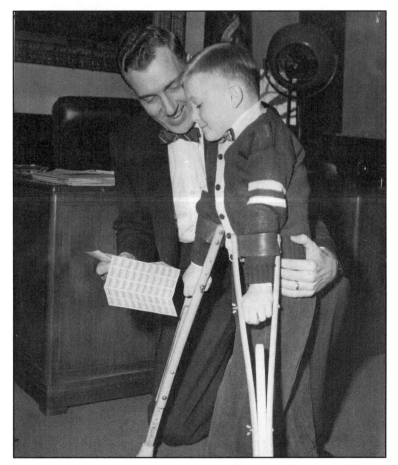

Ed shows his support of Easter Seals with help from the charity's poster boy.

mortgages; a $24,000,000 highway bond; and a $2,500,000 bond for the state-owned ferry service in Penobscot Bay.

Around Thanksgiving, Ed traded turkey for rubber chicken, embarking on a brief promotional tour of the northeast. First he spoke to Boston University's School of Public Relations and Communications about the question "Do Convictions and Politics Mix?," using the issue of integration as an example. After telling his audience, "I am for integration," Ed went on to explain "that all people want 'the right to earn a living, to provide an education and opportunity for their children, to live in dignity and self-respect.'"[97]

The civil rights movement in America had been gaining momentum for the past several years. In 1954 the United States Supreme Court under Chief Justice Earl Warren (an Eisenhower appointee) had unanimously ruled that segregation in public schools was illegal in the case of *Brown* v. *Board of Education of Topeka*. Late the following year, Reverend Martin Luther King, Jr., led a boycott that resulted in the desegregation of the bus system in Montgomery, Alabama. But there was still a long way to go; just two months before Ed's talk, President Eisenhower had needed to dispatch the National Guard to Little Rock, Arkansas, so that nine black students could attend public school there.

From Boston, Ed returned to New York and the Waldorf-Astoria, where he explained "the state's new plan for using its credit to ensure mortgages on new factory space"[98] to a group of financial writers.

> Under the new plan, he said, communities interested in obtaining new industry may create a nonprofit development corporation. When the corporation has an industrial prospect, it will determine the needs for new factory space and raise ten percent or more of the cost. It would then apply through normal financial channels for a loan covering the balance and to the newly created industrial building authority for insurance on this plan.[99]

Politics Never Stops

As had been the case in all other even-numbered years since Maine had achieved statehood in 1820, the year of 1958 began with a flurry of political activity. At the end of January, Ed made official what many observers already suspected: He was not going to run for reelection as governor and would not seek to take advantage of the new four-year term of office. He was keeping "an open mind" about challenging Waldoboro's Frederick Payne for his U.S. Senate seat, but Ed was adamant in his belief that now was the time for Frank Coffin to make his run for the Blaine House.

The Democrats' preconvention platform committee met in Waterville during the subsequent two weeks before the party faithful traveled to Bangor to attend a "Meet Muskie" dinner. Somehow the Democrats always seemed to schedule their bigger winter events to coincide with the arrival of a major snowstorm, and this get-together was no different. In spite of the weather, more than 300 people turned out to meet the governor and his wife at the testimonial dinner. Before giving his prepared talk to the group, Ed did nothing to end the speculation about his political plans for the immediate future. "This is a year of much speculation," he said, "and I am not going to end any of that speculation tonight. That would end the fun too suddenly."[100] His talk that evening consisted of a detailed reprisal of his thoughts on "convictions and politics":

> [A]voiding "yes-men" constitutes one of the important "techniques and tools" in the art of politics. "Profit from those who disagree with you," he told Penobscot County's leaders and partisans at Pilots Grill.
> "Seek advice and counsel. Having obtained the facts, surround yourself with those whose experience and judgment will enable you to weigh them."
> "Get the facts and all points of view, be thorough, be a good listener, be decisive and don't agonize."[101]

Ed let the speculation about his plans continue for another six weeks before announcing five days prior to the Democratic convention in late March that he was, in fact, a candidate for the United States Senate. "So I sort of delayed it, I dragged my feet and I finally made the decision to run for the Senate because if I didn't that would largely be the end of the effort to make Maine a two-party state,"[102] he said later. Even though he had recently been having second thoughts about continuing in politics, the decision to run was ultimately an easy one, he recalled:

> [A]s I approached the end of my second term as governor, I gave some thought to the possibility of. . . . As a matter of fact . . . a very successful Portland law firm made an offer to me, as my gubernatorial term approached its end, to join them. And that would have been probably financially much to my advantage. But I didn't hesitate when I finally decided to run for the Senate, I didn't hesitate about doing that because that offer was available. And I never again considered not running for either family reasons or for professional reasons.[103]

The arrival of another big snowstorm could only mean that it was time for another major gathering of Democrats. This time it was their state convention, which was held in Lewiston for the second time in four years.

Although Ed had been urging him to run for governor, Frank Coffin had decided back in January to seek reelection to his Second District congressional seat. His thinking was "that his work on the Foreign Affairs Committee and in the House was very important and that he was gaining the experience and skill to make a real contribution through his congressional service."[104]

With Coffin out of the picture (though he would not make his plans public until May), the Democratic gubernatorial nomination would be contested by chiropractor and former Waterville mayor Dr. Clinton A Clauson, who had served nearly two decades as Maine's IRS tax collector, and State Grange Master Maynard C. Dolloff of Gray. Frank Coffin and most other party leaders supported Dolloff because they believed he "could expand the base of the party to rural areas, lessening its dependence on the traditional urban core."[105] Ed remained neutral, but most pundits believed that if Frank Coffin, Richard McMahon, and Richard Dubord all supported Maynard Dollof, then so must the governor. "Frank was quite open in his support of Dolloff," said Don Nicoll, and yet "Muskie caught much more hell for his supposed support than Frank did for his open support."[106]

"The press speculated that Dolloff was the Muskie candidate," said Ed when he was running for president years later, "and they never believed me when I said I was neutral. . . . I often think I should have come out and supported a candidate. After all, you get accused of it anyway."[107]

The convention was enlivened by the contest to see who would get to take on Republican Representative Robert Hale in the Second Congressional District. When State Representative Lucia Cormier and Eli Gaudet, both of Rumford, decided against entering the race, former Republican Jim Oliver of Cape Elizabeth and Brunswick Representative Adam Walsh were left to settle the matter in the June 16 primary election.

Three weeks after the convention, Ed was still asserting his neutrality in the upcoming gubernatorial primary—but this time he was being accused of backing Clauson. He told a group at the Bates College Citizenship Laboratory that he had told each candidate in the presence of the other that he was not taking sides in the contest. When asked about a rumor circulating through the Lewiston area that he, Frank Coffin, and Clint Clauson were "a team," Ed replied, "I haven't changed my mind. Neither [State Representative Louis] Jalbert or anyone else can speak for me. I am capable of stating my own position publicly. I have no need of any agents."[109] Jalbert quickly denied starting the rumor and said he'd sue whoever had.

While being governor had its myriad problems, the job also had perks, one of which was flying to Florida on official business. A brief mid-May newspaper article focused on the fact that nine-year-old Stephen Muskie's trip aboard an Air National Guard plane was his first long flight, taking his father to the National Governors Conference in Miami Beach. Stephen was also accompanied on the trip by his mother, sisters, and two grandmothers.

In the June 16 primary, both candidates favored by most party leaders were defeated by their rivals. Jim Oliver's victory over Adam Walsh probably came as less of a surprise than 45-year-old Maynard Dolloff's loss to 62-year-old Clint Clauson, who prevailed with 52 percent of the 40,000 votes cast. In the GOP primary, meanwhile, the specter of the 1952 liquor scandal hung over Frederick Payne's head like the sword of Damocles when he was challenged by the case's central figure, Herman Sahagian, whom he defeated.

The Democrats again held their early summer Jefferson-Jackson Dinner at the Samoset Resort in Rockport. "The featured speaker was Speaker Sam Rayburn, whose trip to Maine at Coffin's invitation was a mark of his regard for the Maine Congressman. The Speaker seldom traveled anywhere except Washington and his home in Texas."[110] Further confirmation that the movement in Maine was attracting widespread attention came in the form of a small piece in the *New York Times*: "Another sign of Democratic cockiness comes from Maine where Governor Edmund Muskie, a Democrat running for the Senate seat of Republican Frederick G. Payne, has adopted the slogan, 'The Payne of Maine is Plainly on the Wane.'"[111]

During the summer, Ed got more mileage out of his "Do Convictions and Politics Mix?" speech, discussing the question at his New York alma mater, Cornell. This time the address was reprinted in the *New York Times Sunday Magazine*, which led publisher Harcourt, Brace & Company to immediately dispatch a representative to Augusta, Maine, to speak with Ed about writing a 90,000-word autobiography. Ed told the representative he'd think it over. "I decided my political future was too uncertain for me to decide one way or the other, but I did say 'maybe,'"[112] he said. Another request by the publisher after Ed had been a senator for four months would elicit the same response. He would eventually write his story, called *Journeys*, for Doubleday & Company in 1972.

In late August Ed debated Senator Payne on the subject of foreign policy. The contest, which was televised on WMTW TV, was considered by most observers to have ended in a tie. Frederick Payne was not a gifted orator. "[He] was a typical politician I guess you'd say, run-of-the-mill politician," said former Deputy Secretary of State Paul McDonald. "I can't say that Fred Payne was outstanding in anything he did, but he was adequate."[113] That Ed, a skilled debater, could have finished in a draw with a merely "adequate" opponent has a simple explanation.

On the day of the election, which was then just two weeks away, Ed would disclose that he had arrived at his debating strategy based on the results of a recent poll. The survey of likely voters had revealed that they were mainly concerned about local issues such as highways and economic development and cared little about national and international affairs. More importantly, the survey revealed that most people just plain liked Ed as a person. It was for this reason that he decided not to challenge Payne on a lot of points during the debate; to win the election, he just had to be himself. "In Maine, where the Republicans lost their first Senate seat on September 8," a *New York Times* reporter would note, "it was the widespread personal popularity of Governor Edmund Muskie, not any particular policies he advocated, that won him his passage to the Senate."[114]

A couple days after the debate, as the candidates were gearing up for the stretch run, there came an August surprise. On television in support of Senator Payne, former U.S. Senator Ralph Owen Brewster (who went by "Owen" because his initials were ROB) touched on a number of subjects including the "charge about the amount of money that unions were pouring into the Maine Democratic campaigns."[115] Brewster's two main targets were Frank Coffin and Ed, who let loose on the former senator at a rally in Waterville, "[thundering] in indignation that Brewster had sunk 'to a mere hatchet man to gain political power and prestige.'"[116]

Brewster's timing was every bit as bad as his choice of targets. Frank Coffin had just suspended his campaign that morning because of the death of his father, Herbert. Brewster apologized the next day, saying he'd been unaware of the passing of Coffin's father, but it was too late. His objective had been to make the Democrats look bad, but instead he had shot the GOP in the foot once again.

Two weeks before the election, a pundit for the *New York Times* wrote, "Popular Democratic Governor Edmund Muskie is trying to unseat incumbent Republican Frederick G. Payne. The Democrats are optimistic, but State-o'Mainers aren't so sure."[117] Maybe a lot of Mainers changed their minds about Ed during the next two weeks, or more likely the writer read the tea leaves wrong, because Ed defeated Frederick Payne by 61,000 votes. Afterward the lame-duck senator seemed almost relieved. "Maybe the voters have done me a favor," he said. "This way I'll probably live longer."[118]

Leaving Augusta

On election night the Muskies entertained Democratic supporters Bette Davis and her fourth husband, Gary Merrill, at the Blaine House. (Davis had recently been sued by her third husband, Rockport artist and former boxer William Sherry, for $1,750 in back alimony he said she owed him. The actress had divorced Sherry on July 4, 1950, while working on the movie *All About Eve*, and married Merrill twenty-four days later.) But neither Ed's big win nor the visiting movie stars could overshadow Jane Muskie's news: "The Muskies are expecting a fourth child on Christmas Day. 'Ed told me not to breathe a word of it,' she said, 'because the voters would say we did this in every campaign.'"[119] Six-pound, four-ounce Martha Muskie (1958–2006) would be delivered by Dr. Richard L. Chasse at 1:00 A.M. on December 17 at Sisters' Hospital in Waterville. She would be a classmate of the author at the University of Maine at Orono.

Supporting his growing family (and buying a bigger camp on the south end of China Lake) was about to become a lot easier for Ed, whose salary would more than double to $22,000 once he took the oath in Washington. He later figured that his senatorial campaign cost as much as $100,000, or more than three times as much as he'd spent in his gubernatorial reelection campaign two years earlier. "I mean what happens in politics," he said, "you spend the money

Though always serious about his religion, Ed was here captured in a lighter moment with two unidentified priests.

that you get. And, of course, by the time I was a Senator, running for reelection as a Senator, you know, you could raise almost as much money as you didn't want."[120]

Maine's last Democratic U.S. senators had both started their terms in 1911—Charles Fletcher Johnson as an election winner and Obadiah Gardiner as an appointee (by Democratic Governor Frederick W. Plaisted) to finish the term of the late Republican William P. Frye.

The other top-ticket Democrats also fared well in the 1958 election. Frank Coffin (1919–2009) was reelected over Neil Bishop by a whopping 15,000-vote margin. Also heading to Washington was "Big Jim" Oliver, who'd defeated Robert Hale by 3,000 votes in the First District. The only major Republican candidate to prevail in the election was Third District U.S. Representative Clifford McIntire, who defeated University of Maine professor Gerald Grady, a political newcomer, by nearly 7,500 votes.

In the gubernatorial contest, the *Boston Herald* gleefully

reported that with 478 of 632 precincts reporting, Republican Horace Hildreth led "Doc" Clauson in the balloting 67,206 votes to 63,154. But Clauson made an amazing comeback in the late tallying, eventually beating Hildreth by fewer than 10,000 votes of the 270,000 cast. Though his victory to become Maine's first four-year governor was widely ascribed to the length of Ed's coattails, Clauson had become a tough campaigner in his own right, ultimately unleashing a series of attacks blaming Hildreth and the entire Republican Party (all the way up to President Eisenhower) for the 1958 recession in particular (which, though short, was the most significant postwar recession prior to 1970) and high unemployment in general. "'Doc' was 'not regarded as a particularly strong candidate and was underestimated by all of us,'" [121] said Don Nicoll.

Like his predecessor in the Blaine House, Clint Clauson also benefited from his "one-on-one empathy with the voters. It was this talent 'to connect' that gave Clauson, a one-time chiropractor, the edge."[122] The state legislature would be one-third Democratic—enough to sustain the incoming governor's vetoes. And this favorable September result proved to be a harbinger, for once following the "As Maine goes" script; Democrats made major gains across the nation in November.

One of Ed's last official acts as Governor of Maine was to appoint Tom Delahanty, who'd recently resigned after two and a half years as chairman of the Public Utilities Commission, to the Superior Court. His first attempt to appoint the Lewiston attorney to the bench had been blocked by the Executive Council, whose members were concerned not so much that he was a Democrat as that his appointment would give Androscoggin County four judges on Maine's Supreme and Superior courts. So Ed decided it was time to play a little political poker with the council.

It was well known around the State House that Senate President Robert Haskell very much wanted to be governor—even if only for a few days. Ed declared that instead of leaving early (as he needed to do to keep from losing seniority and committee assignments to other freshman senators), he was willing to remain in Augusta until the end of his term at midnight on January 7, if need be, to fight for Delahanty's appointment. The Executive Council members knew Ed had to be in Washington on the third of January, but in the end they declined to call his bluff and confirmed Delahanty's appointment. Ed resigned on January 2, and Robert Haskell served as governor until Clint Clauson was sworn in on January 8. (Governor Clauson would die on December 30 after less than a year in office. He was replaced by Senate President John H. Reed, Maine's fourth governor during 1959.)

A governor is the steward of his or her state, and a good governor (like a good homeowner) should leave the thing he's caring for in better shape than he found it, whatever the difficulties. Ed Muskie had been a good governor. He had spearheaded an investment in roads, ports, and other vital infrastructure. He had put the state's future capital improvements on a more sustainable footing by allotting $4 million for a long-range building program instead of relying on whatever money happened to be left over in the budget. He had increased funding for the state's parks and supported the idea of establishing a new one at Cape Elizabeth. And he had established the Maine State Museum in the State House.

Ed had increased subsidies for education at all levels—including public schools, the University of Maine, and state teachers' colleges—and he had increased the pay of teachers. He had commissioned an eight-month study of Maine's governmental institutions by the Chicago research firm Public Administration Service (PAS) that recommended "sweeping changes" to the way things were done in Augusta. (As expected, the study generated more partisan bickering than immediate change, but it was a necessary first step.) He had successfully championed the change of Maine's general election date from the second Monday in September to the November date used by the rest of the country. No longer would the state's politicians be without the support of their national parties because Maine's elections were so early. And he had won an increase in the next governor's term of office from two years to four. No longer would the state's chief executive be forced to spend the second half of his term campaigning for reelection.

By his own admission, Muskie had not made much progress during his years as governor on the anti-pollution plank of the Maine Democratic platform. One factor complicating any effort to combat pollution at the state level was the fear (or threat) of the polluting industry picking up stakes and moving to a more accommodating state. This—and the fact that pollution doesn't observe state boundaries—argued for national solutions. Ed's future identity as a shaper of national anti-pollution legislation was quite likely forged in Augusta as well as his Rumford boyhood.

While big-business interests in the Maine legislature could shield the state's mills and shoe factories from new state pollution laws, they could do precious little to protect those industries from distant competitors. The first of the state's big industries to take a hit from competitors from away were the textile mills. In 1954, the year of Ed's first campaign for governor, Burlington Mills Corporation had purchased the Goodall-Sanford mill, the area's largest employer, only to quickly shut it down. Less than three years later, Lewiston's Bates Manufacturing would lay off 350 people when it was forced to suspend weaving operations at one of its mills due to a "sagging rayon market." Over the next few decades, all of Maine's textile and shoe factories—save for a few specialty shops—would succumb to cheaper products from foreign competitors. Some of the larger paper mills are still hanging on in 2014, but paper machine shutdowns and employee layoffs are now an all-too-common occurrence.

Consider Ed's hometown, Rumford. A century after Stephen Muskie's arrival there, Rumford, like other papermaking towns in Maine, is struggling with a downsized mill and a shrinking population. The town's census held steady at around 10,000 until the early 1970s, when it began a steady decline. By 2010, Rumford had about 6,500 residents and found it hard to attract even a small cinema. Among the many recent ideas put forth to revitalize the town are a soap opera hall of fame, a modern assisted-living center, and several boutique shops located at the town's gateway. In early 2013, town officials even considered the construction of several zip-lines—including one from the top of Falls Hill—that would pass under the beautiful Memorial Bridge, which was built in 1929. The plan was defeated at the polls.

As Ed said, jobs are the most important thing of all, and also the hardest thing for a governor—or a president, for that matter—to create. Muskie championed a constitutional amendment to secure $20 million so the state could guarantee new private-company industrial building loans of up to $500,000 each. He spearheaded the formation of the Department of Development of Industry and Commerce, which would become the Department of Economic Development. A governor can try to maintain a favorable infrastructure and a favorable context in which jobs can be created, and Ed did that.

But perhaps Ed's biggest accomplishment as governor was changing the way Maine voters thought. No longer did they have to settle for the GOP's business-as-usual way of conducting business. No longer was the governorship passed from one Republican to the next as a reward for party service and loyalty. The "dry rot" in Augusta was gone, and people seemed to have a sense that real progress was finally on the way.

Maine during the second half of the 1950s was probably the scene of one of the biggest political turnarounds the country has ever seen. Prior to 1954, the Maine Democratic Party had existed in little more than name only; the old joke about the Democrats in the legislature being able to caucus in a phone booth was based in truth. Ed's election as governor had marked the beginning of a sea change for the party; in 1956 Frank Coffin won the Second District Congressional seat, and two years later, Clint Clauson rode Muskie's coattails to the Blaine House. Of the next nine elected governors after Muskie, four would be Democrats (Clauson, Ken Curtis, Joe Brennan, and John Baldacci), three would be Republicans (John Reed, John McKernan, and Paul LePage), and two would be independents (James Longley and Angus King). It's no exaggeration to say that Ed Muskie, Frank Coffin, Don Nicoll, Dick McMahon, and their supporters ended single-party politics in Maine.

As his second term drew to a close, Governor Muskie was about to become Senator Muskie, but the question of how the seven members of the Executive Council should address him in his final weeks at the Blaine House had been settled right after the election. "One said, 'Congratulations, Governor,' another 'Congratulations, Senator,' and a third told Muskie he didn't know which title to use at this point."

"'What's the matter with continuing to call me 'Ed?' Muskie wanted to know."[124]

Afterword

So ends the story of how Ed Muskie was shaped by Maine, and how, as a young man, he in turn helped reshape his native state. As that story ended, the story of how Senator Muskie crafted our nation's environmental laws and protections was about to begin. It's a big story, and here we can offer only a glimpse.

Ed Muskie's Senate career got off to a rocky start when he antagonized Senate Majority Leader Lyndon Baines Johnson shortly after being sworn in for his first term in January 1959. In a get-acquainted chat, LBJ sought Ed's support for a proposed change to Rule XXII, the Senate cloture rule for ending filibusters. A change was needed in part to overcome Southern opposition to civil rights legislation, and Johnson proposed that debate be ended with the agreement of two-thirds of those present instead of two-thirds of the total Senate membership. Ed, however, favored ending debate with just three-fifths of those present, and he made the mistake of stating his position too freely to LBJ.

What Ed viewed as discussion, LBJ saw as insubordination, and he saw to it that the freshman senator got none of his desired committee assignments. Ed had wanted seats on the Foreign Relations, Commerce, and Judiciary committees but instead was assigned to the Public Works, Banking and Currency, and Government Operations committees. Lyndon Johnson then ignored him for months. Muskie said later of his initiation into the Senate, "I was very frustrated, lonely, disillusioned and disconsolate."

Nevertheless, the new senator made the most of his assignments, writing shortly after his contretemps with LBJ that a senator "should never lose sight of where he wants to go" and that good government in the Jeffersonian tradition was "the enduring polestar." Rejecting standard political labels, Ed wrote that if labels were unavoidable, the one he would accept was "realist." Realistic governance would "[r]ecognize that laws and institutions are not ends in themselves but means of serving the needs and aspirations of our people," and it would "[a]ccept the need for change when the times and circumstances require it." A realist, wrote Muskie, "believes in serving ideals, but he believes in doing so practically." By the time Edmund S. "Ned" Muskie, Jr. was born in 1961—Jane and Ed's fifth child— Ed had become a respected member of the United States Senate. In his autobiography, *Journeys,* Ed wrote of LBJ's retaliation:

> In the long run, perhaps it was just as well. Such committees gave me the chance to work on problems of increasing importance to the country. In fact, the combination of Banking and Currency, Government Operations, and Public Works was unique in the Senate, and working in and between those committees I was caught up in most of the legislative effort to improve the quality of urban life in America. Senator Johnson had done me a favor. Although I don't think he had planned it that way.

Through his work in the Public Works Committee, Ed's environmental awareness continued to evolve and expand. In 1960 he was highly critical of President Eisenhower's veto of legislation that would have increased federal grants for the construction of sewage treatment plants in communities around the nation from $50 million to $90 million. In 1961, during committee hearings on amendments to the Federal Water Pollution Control Act, he was enthusiastic about the prospects for amending and funding the legislation under new President John F. Kennedy.

In 1963, following the deaths of two more senior Democratic committee members, he found himself chair of the Public Works Committee's newly created Special Subcommittee on Air and Water

Pollution—another of those opportunities that Ed would recognize and embrace. The subcommittee, created at his request, reflected an evolving national awareness of environmental health issues. *Silent Spring,* Rachel Carson's groundbreaking book about the dangers of pesticides, had been published in 1962. In 1964 the U.S. Public Health Service would for the first time characterize cigarette smoking as a health hazard.

Five years earlier, in one of a series of talks he called "Do Convictions and Politics Mix?," delivered at his law school alma mater Cornell, Muskie had suggested that "[o]ne is not equipped for leadership in a democracy unless one is willing and able to see problems when they arise, and to understand their nature, to develop judgments in advance of the voters, and to propose the solutions indicated, whatever risk may be involved. . . ." In 1963, Muskie recognized that the time had come to lead on environmental issues. Whereas conservationism had been concerned with the preservation of land, environmentalism would be concerned with the preservation and improvement of public health. Muskie's commitment to the well-being of average Americans and his belief in the beneficial possibilities of an activist government led him to the insight that public health should be the linchpin of environmental policy, and that it argued for a strong federal role.

Hailed by his peers as that rare legislator who could persuade opponents to his point of view, Muskie wrote and guided to passage the nation's first major pollution control laws, the Clean Air Act of 1963 and the Water Quality Act of 1965, then followed these with the Air Quality Act of 1967 (which expanded the research program established by the 1963 bill) and ultimately the landmark Clean Air Act of 1970 (which established regulatory controls for air pollution) and Clean Water Act of 1972. He was also a key figure in the creation of the Environmental Protection Agency. As his hard work paid off and he rose through the ranks in the Senate, Ed became known as "Mr. Clean" for his work to help clean up the environment.

He was considered Lincolnesque not just because of his lanky six-foot-four frame and craggy features, but also because of his plain-spoken honesty, self-deprecating humor, and record of integrity. He was selected by Hubert Humphrey to be his running mate in the 1968 presidential race. Journalist David Broder said years later that this was "perhaps the only ticket in my time on which both men clearly could have been and should have been President. Instead, we got Richard Nixon." The election was extremely tight, and Muskie's effective campaigning added to his national stature. "In politics," Humphrey said later, "I've known people who were brilliant, clever, but he has qualities that are more important—intuition, judgment, wisdom."

Muskie's national profile rose further with a ringing 1970 election-eve rebuke to President Nixon and Vice President Spiro Agnew's strident insistence that Democrats were endangering America by appeasing communism. "There are only two kinds of politics," Muskie said, "the politics of fear and the politics of trust. One says: You are encircled by monstrous dangers. . . . The other says: The world is a baffling and hazardous place, but it can be shaped to the will of men." He came to be regarded as the frontrunner for the Democratic nomination for president in 1972, Senator Edward Kennedy's aspirations having been detoured by the drowning death of a female aide at Chappaquiddick Island in 1969.

But America and the Democratic Party were deeply divided by the Vietnam War in 1972, the one issue about which Muskie was uncharacteristically indecisive. He had been moving by small degrees from support to opposition of the war since 1966, but still had trouble articulating a non-nuanced position in 1972. He was instinctively a moderate in a time that devalued moderation. His candidacy effectively ended in the New Hampshire primary after the *Manchester Union Leader* printed a letter—afterward known as the "Canuck letter"—accusing Muskie of insulting French Americans during a speech in Florida.

The letter was later discovered to have been forged by Nixon operatives waging a "dirty tricks" tactic against a feared opponent. Incensed by the smear, Muskie was further outraged by the *Union Leader*'s publication of allegations—reprinted from *Newsweek* magazine, which had picked up the allegations from yet another publication—that Jane Muskie was an alcoholic given to vile obscenities. In a news conference in a snow squall in front of the *Union Leader* offices, Muskie called publisher William Loeb "a gutless coward . . . who doesn't walk (but) crawls." Enraged, his voice cracking with emotion as he defended his wife, he lost composure in a way that might have been applauded twenty years in the future but was considered unseemly at the time in a candidate for the nation's highest office. Muskie won the New Hampshire primary, but his support slipped from that day forward. He stopped campaigning in April and quit the race in July. George McGovern became the Democratic nominee—largely on the basis of his outspoken opposition to the war—and lost the election to Nixon in a landslide.

Muskie resigned from the Senate in 1980 to become secretary of state under President Carter following the resignation of Cyrus Vance, serving until Carter left office in 1981 (after awarding Muskie the Presidential Medal of Freedom). Ed elected to stay in Washington, saying that "the one thing I have to bear in mind is that I must assume my wife is going to outlive me. . . . She's much younger than me. I have to start building a life that she can continue." In 1981 he joined the Washington office of Chadbourne & Parke, a large New York law firm.

To recognize his achievements and catalog his life, Bates College in Lewiston established the Edmund S. Muskie Archives on September 28, 1985, only hours after Hurricane Gloria had blown through the state. The following year, Ed was appointed to the Tower Commission to investigate the Reagan administration's role in the Iran-Contra Affair, and in 1990 the University of Southern Maine established the Edmund S. Muskie Institute of Public Affairs.

Edmund Sixtus Muskie died at Georgetown University Hospital from heart failure early in the morning of March 26, 1996, two days before his eighty-second birthday. In 2000, a two-year effort led by J. Harold McQuade came to fruition with the dedication of the Edmund S. Muskie Memorial in Rumford. The dedication ceremony was attended by Jane Muskie, who was being cared for in the final years of her life by her daughter Martha. Jane died on December 25, 2004, at the age of seventy-seven, and Martha died a year later, on January 2, 2006, at the age of forty-seven, after a long struggle with lupus.

Senator George Mitchell broke into politics as a member of Muskie's staff from 1961 to 1967, managed Muskie's 1972 presidential campaign, and succeeded Ed to the Senate in 1980. In eulogizing his friend and mentor, Mitchell said, "He changed the way Americans think and the way they live. It would be unthinkable now for someone to suggest that we suddenly let factories and municipalities start dumping all their sewage into rivers—which we did for almost all of American history until he changed laws and changed minds and changed attitudes." (In his eulogy, Mitchell also recalled his first encounter with Muskie's legendary temper. "I couldn't control the shaking of my legs, even though I was sitting down," he said.)

Elsewhere Mitchell said, "Nothing surpasses what he did to protect America's natural environment. It's one thing to write and pass a law. It's another thing to change the way people live. It's yet another and quite difficult thing to change how people think. Ed Muskie did that. Before it was a national cause or even well known, environmental protection was Ed Muskie's passion. Any Maine citizen who wants to appreciate what Ed Muskie did need only drive to the nearest river."

Said journalist Mark Shields: "Before [Ed Muskie] began his work, there were no national laws and no international agreements governing the quality of the country's air and water. None. When he began his work, nearly three-quarters of the nation's rivers were unswimmable and unfishable. The Great Lakes were dying. In too many places, the air was a threat to a child's lungs and even to a community's life. In no small measure because of the laws he wrote, twenty years later three quarters of the nation's rivers were both swimmable and fishable. The Great Lakes were alive—recreationally, economically and spiritually. More than 95 percent of the lead had been removed from the nation's air. But more than the landmark environmental laws he crafted, the legacy of Senator Edmund Muskie of Maine is a truly healthier, safer and more responsible country. Of how many American Presidents can the same be said?"

Not bad for an immigrant tailor's son from Rumford, Maine.

Endnotes

Chapter One. Rumford Beginnings

1. Vito Puiia interviewed by James G. Ross, Rumford, Me., July 1985, MOH 005, transcript, Muskie Oral History Collection, The Edmund S. Muskie Archives and Special Collections Library, www.Bates.edu/Muskie-Archives

2. David Nevin, *Muskie of Maine*, Random House, New York, 1972, p. 43.

3. Nevin, p. 73.

4. Edmund S. Muskie interviewed by Sally Davis and Virginia Ray in Kennebunk, Me., 4 Sept. 1991, MOH 024, transcript, Muskie Oral History Collection, The Edmund S. Muskie Archives and Special Collections Library, www.Bates.edu/Muskie-Archives

5. Edmund S. Muskie interviewed by Don Larrabee in Washington, DC, 28 Nov. 1995, MOH 095, transcript, Muskie Oral History Collection, The Edmund S. Muskie Archives and Special Collections Library, www.Bates.edu/Muskie-Archives

6. Muskie interviewed by Davis and Ray, 4 Sep. 1991, MOH 024, Muskie Oral History Collection.

7. Frances and Austin McInnes interviewed by Andrea L'Hommedieu, Rumford, ME, 13 Sept. 00, MOH 220, transcript, Muskie Oral History Collection, The Edmund S. Muskie Archives and Special Collections Library, www.bates.edu/Muskie-Archives

8. Muskie interviewed by Davis and Ray, 4 Sep. 1991, MOH 024, Muskie Oral History Collection.

9. James M. Naughton, "The Taste of Defeat," *New York Times*, 14 May 1972, p. SM13.

10. Nevin, pp. 56-7.

11. Edmund S. Muskie interviewed by James G. Ross in Kennebunk, Me., 14 Aug. 1985, MOH 001, transcript, Muskie Oral History Collection, The Edmund S. Muskie Archives and Special Collections Library, www.Bates.edu/Muskie-Archives

12. Tom Shields, "Ed Muskie's $14,000 campaign to the Blaine House," *Bangor Daily News Magazine*, 1 Feb. 1984.

13. Nevin, pp. 74-5.

14. Edmund S. Muskie, *Journeys*, Doubleday & Company, Inc. Garden City, NY, 1972, pp. 162-3.

15. Naughton, p. SM13.

16. Posted by Max Znak at http://connect.state.gov/group/muskie/forum/topics/midnight-research-on-edmund-s-muskie-origins, 18 Oct. 2011.

17. Muskie, et al. interviewed by Beam, 6 Aug 1991, MOH 022, Muskie Oral History Collection.

18. Muskie, *Journeys*, p. 73.

19. Muskie interview by Ross, 14 Aug 1985, MOH 001, Muskie Oral History Collection.

20. Ibid.

21. Phil and Frank Anastasio interviewed by Andrea L'Hommedieu, Rumford, Maine, 30 Oct. 00, MOH 235, transcript, Muskie Oral History Collection, The Edmund S. Muskie Archives and Special Collections Library, www.Bates.edu/Muskie-Archives

22. Kenneth Bosworth interviewed by James G. Ross, Mexico, Me., July 1985, MOH 009, transcript, Muskie Oral History Collection, The Edmund S. Muskie Archives and Special Collections Library, www.Bates.edu/Muskie-Archives

23. Nevin, p. 61
24. Phil and Frank Anastasio interviewed by L'Hommedieu, 30 Oct. 2000, MOH 235, Muskie Oral History Collection.
25. Susan Sheehan, "Pro: He's a nice guy. Con: Nice guys don't necessarily make good presidents," *The New York Times.* 22 Nov. 1970, p. 223.
26. Bosworth interviewed by Ross, July 1985, MOH 009, Muskie Oral History Collection.
27. Phil and Frank Anastasio interviewed by L'Hommedieu, 30 Oct. 2000, MOH 235, Muskie Oral History Collection.
28. Irene (Muskie) Chaisson and Lucy (Muskie) Paradis interviewed by James G. Ross, location unknown, 14 May 1985, MOH 003, transcript, Muskie Oral History Collection, The Edmund S. Muskie Archives and Special Collections Library, www.Bates.edu/Muskie-Archives
29. Muskie, *Journeys*, p. 70.
30. Muskie interviewed by Ross, 14 Aug. 1985, MOH 001, Muskie Oral History Collection.
31. Ibid.
32. Nevin, p. 83.
33. Muskie, *Journeys*, p. 112.
34. Bosworth interviewed by Ross, July 1985, MOH 009, Muskie Oral History Collection.
35. David A. Sargent, "River Views," *Lewiston Sun Journal*, 28 April, 2009, p. B1.
36. Nevin, p. 58
37. Muskie interviewed by Ross, 14 Aug. 1985, MOH 001, Muskie Oral History Collection.
38. Puiia interviewed by Ross, July 1985, MOH 005, Muskie Oral History Collection.
39. Muskie interviewed by Ross, 14 Aug. 1985, MOH 001, Muskie Oral History Collection.
40. Phil and Frank Anastasio interviewed by L'Hommedieu, 30 Oct. 2000, MOH 235, Muskie Oral History Collection.
41. Frances and Austin McInnis interviewed by L'Hommedieu, 13 Sept. 2000, MOH 220, Muskie Oral History Collection.
42. Muskie interviewed by Ross, 14 Aug. 1985, MOH 001, Muskie Oral History Collection.
43. Bosworth interviewed by Ross, July 1985, MOH 009, Muskie Oral History Collection.
44. Muskie, *Journeys*, pp. 74-5.
45. Puiia interviewed by Ross, July 1985, MOH 005, Muskie Oral History Collection.
46. Ibid.
47. Muskie interviewed by Ross, 14 Aug. 1985, MOH 001, Muskie Oral History Collection.
48. Phil and Frank Anastasio interviewed by L'Hommedieu, 30 Oct. 2000, MOH 235, Muskie Oral History Collection.
49. Theo Lippman, Jr. and Donald C. Hansen, *Muskie*, W. W. Norton and Co., New York, 1971, pp. 39-40.
50. Diana and Frank Anastasio interviewed by James G. Ross, Mexico, Me., 24 June 1985, MOH 007, transcript, Muskie Oral History Collection, The Edmund S. Muskie Archives and Special Collections Library, www.Bates.edu/Muskie-Archives
51. Muskie, *Journeys*, p. 76.
52. Bosworth interviewed by Ross, July 1985, MOH 009.
53. Phil and Frank Anastasio interviewed by L'Hommedieu, 30 Oct. 2000, MOH 235, Muskie Oral History Collection.
54 Edmund Muskie, introduction to diary, summer 1933, p. 4, The Edmund S. Muskie Archives and Special Collections Library, Series 1, Box 31, Folder 2.

55. An error on page 76 of Muskie's 1972 autobiography, *Journeys*, has the sentence reading, in part, that Miss Hicks "later became Mrs. Warren," instead of Mrs. Warren S. Abbott.

56. Nevin, p. 58.

57. James G. Ross, *As Maine Goes*, (Senior Thesis, Bates College), 1986, pp. 92-3, The Edmund S. Muskie Archives and Special Collections Library, Bates College, Lewiston, Me.

58. Muskie interviewed by Ross, 14 Aug. 1985, MOH 001, Muskie Oral History Collection.

59. Nevin, p. 82.

60. Nevin, p. 59.

61. Frances and Austin McInnis interviewed by L'Hommedieu, 13 Sept. 2000, MOH 220, Muskie Oral History Collection.

62. "Stephens Seniors Awarded Diplomas on Thursday Night," *Rumford Falls Times*, 23 June 1932.

63. Also called the Pact of Paris or the Treaty for the Renunciation of War, the pact had been drafted in 1928 by U.S. Secretary of State Frank B. Kellogg and French Foreign Minister Aristide Briand. The following year Kellogg was awarded the Nobel Peace Prize for the pact, which had been signed by 15 nations. Aggressions that led up to World War II made the treaty useless for preventing wars. It did, however, remain useful for its establishment of the concept of war as an outlaw act by an aggressor state on a victim state.

64. Muskie, *Journeys*, p. 150.

Chapter Two. College, Law School, War

1. Edmund Muskie, Shep Lee, Don Nicoll, and Frank Coffin interviewed by Chris Beam in Kennebunk, ME, 6 August 1991, MOH 022, transcript, Muskie Oral History Collection, The Edmund S. Muskie Archives and Special Collections Library, www.Bates.edu/Muskie-Archives

2. Letter from Harry Rowe to George Lord, 1 Dec. 1931, The Edmund S. Muskie Archives and Special Collections Library, Series 1, Box 11, Folder 5.

3. Muskie interviewed by Ross, 14 Aug. 1985, MOH 001, Muskie Oral History Collection.

4. Ibid.

5. Betty Winston Scott interviewed by Don Nicoll in Cape Elizabeth, ME, 6 Sept. 2006, MOH 230, transcript, Muskie Oral History Collection, The Edmund S. Muskie Archives and Special Collections Library, www.Bates.edu/Muskie-Archives

6. Lucy (Muskie) Paradis and Irene (Muskie) Chaisson interviewed by Ross, 14 May 1985, MOH 003, Muskie Oral History Collection.

7. "Heavy Losses Caused by Sunday Morning Fire on Congress Street.," *Rumford Falls Times*, 16 Feb. 1933, p. 1.

8. Muskie diary entry, 26 July 1933. Series 1, Box 31, Folder 2, Muskie Papers.

9. Muskie diary entry, 13 Sept 1933. Series 1, Box 31, Folder 2, Muskie Papers.

10. Muskie diary entry, 19 July 1933. Series 1, Box 31, Folder 2, Muskie Papers.

11. Vincent McKusick interviewed by Andrea L'Hommedieu in Portland, ME, 23 July 2001, MOH 311, transcript, Muskie Oral History Collection The Edmund S. Muskie Archives and Special Collections Library, www.Bates.edu/Muskie-Archives

12. Ruth Rowe Wilson interviewed by Don Nicoll, Rob Chavira, and Stuart O'Brien in Lewiston, ME, 22 July 1998, MOH 034, transcript, Muskie Oral History Collection, The Edmund S. Muskie Archives and Special Collections Library, www.Bates.edu/Muskie-Archives

13. Nevin, p. 60.

14. Nicoll interview of Betty Winston Scott, MOH 230.

15. Robert G. Wade, Sr. interviewed by Andrea L'Hommedieu, Auburn, ME, 15 Dec. 1999, MOH 163, transcript, Muskie Oral History Collection, The Edmund S. Muskie Archives and Special Collections Library, www.Bates.edu/Muskie-Archives

16. Robert York interviewed by Rob Chavira, and Stuart O'Brien, Orr's Island, ME, 13 Aug. 1998, MOH 040, transcript, Muskie Oral History Collection, The Edmund S. Muskie Archives and Special Collections Library, www.Bates.edu/Muskie-Archives

17. "Rare photos of Muskie now on display at Bates," (Lewiston) *Sun Journal*, 1 April 2008, p. C13.

18. Edmund S. Muskie to his sister Lucy, March 1935, Series 1, (Personal and Family), Box 4, Folder 2. Edmund S. Muskie Papers, The Edmund S. Muskie Archives and Special Collections Library, Bates College, Lewiston, ME.

19. Stan Franczyk, "Muskie at Bates," *Am-Pol Eagle*, 13 Oct. 1988, p. 11. Series 1 (Personal and Family), Box 25, Folder 2A, Edmund S. Muskie Papers, The Edmund S. Muskie Archives and Special Collections Library, Bates College, Lewiston, ME.

20. Edmund S. Muskie to his sister Lucy, May 1935, Series 1 (Personal and Family), Box 4, Folder 2. Edmund S. Muskie Papers, The Edmund S. Muskie Archives and Special Collections Library, Bates College, Lewiston, ME.

21. Muskie, *Journeys*, p. 113.

22. Ibid.

23. Edmund S. Muskie to his sister Lucy, 6 Oct. 1935, Series 1 (Personal and Family), Box 4, Folder 2. Edmund S. Muskie Papers, The Edmund S. Muskie Archives and Special Collections Library, Bates College, Lewiston, ME.

24. Joe Biernacki and Pricilla Biernacki Clark interviewed by Meredith Gethin-Jones, Naugatuck, CT, 18 Feb. 1999, MOH 065, transcript, Muskie Oral History Collection, The Edmund S. Muskie Archives and Special Collections Library, www.Bates.edu/Muskie-Archives

25. Winston Scott interviewed by Nicoll, 6 Sept. 2006, MOH 230, Muskie Oral History Collection.

26. Ruth Rowe Wilson interviewed by Nicoll, et al., 22 July 1998, MOH 034, Muskie Oral History Collection.

27. Ibid.

28. Muskie interviewed by Ross, 14 Aug. 1985, MOH 001, Muskie Oral History Collection.

29. Edmund S. Muskie to Stephen Muskie, June 1936, Series 1 (Personal and Family), Box 4, Folder 2. Edmund S. Muskie Papers, The Edmund S. Muskie Archives and Special Collections Library, Bates College, Lewiston, ME.

30. Stan Franczyk, "Muskie at Cornell," *Am-Pol Eagle*, 27 Oct. 1988, p. 14. Series 1 (Personal and Family), Box 25, Folder 2A, Muskie Papers.

31. Muskie interviewed by Davis and Ray, 4 Sept. 1991, MOH 024, Muskie Oral History Collection.

32. Lippman and Hansen, p. 42.

33. Muskie interviewed by Ross, 14 Aug. 1985, MOH 001, Muskie Oral

History Collection.

34. George B. Farnsworth, M.D. to Edmund S. Muskie, 5 Feb. 1945, Series 1 (Personal and Family), Box 4, Folder 13. Edmund S. Muskie Papers, The Edmund S. Muskie Archives and Special Collections Library, Bates College, Lewiston, ME.

35. George B. Farnsworth, M.D. to Edmund S. Muskie, 13 May 1938, Series 1 (Personal and Family), Box 13, Folder 5. Edmund S. Muskie Papers, The Edmund S. Muskie Archives and Special Collections Library, Bates College, Lewiston, ME.

36. Winston Scott interviewed by Nicoll, 6 Sept. 2006, MOH 230, Muskie Oral History Collection.

37. Frances and Austin McInnis interviewed by L'Hommedieu, 13 Sept. 2000, MOH 220, Muskie Oral History Collection.

38. George B. Farnsworth, M.D., letter to Edmund S. Muskie, 27 March 1940, Series 2 (Waterville Law Practice), Box 2. Edmund S. Muskie Papers, The Edmund S. Muskie Archives and Special Collections Library, Bates College, Lewiston, ME.

39. Muskie, et al. interviewed by Beam, 6 Aug. 1991, MOH 022, Muskie Oral History Collection.

40. Lippman and Hansen, p. 43.

41. Muskie, et al. interviewed by Beam, 6 Aug. 1991, MOH 022, Muskie Oral History Collection.

42. Nevin, p. 91.

43. Ibid.

44. Lippman and Hansen, p. 44.

45. Muskie, et al. interviewed by Beam, 6 Aug. 1991, MOH 022, Muskie Oral History Collection.

46. Ibid.

47. John Roger Fredland to Edmund S. Muskie, 19 Nov. 1940, Series 1 (Personal and Family), Box 4, Folder

4. Edmund S. Muskie Papers, The Edmund S. Muskie Archives and Special Collections Library, Bates College, Lewiston, ME.

48. Muskie interviewed by Ross, 14 Aug. 1985, MOH 001, Muskie Oral History Collection.

49. Lippman and Hansen, p. 44.

50. Edmund S. Muskie to Stephen Muskie, 4 Sept. 1942, Series 1 (Personal and Family), Box 16, Folder 1. Edmund S. Muskie Papers, The Edmund S. Muskie Archives and Special Collections Library, Bates College, Lewiston, ME.

51. Ibid.

52. Francis Mascianica interviewed by Greg Beam, Saugus, MA, 14 Aug. 2000, MOH 227, transcript, Muskie Oral History Collection, The Edmund S. Muskie Archives and Special Collections Library, www.Bates.edu/Muskie-Archives

53. Ibid.

54. Letter of recommendation from Edmund S. Muskie's commanding officer, 11 Nov. 1943, Series 1 (Personal and Family), Box 17, Folder 3. Edmund S. Muskie Papers, The Edmund S. Muskie Archives and Special Collections Library, Bates College, Lewiston, ME.

55. United States Navy orders for Lt. (jg) Edmund S. Muskie, April 1944, Series 1 (Personal and Family), Box 17, Folder 3. Edmund S. Muskie Papers, The Edmund S. Muskie Archives and Special Collections Library, Bates College, Lewiston, ME.

56. Muskie, *Journeys*, pp. 113-14.

57. Ibid., p. 114.

58. Professor Brooks Quimby to Edmund S. Muskie, 30 September 1944, Series 1 (Personal and Family), Box 5, Folder 1. Edmund S. Muskie Papers, The Edmund S. Muskie Archives and Special Collections Library, Bates College,

Lewiston, ME.

59. Unknown Navy buddy to Edmund
S. Muskie, 23 Jan. 1945, Series
1 (Personal and Family), Box 5,
Folder 1. Edmund S. Muskie
Papers, The Edmund S. Muskie
Archives and Special Collections
Library, Bates College, Lewiston,
ME.

60. Martha Blackington to Edmund S.
Muskie, 25 July 1945, Series 1 (Per-
sonal and Family), Box 5, Folder
1. Edmund S. Muskie Papers, The
Edmund S. Muskie Archives and
Special Collections Library, Bates
College, Lewiston, ME.

61. Edmund S. Muskie to his com-
manding officer, 8 Sept. 1945,
Series 1 (Personal ad Family), Box
17, Folder 3. Edmund S. Muskie
Papers, The Edmund S. Muskie
Archives and Special Collections
Library, Bates College, Lewiston,
ME.

Chapter Three. Rising Star

1. Lippman and Hansen, p. 46.
2. Edmund S. Muskie to his parents,
18 Jan. 1946, Series 1 (Personal and
Family), Box 5, Folder 1. Edmund
S. Muskie Papers, The Edmund
S. Muskie Archives and Special
Collections Library, Bates College,
Lewiston, ME.
3. Edmund S. Muskie interviewed
by Chris Beam, Kennebunk, ME,
3 Sept. 1991, MOH 013, transcript, Muskie Oral History Collection, The Edmund S. Muskie
Archives and Special Collections
Library, www.Bate.edu/Musk-
ie-Archives
4. Lippman and Hansen, p. 45.
5. Muskie, Journeys, p. 132.
6. Nevin, p. 147.
7. Jane Muskie interviewed by Don
Nicoll, Bethesda, Maryland, 3

May 2000, MOH 189, transcript,
Muskie Oral History Collection,
The Edmund S. Muskie Archives
and Special Collections Library,
www.Bate.edu/Muskie-Archives
8. Ibid.
9. Ibid.
10. Judy Klemesrud, "It was love that
made Mrs. Muskie join the Democratic Party," New York Times,
30 Aug. 1968, p. 36.
11. Klemesrud, p. 35.
12. Ibid.
13. J. Muskie interviewed by Nicoll, 3
May 2000, MOH 189, Muskie Oral
History Collection.
14. Ibid.
15. Ibid.
16. Klemesrud, p. 35.
17. Nevin, p. 94
18. Franczyk, "Ed Muskie enters politics," Am-Pol Eagle, 1 Dec. 1988, p.
8. Series 1 (Personal and Family),
Box 25, Folder 2A, Muskie Papers.
19. Bob Thomas, "Rudy Vallée eyes
politics," Nashua Telegraph, 2 Jan.
1968, p. 9.
20. Edmund S. Muskie, mayoral
candidate speech on WTVL Radio,
27 Nov. 1947, Series 3 (Early Public
Service), Box 1, Folder 7. Edmund
S. Muskie Papers, The Edmund
S. Muskie Archives and Special
Collections Library, Bates College,
Lewiston, ME.
21. Edmund S. Muskie, speech to the
Maine Democratic preconvention conference, Bangor, ME, 29
Nov. 1947, Series 3 (Early Public
Service), Box 1, Folder 10. Edmund
S. Muskie Papers, The Edmund
S. Muskie Archives and Special
Collections Library, Bates College,
Lewiston, ME.
22. Lippman and Hansen, p. 48.
23. Nevin, pp. 101-02.
24. Susan Sheehan, "Pro: He's a nice
guy. Con: Nice guys don't necessar-
ily make good presidents," The New

York Times, 22 Nov. 1970, p. 223.

25. Klemesrud, p. 36.

26. Nicoll interview of Jane Muskie, MOH 189.

27. "Muskie-Gray," Rumford Falls Times, 27 May 1948.

28. Joe Biernacki and Pricilla Biernacki Clark interviewed by Gethin-Jones, 18 Feb. 1999, MOH 065, Muskie Oral History Collection.

29. Postcard from Ed and Jane Muskie to Stephen Muskie, 3 June 1948, Series 1 (Personal and Family), Box 5, Folder 2. Edmund S. Muskie Papers, The Edmund S. Muskie Archives and Special Collections Library, Bates College, Lewiston, ME.

30. Muskie, Journeys, p. 132.

31. L. A. "Lal" Lemieux, "Feel no district in state is hopeless," Lewiston Evening Journal, 24 March 1950, p. 1.

32. Don Nicoll and Frank Coffin interviewed by Chris Beam and Erin Griffiths, Portland, ME, 20 Nov. 1996, MOH 011, transcript, Muskie Oral History Collection, The Edmund S. Muskie Archives and Special Collections Library, www.Bate.edu/Muskie-Archives

33. Frank M. Coffin, Life and Times in Three Branches, 2004, (unpublished), p. 261. Cited by Don Nicoll in "Frank Morey Coffin's Political Years: Prelude to a Judgeship," Maine Law Review, Vol. 63:2, 2004, p. 399.

34. Don Nicoll, "Frank Morey Coffin's Political Years: Prelude to a Judgeship," Maine Law Review, Vol. 63:2, 2004, p. 399.

35. Lorin "Doc" Arnold, Bangor Daily News, 25 March 1950, cited by Don Nicoll in "Frank Morey Coffin's Political Years: Prelude to a Judgeship," Maine Law Review, Vol. 63:2, 2004, p. 399.

36. Muskie, et al. interviewed by Beam, 6 Aug. 1991, MOH 022, Muskie Oral History Collection.

37. Muskie, Journeys, p. 132.

38. Muskie, et al. interviewed by Beam, 6 Aug. 1991, MOH 022, Muskie Oral History Collection.

39. Edmund S. Muskie, letter to William Silsby, Speaker of the House, Legislative Record—House, 8 February 1951, p. 219.

40. Muskie, et al. interviewed by Beam, 6 Aug. 1991, MOH 022, Muskie Oral History Collection.

41. Milton Wheeler interviewed by Greg Beam, Portland, ME, 5 July 2000, MOH 201, transcript, Muskie Oral History Collection, The Edmund S. Muskie Archives and Special Collections Library, www.Bate.edu/Muskie-Archives

43. J. Muskie interviewed by Nicoll, 3 May 2000, MOH 189, Muskie Oral History Collection.

44. Lippman and Hansen, p. 51.

45. Lippman and Hansen, p. 52.

46. Muskie, Journeys, p. 133.

47. Floyd L. Harding interviewed by Don Nicoll, Presque Isle, ME, 9 October 1998, MOH 049, transcript, Muskie Oral History Collection, The Edmund S. Muskie Archives and Special Collections Library, www.Bate.edu/Muskie-Archives

48. Michael V. DiSalle, "Balance from the bottom up," New York Times, 17 April 1973, p. 41.

49. L. A. Lemieux, "Muskie won't run; Demos write-in plan falls through," Lewiston Evening Journal, 9 June 1952, p. 1.

50. John E. "Jeb" Byrne interviewed by Don Nicoll, Alexandria, VA, 5 Dec. 2000, MOH 253, transcript, Muskie Oral History Collection, The Edmund S. Muskie Archives and Special Collections Library, www.Bate.edu/Muskie-Archives

51. Nicoll, Maine Law Review, p. 400.

52. Frank Morey Coffin interviewed by Don Nicoll, Stuart O'Brian,

and Rob Chavira, Portland, ME, 21 July 1998, MOH 033, transcript, Muskie Oral History Collection, The Edmund S. Muskie Archives and Special Collections Library, www.Bate.edu/Muskie-Archives

53. Nicoll, Maine Law Review, pp. 399-400.

54. Wheeler interviewed by Beam, 5 July 2000, MOH 201, Muskie Oral History Collection.

55. Muskie, et al. interviewed by Beam, 6 Aug. 1991, MOH 022, Muskie Oral History Collection.

56. Wheeler interviewed by G. Beam, 5 July 2000, MOH 201, Muskie Oral History Collection.

57. McKusick interviewed by L'Hommedieu, 23 July 2001, MOH 311, Muskie Oral History Collection.

58. Muskie interviewed by Beam, 3 Sept. 1991, MOH 013, Muskie Oral History Collection.

59. Muskie, et al. interviewed by Beam, 6 Aug. 1991, MOH 022, Muskie Oral History Collection.

60. Nicoll, Maine Law Review, p. 401.

61. Muskie, Journeys, p.134.

62. J. Muskie interviewed by Nicoll, 3 May 2000, MOH 189, Muskie Oral History Collection.

63. Muskie, Journeys, p. 134.

64. Jere Clifford interviewed by Marisa Burnham-Bestor, Lewiston, ME, 12 May 1999, MOH 093, transcript, Muskie Oral History Collection, The Edmund S. Muskie Archives and Special Collections Library, www.Bate.edu/Muskie-Archives

65. Muskie, et al. interviewed by Beam, 6 Aug. 1991, MOH 022, Muskie Oral History Collection.

66. Christopher Williams, "Judge an outspoken agent of change," Lewiston Sun Journal, 11 Nov. 2008, p. A1.

67. Frank Morey Coffin interviewed by Nicoll, et al., 21 July 1998, MOH 033, Muskie Oral History

Collection.

68. Williams, p. A1.

69. Nicoll, Maine Law Review, p. 402.

70. "Maine democrats to hold convention in Lewiston," Lewiston Evening Journal, 5 Oct. 1953.

71. Lippman and Hansen, p. 53.

Chapter Four. Improbable Victory

1. "Gov. Cross decides to seek reelection," Lewiston Evening Journal, 7 Jan. 1954.

2. Frank Morey Coffin interviewed by Nicoll, et al., 21 July 1998, MOH 033, Muskie Oral History Collection.

3. Nicoll, Maine Law Review, p. 402.

4. Don Nicoll, interview with author, Portland, ME, 18 Jan 2013.

5. Ibid.

6. Muskie, et al. interviewed by Beam, 6 Aug. 1991, MOH 022, Muskie Oral History Collection.

7. Ibid.

8. "Democrats seek 'Ground Roots' for platform in six-page questionnaires," Lewiston Evening Journal (AP), March 1954, p. 1.

9. Don Nicoll, interview with author, Portland, ME, 18 Jan 2013.

10. Muskie, et al. interviewed by Beam, 6 Aug. 1991, MOH 022, Muskie Oral History Collection.

11. Lippman and Hansen, p. 80.

12. Muskie, et al. interviewed by Beam, 6 Aug. 1991, MOH 022, Muskie Oral History Collection.

13. Ibid.

14. Muskie, Journeys, p. 52.

15. Nicoll and Coffin interviewed by Beam and Griffiths, 20 Nov. 1996, MOH 011, Muskie Oral History Collection.

16. Ibid.

17. L. A. Lemieux, "Maine Politics: Demos find convention interest lags," Lewiston Evening Journal, 6

March 1954, p. 1.

18. L. A. Lemieux, "Sills can't be governor, was born in Nova Scotia," Lewiston Evening Journal, 24 March 1954, p. 1.

19. "Meyer tells Rotarians of Mt. Washington TV," Lewiston Evening Journal, 25 March 1954.

20. Edward Schlick, "Speaks on two-party system," Lewiston Daily Sun, 26 March 1954.

21. "Public platforms publicly arrived at," clipping on microfilm, no newspaper cited, 27 March 1954. News Clipping Scrapbook, Senator Edmund Muskie, 1950-1955 (microfilm), Albums and Scrapbooks, Edmund S. Muskie Archives and Special Collections Library, Bates College, Lewiston, ME.

22. Muskie, Journeys, p. 81.

23. L. A. Lemieux, "Anti-McCarthy resolve to be offered Saturday," Lewiston Evening Journal, 26 March 1954, p. 1.

24. "Plan style show and tea [for] Maine democratic women," Lewiston Evening Journal, 23 March 1954, p. 4.

25. "Colby Professor says his candidacy result of teaching," Lewiston Evening Journal (AP), 17 April 1954, p. 8.

26. L. A. Lemieux, "Fear of serious party split over issue of McCarthyism," Lewiston Evening Journal, 1 April, 1954, p. 1.

27. "Maine politics," Lewiston Evening Journal, 12 June 1954, p. 6.

28. "Muskie obtains petition forms," Portland Evening Express (AP), 11 March 1954. News Clipping Scrapbook, Senator Edmund Muskie, 1950-1955 (microfilm), Albums and Scrapbooks, Edmund S. Muskie Archives and Special Collections Library, Bates College, Lewiston, ME.

29. Muskie, et al. interviewed by Beam, 6 Aug. 1991, MOH 022, Muskie Oral History Collection.

30. Ibid.

31. Peter M. Damborg, "Muskie for governor?," Portland Press Herald, 7 April 1954. News Clipping Scrapbook, Senator Edmund Muskie, 1950-1955 (microfilm), Albums and Scrapbooks, Edmund S. Muskie Archives and Special Collections Library, Bates College, Lewiston, ME.

32. J. Muskie interviewed by Nicoll, 3 May 2000, MOH 189, Muskie Oral History Collection.

33. Don Nicoll, interview with the author, Portland, ME, 18 Jan. 2013.

34. Ibid.

35. Vincent F. X. Belleau, "Delahanty runs for congress," Lewiston Evening Journal, 10 April 1954, p. 1.

36. Don Nicoll, interview with the author, Portland, ME, 18 Jan. 2013.

37. Jeanne Delahanty interviewed by Don Nicoll, Lewiston, ME, 22 March 2000, MOH 181, transcript, Muskie Oral History Collection, The Edmund S. Muskie Archives and Special Collections Library, www.Bates.edu/Muskie-Archives

38. Don Nicoll, interview with the author, Portland, ME, 18 Jan. 2013.

39. Ibid.

40. Ibid.

41. "Colby professor says his candidacy result of teaching," Lewiston Evening Journal (AP), 17 April 1954, p. 8.

42. Muskie, et al. interviewed by Beam, 6 Aug. 1991, MOH 022, Muskie Oral History Collection.

43. Lippman and Hansen, p. 63.

44. L. A. Lemieux, "Big rush to file nomination papers at last minute," Lewiston Evening Journal, 19 April 1954, p. 1.

45. Paul A. MacDonald interviewed by Don Nicoll, Bath, ME, 20 Aug. 1998, MOH 045, transcript,

Muskie Oral History Collection,
The Edmund S. Muskie Archives
and Special Collections Library,
www.Bates.edu/Muskie-Archives

46. John Orestis interviewed by Mike
Richard, Lewiston, ME, 20 August
1999, MOH 145, transcript, Muskie
Oral History Collection, The
Edmund S. Muskie Archives and
Special Collections Library, www.
Bates.edu/Muskie-Archives

47. L. A. Lemieux, "GOP watches
Democrats, keeps quiet," Lewiston
Evening Journal, 29 May 1954, p. 1.

48. Nicoll and Coffin interviewed by
Beam and Griffiths, 20 Nov. 1996,
MOH 011, Muskie Oral History
Collection.

49. "County Democrats choose officers," Lewiston Evening Journal,
28 April 1954, p. 1.

50. Nicoll and Coffin interviewed by
Beam and Griffiths, 20 Nov. 1996,
MOH 011, Muskie Oral History
Collection.

51. Peter Damborg, "Ed Muskie
promises hard-hitting campaign,"
Portland Press Herald, 26 April
1954. News Clipping Scrapbook,
Senator Edmund Muskie, 1950-
1955 (microfilm), Albums and
Scrapbooks, Edmund S. Muskie
Archives and Special Collections
Library, Bates College, Lewiston,
ME.

52. "The minority's Muskie launches
his campaign," Portland Press
Herald editorial, 28 April 1954.
News Clipping Scrapbook,
Senator Edmund Muskie, 1950-
1955 (microfilm), Albums and
Scrapbooks, Edmund S. Muskie
Archives and Special Collections
Library, Bates College, Lewiston,
ME.

53. Edgar Comee interviewed by
Jeremy Robitaille, Brunswick, ME.
30 May 2001, MOH 273, transcript,
Muskie Oral History Collection,

The Edmund S. Muskie Archives
and Special Collections Library,
www.Bates.edu/Muskie-Archives

54. Bill Langzettel, "Maine Dem-
ocratic leaders scorn Cross'
party-building advice as split-
ting tactic," Portland Evening
Express (AP), 28 April 1954, p.
1. News Clipping Scrapbook,
Senator Edmund Muskie, 1950-
1955 (microfilm), Albums and
Scrapbooks, Edmund S. Muskie
Archives and Special Collections
Library, Bates College, Lewiston,
ME.

55. Ibid.

56. "Governor Cross and Eastport editor differ on whether 'depression'
afflicting Washington County,"
Lewiston Evening Journal (AP), 3
Feb. 1954, p. 1.

57. Stanley Tupper interviewed by Don
Nicoll, Rob Chavira, and Stuart
O'Brien, Boothbay Harbor, ME,
20 July 1998, MOH 031, transcript,
Muskie Oral History Collection,
The Edmund S. Muskie Archives
and Special Collections Library,
www.Bates.edu/Muskie-Archives

58. Floyd Harding interviewed by Don
Nicoll, 9 Oct. 1998, MOH 049,
Muskie Oral History Collection.

59. "Muskie challenges Cross to
debate on any subject," Water-
ville Morning Sentinel, 16 May
1954. News Clipping Scrapbook,
Senator Edmund Muskie, 1950-
1955 (microfilm), Albums and
Scrapbooks, Edmund S. Muskie
Archives and Special Collections
Library, Bates College, Lewiston,
ME.

60. Ibid.

61. "Coffin says Demos need executive," Lewiston Evening Journal
(AP), 19 April 1954.

62. "Maine Democrats to wage mass
sticker campaign in areas lacking
candidates," Portland Press Her-

ald, 18 May 1954. News Clipping Scrapbook, Senator Edmund Muskie, 1950-1955 (microfilm), Albums and Scrapbooks, Edmund S. Muskie Archives and Special Collections Library, Bates College, Lewiston, ME.

63. Muskie, et al. interviewed by Beam, 6 Aug. 1991, MOH 022, Muskie Oral History Collection.

64. Don Nicoll interview with author Portland, 18 Jan. 2013.

65. Nicoll and Coffin interviewed by Beam and Griffiths, 20 Nov. 1996, MOH 011, Muskie Oral History Collection.

66. "Democratic State Committee opens state headquarters here," Lewiston Evening Journal, 13 July 1954, p. 1.

67. "Maine Democrats to wage mass sticker campaign in areas lacking candidates," Portland Press Herald, 18 May 1954. News Clipping Scrapbook, Senator Edmund Muskie, 1950-1955 (microfilm), Albums and Scrapbooks, Edmund S. Muskie Archives and Special Collections Library, Bates College, Lewiston, ME.

68. Nicoll, Maine Law Review, p. 404.

69. Edmund S. Muskie to Charles F. Taylor, 21 May 1954, Series IV (Governor), Box 1, Folder 7. Edmund S. Muskie Papers, The Edmund S. Muskie Archives and Special Collections Library, Bates College, Lewiston, ME.

70. L. A. Lemieux, "Maine Democrats must stand on own feet—Mitchell," Lewiston Evening Journal, 25 May 1954, p. 1.

71. Muskie, et al. interviewed by Beam, 6 Aug. 1991, MOH 022, Muskie Oral History Collection.

72. Ibid.

73. Ibid.

74. "The busy Democrats," (editorial), Portland Evening Express, 27 May 1954. News Clipping Scrapbook, Senator Edmund Muskie, 1950-1955 (microfilm), Albums and Scrapbooks, Edmund S. Muskie Archives and Special Collections Library, Bates College, Lewiston, ME.

75. L. A. Lemieux, GOP watches Democrats, keeps quiet," Lewiston Evening Journal, 29 May 1954, p. 1.

76. Nicoll and Coffin interviewed by Beam and Griffiths, 20 Nov. 1996, MOH 011, Muskie Oral History Collection.

77. Muskie interviewed by Beam, 3 Sept. 1991, MOH 013, Muskie Oral History Collection.

78. Nicoll and Coffin interviewed by Beam and Griffiths, 20 Nov. 1996, MOH 011, Muskie Oral History Collection.

79. Shep Lee interviewed by Chris Beam, Lewiston, ME, 17 Sept. 1991, MOH 012, transcript, Muskie Oral History Collection, The Edmund S. Muskie Archives and Special Collections Library, www.Bates.edu/Muskie-Archives

80. J. Muskie interviewed by Nicoll, 3 May 2000, MOH 189, Muskie Oral History Collection.

81. Don Nicoll, interview with author, Portland, ME, 18 Jan. 2013.

82. Muskie interviewed by Beam, 3 Sept. 1991, MOH 013, Muskie Oral History Collection.

83. Edward Penley, "Magnuson hits GOP policies," Lewiston Daily Sun, 21 June 1954.

84. L. A. Lemieux, "Maine Democrats must stand on own feet—Mitchell," Lewiston Evening Journal, 25 May 1954, p. 1.

85. Edward Penley, "Magnuson hits GOP policies," Lewiston Daily Sun, 21 June 1954.

86. Note from Alton A. Lessard to Edmund S. Muskie, 14 June 1954, Series IV (Governor), Box 1, Folder

7. Edmund S. Muskie Papers, The Edmund S. Muskie Archives and Special Collections Library, Bates College, Lewiston, ME.

87. Edward L. Penley, "Magnuson hits GOP policies," Lewiston Daily Sun, 21 June 1954.

88. Muskie, Journeys, p. 136.

89. Don Nicoll, interview with Author, Portland, ME, 18 Jan. 2013.

90. Muskie, et al. interviewed by Beam, 6 Aug. 1991, MOH 022, Muskie Oral History Collection.

91. Nicoll and Coffin interviewed by Beam and Griffiths, 20 Nov. 1996, MOH 011, Muskie Oral History Collection.

92. Don Nicoll, interview with author, Portland, ME, 18 Jan 2013.

93. Muskie, et al. interviewed by Beam, 6 Aug. 1991, MOH 022, Muskie Oral History Collection.

94. Muskie, Journeys, p. 56.

95. Don Nicoll, interview with the author, Portland, ME, 18 Jan. 2013.

96. Byrne interviewed by Nicoll, 5 Dec. 2000, MOH 253, Muskie Oral History Collection.

97. Lippman and Hansen, p. 73.

98. Phillip Johnson interviewed by Andrea L'Hommedieu, Lewiston, ME, 27 October 2000, MOH 225, transcript, Muskie Oral History Collection, The Edmund S. Muskie Archives and Special Collections Library, www.Bates.edu/Muskie-Archives

99. Ibid.

100. Lippman and Hansen, p. 73.

101. Roger Snow interviewed by Don Nicoll and Mike Richard, Falmouth Foreside, ME, 23 June 1999, MOH 111, transcript, Muskie Oral History Collection, The Edmund S. Muskie Archives and Special Collections Library, www.Bates.edu/Muskie-Archives

102. L&H, p. 70.

103. Nicoll and Coffin interviewed by Beam and Griffiths, 20 Nov. 1996, MOH 011, Muskie Oral History Collection.

104. Muskie, et al. interviewed by Beam, 6 Aug. 1991, MOH 022, Muskie Oral History Collection.

105. Nicoll and Coffin interviewed by Beam and Griffiths, 20 Nov. 1996, MOH 011, Muskie Oral History Collection.

106. Nevin, p. 154.

107. L. A. Lemieux, "Hussey willing [to] endorse GOP ticket," Lewiston Evening Journal, 10 July 1954, p. 1.

108. Lippman and Hansen, p. 71.

109. "Journal political writer tells Kiwanis Democratic resurgence is just a ripple," Lewiston Evening Journal, 14 July 1954, p. 1.

110. Lionel A. "Lal" Lemieux interviewed by Brian O'Doherty, Lewiston, ME, 15 Nov. 1999, MOH 162, transcript, Muskie Oral History Collection, The Edmund S. Muskie Archives and Special Collections Library, www.Bates.edu/Muskie-Archives

111. Nicoll interview of Paul A. McDonald, MOH 045.

112. J. Muskie interviewed by Nicoll, 3 May 2000, MOH 189, Muskie Oral History Collection.

113. Ibid.

114. Nevin, Muskie of Maine, p. 150.

115. Muskie, et al. interviewed by Beam, 6 Aug. 1991, MOH 022, Muskie Oral History Collection.

116. Nevin, p. 151.

117. Muskie, et al. interviewed by Beam, 6 Aug. 1991, MOH 022, Muskie Oral History Collection.

118. Muskie, Journeys, p. 61.

119. Edmund S. Muskie to Elliot Newcomb, 30 July 1954, Series 4 (Governor), Box 1, Folder 7. Edmund S. Muskie Papers, The Edmund S. Muskie Archives and Special Collections Library,

Bates College, Lewiston, ME. The Edmund S. Muskie Archives and Special Collections Library, Governor Series, Box 1, Folder 7.

120. "Muskie urges state concern over Sanford economy," Lewiston Evening Journal (AP), 3 Aug. 1954, p. 10.

121. Ibid.

122. Mary Ellen (Kiah) Johnson interviewed by Don Nicoll, Brewer, ME, 22 March 2004, MOH 431, transcript, Muskie Oral History Collection, The Edmund S. Muskie Archives and Special Collections Library, www.Bates.edu/Muskie-Archives

123. "Muskie says industry rating low," Lewiston Evening Journal (AP), 3 Aug. 1954, p. 1.

124. L. A. Lemieux, "Muskie ill-informed says Cross," Lewiston Evening Journal, 4 Aug. 1954, p. 1.

125. Ibid.

126. Lippman and Hansen, p. 56.

127. Muskie, Journeys, pp. 135-36.

128. Muskie urges governor to get off his cloud," Lewiston Evening Journal (AP), 6 Aug. 1954, p. 9.

129. Ibid.

130. L. A. Lemieux, "Campaign livens up as Cross answers Muskie's charges," Lewiston Evening Journal, 7 August 1954, p. 1.

131. Ibid.

132. "Muskie takes issue with governor on sanatoria consolidation," Lewiston Evening Journal (AP), 9 Aug. 1954, p. 9.

133. "Muskie charges Cross trying to obscure lack of past progress," Lewiston Evening Journal (AP), 14 Aug. 1954, p. 2

134. Ibid.

135. "Coffin says major candidates to start swinging hard," Lewiston Evening Journal (AP), 16 Aug. 1954, p. 6.

136. Clarke Canfield, "125-year-old Grange folds," Lewiston Sun Journal (AP), 3 Sept. 2013, p. A3.

137. L. A. Lemieux, "Muskie proposes experimental textile plant to prove industry can run profitably in Maine," Lewiston Evening Journal, 18 Aug. 1954, p. 1.

138. Ibid.

139. "You attend Exchange Club meetings or else!" (Photo caption), staff photo by Philbrick, Lewiston Evening Journal, 18 Aug. 1954, p. 5.

140. "Cross declines Muskie debate challenge," Lewiston Evening Journal (AP), 19 August 1954, p. 10.

141. Ibid.

142. Nevin, p. 155.

143. Don Nicoll, interview with author, Portland, ME, 18 Jan 2013.

144. Muskie, Journeys, p. 44.

145. Don Nicoll, interview with author, Portland, ME, 18 Jan 2013.

146. L. A. Lemieux, "Some old-time Republicans at Muskie West Minot rally; resent Cross proposal on 'san,'" Lewiston Evening Journal, 24 Aug. 1954, p. 1.

147. Ibid.

148. Larry Harpe interviewed by Nicholas Christie, Rumford, ME, 5 June 2001, MOH 276, transcript, Muskie Oral History Collection, The Edmund S. Muskie Archives and Special Collections Library, www.Bates.edu/Muskie-Archives

149. "Muskie says GOP refuses to admit pollution problem," Lewiston Evening Journal, 27 Aug. 1954, p. 6.

150. "Maine Democrats to put Kennedy on TV ahead of GOP's Nixon," Lewiston Evening Journal, 28 Aug. 1954, p. 2.

151. Nicoll and Coffin interviewed by Beam and Griffiths, 20 Nov. 1996, MOH 011, Muskie Oral History Collection.

152. Stanley Tupper interviewed by
Nicoll, et al., 20 July 1998, MOH
031, Muskie Oral History Collection.
153. L. A. Lemieux, "Muskie expected
to get good vote, but win unlikely,"
Lewiston Evening Journal, 11
Sept. 1954, p. 1.
154. Muskie, et al. interviewed by
Beam, 6 Aug. 1991, MOH 022,
Muskie Oral History Collection.
155. Lippman and Hansen, p. 74.
156. Lippman and Hansen, p. 75.
157. James M. Naughton, "The taste of
defeat," New York Times, 14 May
1972, p. SM13.
158. J. Muskie interviewed by Nicoll,
3 May 2000, MOH 189, Muskie
Oral History Collection.
159. Jane Muskie as told to Roul
Tunley, "So we moved into the
governor's mansion," Saturday
Evening Post, vol. 229, issue 47, 25
May 1957, P. 135.
160. Edmund S. Muskie speech in
Texas, 1968, cited in Nevin,
Muskie of Maine, p. 156.
161. Comee interviewed by Robitaille,
30 May 2001, MOH 273, Muskie
Oral History Collection.
162. Muskie and Tunley, p. 27.
163. "Maine's governor-elect had defied
tradition," New York Times, 15
Sept. 1954, p. 24.
164. W. H. Lawrence, "Save Eisenhower from G.O.P. evils, Truman
exhorts," New York Times, 18
Sept. 1954, p. 1.
165. Ibid.
166. Muskie, Journeys, p. 144.
167. "Coffin would give governors-elect
appropriations before they take
office. Sees it as thrifty move,"
Lewiston Evening Journal (AP),
30 Nov. 1954, p. 14.
168. "Close vote to keep parties on toes
for '56—Muskie," Lewiston Evening Journal (AP), 2 Nov. 1954, p. 2.
169. "Muskie and St. Dominic's Glee

Club to be among attractions at
Dr. Gard Twaddle testimonial,"
Lewiston Evening Journal, 28 Oct.
1954, p. 26
170. Byrne interviewed by Nicoll, 5
Dec. 2000, MOH 253, Muskie
Oral History Collection.
171. Joan Arnold interviewed by Marisa
Burnham-Bestor, Belgrade,
ME, 20 Nov. 1998, MOH 060,
transcript, Muskie Oral History
Collection, The Edmund S. Mu
skie Archives and Special Collec-
tions Library, www.Bates.edu/
Muskie-Archives
172. Muskie, et al. interviewed by
Beam, 6 Aug. 1991, MOH 022,
Muskie Oral History Collection.
173. "Muskie wins biggest news story,"
Lewiston Evening Journal (AP),
24 Dec. 1954, p. 8.

Chapter Five. Governor Muskie

1. Ruth Henderson, "Muskies arrive
Monday," Kennebec Journal, 30
Dec. 1954. Senator Edmund S.
Muskie Scrapbooks, September
14, 1954 to May 15, 1958 (microfilm, roll 1), Edmund S. Muskie
Archives and Special Collections
Library, Bates College Lewiston,
Me.
2. Cecil Burns interviewed by Andrea
L'Hommedieu, Rumford, ME, 4
Sept. 2002, MOH 362, transcript,
Muskie Oral History Collection,
The Edmund S. Muskie Archives
and Special Collections Library,
www.Bates.edu/Muskie-Archives
3. Rose O'Brien, "Muskie's son stops
show at Augusta," Lewiston Evening Journal, 6 Jan. 1955, p. 1.
4. The full text of Governor Muskie's first inaugural address can be
found in the Lewiston Evening
Journal, 6 January 1955, pp. 6-8.
5. Bosworth interviewed by Ross,
July 1985, MOH 009, Muskie Oral

History Collection.

6. Muskie, Journeys, p. 143

7. Lippman and Hanson, p. 84.

8. McKusick interviewed by L'Hom-medieu, 23 July 2001, MOH 311, Muskie Oral History Collection.

9. Robert M. Crocker, "Ability to manage people key to successful handling of governorship, Muskie finds," Lewiston Evening Journal, 21 April 1955, p. 16.

10. Jane Muskie interviewed by Don Nicoll, Bethesda, MD, 4 Dec. 2000, MOH 251, transcript, Muskie Oral History Collection, The Edmund S. Muskie Archives and Special Collections Library, www.Bates.edu/Muskie-Archives

11. Muskie, Journeys, pp. 144-45.

12. The full text, of the governor's budget address can be found in the Lewiston Evening Journal, 13 January 1955, pp. 5-7.

13. "Pollution report recommends classifying thousands of miles of Maine waters by degrees," Lewiston Evening Journal, 27 Jan. 1955, p. 1.

14. Nevin, p. 161.

15. Don Nicoll, interview with author, Portland, ME, 18 Jan. 2013.

16. Nevin, p. 160.

17. Edward C. Schlick, "Haskell, Muskie compromise on Indus-try-Commerce Department," Lewiston Evening Journal, 6 April 1955, p. 1.

18. Lippman and Hansen, p. 86.

19. Nevin, p. 171.

20. Ibid.

21. Nevin, p. 166.

22. McDonald interviewed by Nicoll, 20 Aug. 1998, MOH 045, Muskie Oral History Collection.

23. Don Nicoll, interview with author, Portland, ME, 18, Jan. 2013.

24. Crocker, "Ability to manage . . . ."

25. Arnold interviewed by Burn-ham-Bestor, 20 Nov. 1998, MOH

060, Muskie Oral History Collection.

26. Muskie, Journeys, p. 49.

27. Nevin, p. 71.

28. Headliners at Democratic gath-ering" (photo caption), Lewiston Evening Journal, 31 May 1955, p. 11.

29. L. A. Lemieux, "Governor Muskie says community service part of the duty of college men and women," Lewiston Evening Journal, 13 June 1955, p. 12.

30. Ann Davis, "Governor gives extemporaneous tribute to Fullam at university," Bangor Daily News, 23 June 1955. Senator Edmund S. Muskie Scrapbooks, September 14, 1954 to May 15, 1958 (micro-film, roll 1), Edmund S. Muskie Archives and Special Collections Library, Bates College Lewiston, Me.

31. Trout or lobster for Ike?" Lewiston Daily Sun (editorial), 21 June 1955.

32. Ed Dodd and Jack Elrod, "Mark Trail," Lewiston Sun Journal, 29 Sept. 2013, comics section.

33. John Gould, "Memo to Ike: On fishing in Maine," New York Times Magazine, 12 June 1955, p. 55.

34. Bruce Verrill, Chesterville, ME, letter to the author, 1 Feb. 2013.

35. W. H. Lawrence, "President lands 18-inch salmon," New York Times, 27 June 1955, p. 4.

36 "Eisenhower sees progress in world quest for peace," New York Times, 28 June 1955, p. 1.

37. "Governor Muskie looks tanned and rested after vacation," Lewis-ton Evening Journal (AP), 28 July 1955, p. 2.

38. "Frank Coffin calls Millett rejection party politics," Lewiston Evening Journal, 5 August 1955.

39. "Muskie says 'start' all disabled veterans want," Lewiston Evening Journal (AP), 12 August 1955, p.9.

40. "Orders crackdown on speeders, drunken, and reckless drivers," Lewiston Evening Journal (AP), 24 August 1955, p. 1.

41. Ibid.

42. "Muskie apologizes to magazine for ad cancellation," Bath Daily Times (AP), 10 Nov. 1955. Senator Edmund S. Muskie Scrapbooks, September 14, 1954 to May 15, 1958 (microfilm, roll 1), Edmund S. Muskie Archives and Special Collections Library, Bates College Lewiston, Me.

43. Ibid.

44. The governor pinpoints need for four-year term," Portland Press Herald (editorial), 30 December 1955. Senator Edmund S. Muskie Scrapbooks, September 14, 1954 to May 15, 1958 (microfilm, roll 1), Edmund S. Muskie Archives and Special Collections Library, Bates College Lewiston, Me.

45. Ibid.

46. "Prepare for 1956 platform," Lewiston Daily Sun, 31 Oct. 1955.

47. Ibid.

48. Lorin L. Arnold, "Lewiston's Coffin seen as Democratic candidate for Congress against Nelson," Bangor Daily News, 26 Nov. 1955. Senator Edmund S. Muskie Scrapbooks, September 14, 1954 to May 15, 1958 (microfilm, roll 1), Edmund S. Muskie Archives and Special Collections Library, Bates College Lewiston, Me.

49. "The 'Indian problem' one of Maine's hardy perennials," (editorial), Portland Press Herald, 11 Jan. 1956. Senator Edmund S. Muskie Scrapbooks, September 14, 1954 to May 15, 1958 (microfilm, roll 1), Edmund S. Muskie Archives and Special Collections Library, Bates College Lewiston, Me.

50. Peter M. Damborg, "Clears way for second term by quitting national post," Portland Press Herald, 18 Jan. 1956. Senator Edmund S. Muskie Scrapbooks, September 14, 1954 to May 15, 1958 (microfilm, roll 1), Edmund S. Muskie Archives and Special Collections Library, Bates College Lewiston, Me.

51. "Governor Muskie seen as possible opponent for Nelson." Waterville Morning Sentinel, 2 Feb. 1956. Senator Edmund S. Muskie Scrapbooks, September 14, 1954 to May 15, 1958 (microfilm, roll 1), Edmund S. Muskie Archives and Special Collections Library, Bates College Lewiston, Me.

52. Bud Leavitt, "Muskie, Cobb, Broggi featured today in Boston Sportsmen's Show dinners," Bangor Daily News, 8 Feb. 1956. Senator Edmund S. Muskie Scrapbooks, September 14, 1954 to May 15, 1958 (microfilm, roll 1), Edmund S. Muskie Archives and Special Collections Library, Bates College Lewiston, Me.

53. Nevin, p. 84.

54. Chaisson and Paradis interviewed by Ross, 14 May 1985, MOH 003, Muskie Oral History Collection.

55. "Observers say Muskie wants second term to push program," Portland Evening Express, 7 March 1956. Senator Edmund S. Muskie Scrapbooks, September 14, 1954 to May 15, 1958 (microfilm, roll 1), Edmund S. Muskie Archives and Special Collections Library, Bates College Lewiston, Me.

56. Nicoll, Maine Law Review, p. 406.

57. "The Democrats' platform," Bangor Daily News, 27 March 1956. Senator Edmund S. Muskie Scrapbooks, September 14, 1954 to May 15, 1958 (microfilm, roll 1), Edmund S. Muskie Archives and Special Collections Library, Bates College Lewiston, Me.

58. "Bangor man urges favorite son

backing for Governor," Kennebec Journal, 22 March 1956. Senator Edmund S. Muskie Scrapbooks, September 14, 1954 to May 15, 1958 (microfilm, roll 1), Edmund S. Muskie Archives and Special Collections Library, Bates College Lewiston, Me.

59. "Muskie answers GOP charges in Bates talk," Lewiston Evening Journal, 13 April 1956.

60. Peter M. Damborg, "Coffin campaigning like veteran in first attempt for major office," Kennebec Journal, 14 May 1956. Senator Edmund S. Muskie Scrapbooks, September 14, 1954 to May 15, 1958 (microfilm, roll 1), Edmund S. Muskie Archives and Special Collections Library, Bates College Lewiston, Me.

61. Ibid.

62. Nicoll, Maine Law Review, p. 406.

63. Muskie, et al. interviewed by Beam, 6 Aug. 1991, MOH 022, Muskie Oral History Collection.

64. Ibid.

65. J. Muskie interviewed by Nicoll, 4 Dec. 2000, MOH 251, Muskie Oral History Collection.

66. Lippman and Hansen, p. 46.

67. "Oh, Governor" (editorial), Lewiston Evening Journal, 6 Sept. 1956.

68. Muskie, et al. interviewed by Beam, 6 Aug. 1991, MOH 022, Muskie Oral History Collection.

69. "Oh, Governor."

70. Denis Blais interviewed by Don Nicoll, Stuart O'Brien, and Rob Chavira, Lewiston, ME, 22 June 1998, MOH 028, transcript, Muskie Oral History Collection, The Edmund S. Muskie Archives and Special Collections Library, www.Bates.edu/Muskie-Archives

71. Wade interviewed by L'Hommedieu, 15 Dec. 1999, MOH 163, Muskie Oral History Collection.

72. Arnold interviewed by Burn-ham-Bestor, 20 Nov. 1998, MOH 060, Muskie Oral History Collection.

73. Nicoll, Maine Law Review, p. 408

74. "Dr. Donovan heads Maine Democrats," Portland Press Herald, 10 Dec. 1956. Senator Edmund S. Muskie Scrapbooks, September 14, 1954 to May 15, 1958 (microfilm, roll 1), Edmund S. Muskie Archives and Special Collections Library, Bates College Lewiston, Me.

75. Catherine Rines interviewed by Andrea L'Hommedieu, Chamberlain, ME, 11 July 2001, MOH 293, transcript, Muskie Oral History Collection, The Edmund S. Muskie Archives and Special Collections Library, www.Bates.edu/Muskie-Archives

76. Lippman and Hansen, p 90

77. "One out of 36 a poor average, but it'd satisfy Democrats," Portland Evening Express (AP), 17 Jan. 1957. Senator Edmund S. Muskie Scrapbooks, September 14, 1954 to May 15, 1958 (microfilm, roll 1), Edmund S. Muskie Archives and Special Collections Library, Bates College Lewiston, Me.

78. Edward C. Schlick, "Muskie hedges on whether he will seek third term," Lewiston Daily Sun, 13 March 1957.

79. "Muskie tax plan, Budgets generally well received," Portland Press Herald (AP), 11 Jan. 1957. Senator Edmund S. Muskie Scrapbooks, September 14, 1954 to May 15, 1958 (microfilm, roll 1), Edmund S. Muskie Archives and Special Collections Library, Bates College Lewiston, Me.

80. Nevin, p. 40.

81. Muskie interviewed by Larrabee, 28 Nov. 1995, MOH 095, Muskie Oral History Collection.

82. Andrea L'Hommedieu interview of Virginia "Ginny" (Gray) Harvey

and Judy Harvey, Waterville, ME, 3 April 2004, MOH 428.

83. J. Muskie interviewed by Nicoll, 4 Dec. 2000, MOH 251, Muskie Oral History Collection.

84. "Won't carry a tune," unknown newspaper (AP), 6 Feb. 1957. Senator Edmund S. Muskie Scrapbooks, September 14, 1954 to May 15, 1958 (microfilm, roll 1), Edmund S. Muskie Archives and Special Collections Library, Bates College Lewiston, Me.

85. "Results of first meeting with solons please Muskie," Portland Press Herald (AP), 7 Feb. 1957. Senator Edmund S. Muskie Scrapbooks, September 14, 1954 to May 15, 1958 (microfilm, roll 1), Edmund S. Muskie Archives and Special Collections Library, Bates College Lewiston, Me.

86. "Muskie says Maine's future industrial growth hinges on building authority," Portland Press Herald, 27 Feb. 1957. Senator Edmund S. Muskie Scrapbooks, September 14, 1954 to May 15, 1958 (microfilm, roll 1), Edmund S. Muskie Archives and Special Collections Library, Bates College Lewiston, Me.

87. "They saved the bill," Portland Sunday Telegram, circa 2 June 1957. Senator Edmund S. Muskie Scrapbooks, September 14, 1954 to May 15, 1958 (microfilm, roll 1), Edmund S. Muskie Archives and Special Collections Library, Bates College Lewiston, Me.

88. "Looking back: 50 years ago, 1957," Lewiston Sun Journal, 15 March 2007.

89. "Governor may have extra role in Peyton Place," Kennebec Journal, 7 June 1957. Senator Edmund S. Muskie Scrapbooks, September 14, 1954 to May 15, 1958 (microfilm, roll 1), Edmund S. Muskie Archives and Special Collections Library,

Bates College Lewiston, Me.

90. "While the elephant snores on," Bangor Daily News (editorial), 20 June 1957. Senator Edmund S. Muskie Scrapbooks, September 14, 1954 to May 15, 1958 (microfilm, roll 1), Edmund S. Muskie Archives and Special Collections Library, Bates College Lewiston, Me.

91. Ibid.

92. Byrne interviewed by Nicoll, 5 Dec. 2000, MOH 253, Muskie Oral History Collection.

93. Virginia and Judy Harvey interviewed by Andrea L'Hommedieu, Waterville, ME, 3 April 2004, MOH 428, transcript, Muskie Oral History Collection, The Edmund S. Muskie Archives and Special Collections Library, www.Bates. edu/Muskie-Archives

94. "Senator Payne protests government's action in lobster dispute," Portland Press Herald (AP), 17 Oct. 1957. Senator Edmund S. Muskie Scrapbooks, September 14, 1954 to May 15, 1958 (microfilm, roll 1), Edmund S. Muskie Archives and Special Collections Library, Bates College Lewiston, Me.

95. Ibid.

96. Tupper interviewed by Nicoll, et al., 20 July 1998, MOH 031, Muskie Oral History Collection.

97. "Muskie speaks on political views at BU," Portland Press Herald (AP), 26 Nov. 1957. Senator Edmund S. Muskie Scrapbooks, September 14, 1954 to May 15, 1958 (microfilm, roll 1), Edmund S. Muskie Archives and Special Collections Library, Bates College Lewiston, Me.

98. "Muskie in New York seeking industries," Waterville Morning Sentinel (AP), 27 Nov. 1957. Senator Edmund S. Muskie Scrapbooks, September 14, 1954 to May 15, 1958 (microfilm, roll 1), Edmund S. Muskie Archives and

Special Collections Library, Bates College Lewiston, Me.

99. Ibid.

100. Lorin L. Arnold, "Muskie urges party workers keep ideals," Bangor Daily News, 14 Feb. 1958. Senator Edmund S. Muskie Scrapbooks, September 14, 1954 to May 15, 1958 (microfilm, roll 1), Edmund S. Muskie Archives and Special Collections Library, Bates College Lewiston, Me.

101. Ibid.

102. Muskie interviewed by Beam, 3 Sept. 1991, MOH 013, Muskie Oral History Collection.

103. Ibid.

104. Nicoll, Maine Law Review, p. 410.

105. Ibid.

106. Lippman and Hansen, p. 95.

107. Ibid.

108. Lorin L. Arnold, "Storm deals hard blow, convention at near halt," Bangor Daily News, 22 March 1958, p. 1. Senator Edmund S. Muskie Scrapbooks, September 14, 1954 to May 15, 1958 (microfilm, roll 1), Edmund S. Muskie Archives and Special Collections Library, Bates College Lewiston, Me.

109. Edward C. Schlick, "Governor Muskie is 'neutral,'" Lewiston Daily Sun, 18 April 1958

110. Nicoll, Maine Law Review, p. 410.

111. "Random notes in Washington: Johnson sows, President reaps." New York Times, 28 July 1958, p. 11. Senator Edmund S. Muskie Scrapbooks, May 14, 1958 to December 12, 1960 (microfilm, roll 2), Edmund S. Muskie Archives and Special Collections Library, Bates College Lewiston, Me.

112. "Muskie to 'think about' writing his autobiography," Portland Press Herald, 27 March 1959, p. 11. Senator Edmund S. Muskie

Scrapbooks, May 14, 1958 to December 12, 1960 (microfilm, roll 2), Edmund S. Muskie Archives and Special Collections Library, Bates College Lewiston, Me.

113. McDonald interviewed by Nicoll, 20 Aug. 1998, MOH 045, Muskie Oral History Collection.

114. Allen Drury, "Election: pocket-book big issue," New York Times, 2 Nov. 1958, p. E5.

115. Lippman and Hansen, p. 95.

116. Nicoll, Maine Law Review, p. 411.

117. Allen Drury, "Political prognosis favors Democrats," New York Times, 24 Aug. 1958, p. E6.

118. Lippman and Hansen, p. 96.

119. "Demos score historic triumph in Maine," Arizona Daily Star (AP), 9 Sept. 1958. Senator Edmund S. Muskie Scrapbooks, May 14, 1958 to December 12, 1960 (micro-film, roll 2), Edmund S. Muskie Archives and Special Collections Library, Bates College Lewiston, Me.

120. Muskie, et al. interviewed by Beam, 6 Aug. 1991, MOH 022, Muskie Oral History Collection.

121. Paul Mills, "Inside Maine: Remembering 'Doc' Clauson, the healing governor," Lewiston Sun journal, 27 Dec. 2009, p. C10.

122. Ibid.

123. "Governor Muskie to realize dream of boyhood in trip to Alaska," Lewiston Evening Jour-nal (AP), 18 Oct. 1958, p. 9.

124. "Muskie settles question of what to say," Lewiston Evening Journal (AP), 10 Sept. 1958. Senator Edmund S. Muskie Scrapbooks, May 14, 1958 to December 12, 1960 (microfilm, roll 2), Edmund S. Muskie Archives and Special Collections Library, Bates College Lewiston, Me.

Bibliography

Archives

Edmund S. Muskie Archives and
Special Collections Library, Bates
College, Lewiston, ME.
Olin Science Center Library, Colby
College, Waterville, ME.
Portland Room, Portland Public
Library, Portland, ME.
Rumford Historical Society, Rumford,
ME.

Correspondence

Bruce Verrill, Chesterville, ME to the
author, 1 Feb. 2013.

Diary

Edmund S. Muskie, summer 1933,
The Edmund S. Muskie Archives
and Special Collections Library,
Series 1, Box 31, Folder 2.

Internet Source

Max Znak at http://connect.state.gov/
group/muskie/forum/topics/
midnight-research-on-
edmund-s-muskie-origins,
18 Oct. 2011.

Interview

Donald Nicoll interviewed by the
author, Portland, ME, 18 Jan. 2013.

Manuscripts

Frank M. Coffin, Life and Times in
the Three Branches (unpublished),
cited in Don Nicoll, "Frank Morey
Coffin's Political Years: Prelude to
a Judgeship," Maine Law Review,
vol. 63:2, pp. 398-416.
James G. Ross, As Maine Goes
(unpublished), Senior Thesis, Bates
College, 1986.

Newspapers and Journals

Am-Pol Eagle
Arizona Daily Star
Bangor Daily News
Bath Daily Times
Kennebec Journal
Lewiston Daily Sun
Lewiston Evening Journal
Lewiston Sun Journal
Maine Law Review
Nashua Telegraph
New York Times
Portland Evening Express
Portland Press Herald
Portland Sunday Telegram
Rumford Falls Times
Waterville Morning Sentinel

Oral Histories

(All oral histories are from the Muskie
Oral History Collection, Edmund
S. Muskie Archives and Special
Collections Library, Bates College,
Lewiston, ME, www.bates.edu/
muskie-archives)

Diana and Frank Anastasio interviewed
by James G. Ross, MOH 007.
Phil and Frank Anastasio interviewed
by Andrea L'Hommedieu, MOH
235.
Joan Arnold interviewed by Marisa
Burnham-Bestor, MOH 060.
Joe Biernacki and Pricilla (Biernacki)
Clark interviewed by Meredith
Gethin-Jones, MOH 065.
Denis Blais interviewed by Don Nicoll,
Rob Chavira, and Stuart O'Brien,
MOH 028.
Kenneth Bosworth interviewed by
James G. Ross, MOH 009.
Cecil Burns interviewed by Andrea
L'Hommedieu, MOH 362.
John Byrne interviewed by Don Nicoll,
MOH 253.
Irene (Muskie) Chaisson and Lucy
(Muskie) Paradis interviewed by
James G. Ross, MOH 003.
Jere Clifford interviewed by Marisa
Burnham-Bestor, MOH 093.

Frank M. Coffin interviewed by Don Nicoll, Rob Chavira, and Stuart O'Brien, MOH 033.

Edgar Comee interviewed bt Jeremy Robitaille, MOH 273.

Jean Delahanty interviewed by Don Nicoll, MOH 181.

Floyd Harding interviewed by Don Nicoll, MOH 049.

Larry Harpe interviewed by Nicholas Christie, MOH 276.

Mary Ellen (Kiah) Johnson interviewed by Don nicoll, MOH 431.

Philip Johnson interviewed by Andrea L'Hommedieu, MOH 225.

Shep Lee interviewed by Chris Beam, MOH 012.

Lionel Lemieux interviewed by Brian O'Doherty, MOH 162.

Francis Mascianica interviewed by Greg Beam, MOH 227.

Paul McDonald interviewed by Don Nicoll, MOH 045.

Frances and Austin McInnis interviewed by Andrea L'Hommedieu, MOH 220.

Vincent McKusick interviewed by Andrea L'Hommedieu, MOH 311.

Edmund S. Muskie interviewed by James G. Ross, MOH 001.

Edmund S. Muskie interviewed by Chris Beam, MOH 013.

Edmund S. Muskie interviewed by Sally Davis and Virginia Ray, MOH 024.

Edmund S. Muskie interviewed by Don Larrabee, MOH 095.

Edmund S. Muskie, Shep Lee, Don Nicoll, and Frank Coffin interviewed by Chris Beam, MOH 022.

Jane (Gray) Muskie interviewed by Don Nicoll, MOH 189.

Jane (Gray) Muskie interviewed by Don Nicoll, MOH 251.

Don Nicoll and Frank Coffin interviewed by Chris Beam, MOH 011.

John Orestis interviewed by Mike Richard, MOH 145.

Catherine Rines interviewed by Andrea L'Hommedieu, MOH 293.

Betty (Winston) Scott interviewed by Don Nicoll, MOH 230.

Roger Snow interviewed by Don Nicoll and Mike Richard, MOH 111.

Stanley Tupper interviewed by Don nicoll, Rob Chavira, and Stuart O'Brien, MOH 031.

Vito Puiia interviewed by James G. Ross, MOH 005.

Robert Wade, Sr., interviewed by Andrea L'Hommedieu, MOH 163.

Milton Wheeler interviewed by Greg Beam, MOH 201.

Ruth (Rowe) Wilson interviewed by Don Nicoll, Rob Chavira, and Stuart O'Brien, MOH 034.

Robert York interviewed by Rob Chavira and Stuart O'Brien, MOH 040.

Periodicals

Saturday Evening Post, vol. 229, issue 47, May 25, 1957.

Primary Sources

Edmund S. Muskie, Journeys, Doubleday & Company, Inc. Garden City, NY, 1972.

Secondary Sources

David Nevin, Muskie of Maine, Random House, New York, 1972.

Dr. John C. Donovan, Congressional Campaign: Maine Elects a Democrat (Henry Holt & Company, New York, 1958).

Dr. Ron Formisano, The Great Lobster War, (University of Massachusetts Press, 1997).

Theo Lippman, Jr. and Donald C. Hansen, Muskie, W. W. Norton and Co., New York, 1971.

Index

A

Aldrich, Rupert F., 60, 62, 64, 65, 73
AMVETS (American Veterans), 74, 77, 81, 82, 85, 94, 97, 154, 160
Androscoggin River, 1, 10, 12, 20
Arnold, Joan, 184, 197–98
Arnold, Lorin "Doc," 118

B

Baldacci, John, 244
Bates College, 35, 36, 37, 38, 41, 43, 44, 45, 51, 52, 53, 54, 58, 72, 98, 121, 158, 182, 199, 218, 236; history of, 38–39
Baxter, Percival P., 102, 192, 228
Baxter State Park, 192, 208
Bean, L. L., 202, 213
Benoit, Henry, 125, 138, 141, 150, 223
Bevalaqua, Nicola, 14, 40
Biernacki, Joe, 48, 50, 51, 87, 88
Bingham, William 2nd, 55, 57, 60
Bishop, Neil S., 105, 155–56, 240
Blackington, Doris, 60, 94
Blackington, Martha, 62, 73, 80
Blaine House, 186, 187, 231, 239, 244 245; at Christmas, 210; repairs to, 227–28
Blaine, James G., 227
Blais, Denis, 193, 222–23
Bonus Expeditionary Force, 34
Boston Herald cropped photo, 193, 222–23
Brann, Louis J., 35, 135, 143
Brennan, Joseph, 244
Brewster, Ralph Owen, 79, 102, 106, 125, 238
Broggi, Carl, 206, 216–17
Buffalo, NY, 9, 19, 54

C

Cameron, Don, 201
Camp Anacosta, 34
Camp at China Lake, 77, 78, 83, 84, 89, 110–11, 187, 205, 239
Campaign budget for 1954, 158–59
Carter, James E., 250

Chisholm, Hugh J., 10, 11, 12, 23
Clary, Celia, 27, 28, 30, 44
Clauson, Clinton, 125, 210, 235, 236, 237, 241, 242, 244
Coffin, Frank Morey, 92, 93, 98, 102, 103, 108, 109, 111, 116, 117, 118, 119, 120, 124, 125, 126, 127, 129, 131, 132, 133, 136, 137, 139, *140*, 141, 142, 144, 147, 148, 150, 154, 156, 158, 160, 169, 183, 184, 209, 210, 212, 213, 217, 218, *219*, 224, 225, 231, 234, 235, 236, 238, 240, 244
Colbath, Kenneth, 129, 149, 165, 174, 179
Cold War, 203
Compromising to get results, 195–97
Coolidge, Calvin, 34
Corliss, Edgar, 89, 125, 130, 209
Cormier, Lucia, 105, 122, 124, 236
Cornell Law School, 53, 54, 55, 56, 57, 58, 237, 247
Cornell University, 20
Cross Burton M., 105, 114, 118–19, 125, 129, 133, 134, 135, 136, 146, 148, 151, 152, 155, 156, 159, 162, 164, 165, 168–70, 172, 173, 174, 175, 178, 179, 180, 187, 200
Curtis, Kenneth, 191, 244

D

Damborg, Peter, 116, 118, 127, 133, 153
Davis, Bette, 217, 223, 239
Death threat to Governor Muskie, 231
Debating, high school, 27, 28; college, 39, 44, 47, 51, 59; challenging Governor Cross, 152–53, 162, 163, 168–70
Delahanty, Thomas E., 97, 127, 129, 130, 136, 149, 158, 169, *173*,174, 179, 184, 241, 242
DeVoto, Bernard, 207–08
Dolloff, Maynard C., 235, 236, 237
Donovan, Dr. John C., 98, 105, 121, 224

Dubord, F. Harold, 74, 75, 125, 128, 199
Dubord, Richard, 122, 128, 184, 199, 210, 236

E
Eaton, Harvey D., 60, 94
Edmund S. Muskie Archives and Special Collections Library, 250
Eisenhower, Dwight D., 106, 107, 146, 180, 181, 183, 198–99; visit to Maine, 200–05, 213, 230

F
Farnsworth, Dr. George B., 55–56, 57, 60, 64
Fire at Muskie & Glover law offices, 79
Flood of 1936, 52
Fredland, John "Roger," 58, 63
Furbush, Perry, 125, 126, 127, 182
Fullam, Paul, 124, 130, 136, 148, 149, 150, 161, 165, 172, *173*, 174, 179, 199–200

G
Gannett, Guy, 116, 134, 182
Glover, James, 75, 76, 88
Goodbout, Marjorie, 42, 45, 49, 50
Gould, John, 200
Gould, Raymond R. N., 47, 48
Governor's Executive Council, 190, 225, 241, 245
Great Depression, 24, 33, 34, 35, 36
Greaton, Everett F., 207
Guite, Roland, 117

H
Harriman, W. Averill, 123
Harvey, Pearl, 29, 31, 32
Haskell, Nathaniel, 114
Haskell, Robert N., 194–95, 229, 241, 242
Haynesville Woods, 145
Hicks, Lucille, 30, 33, 48
Highway improvements, 188, 205, 227, 232
Hildreth, Horace, 78, 79, 89, 150, 241
Hiscock, Edmund S., 119, 120, 131
Home at 17 Silvermount Street in Waterville, *91*

Hoover, Herbert, 34
Hooverville shantytowns, 24, 33
Hughes, Howard, 102
Humphrey, Hubert H., 151, 249
Hussey, Leroy, 154–55
Hutchinson, Marjorie, 63, 73, 110, 184
Hurricane Carol, 173, 185
Hurricane Edna, 174, 176, 185

I
Industrial development, 188, 193–95, 206, 229, 231, 233, 244
Internal Revenue Service, 104
Isaacson, Irving, 51–52

J
Jackson, Henry "Scoop," 217
Jalbert, Louis, 112, 115, 225, 236
Johnson, Lyndon B., 246

K
Kennedy, John F., 172, 205, 219, 231
Korean Conflict, 95–96, 202–03

L
Lane, George, 52–53
Lee, Sheperd "Shep," 93, 144
Lemieux, Lionel A. "Lal," 116, 118, 119, 120, 125, 132, 156, 157, 164, 175
Lessard, Alton, 115, 124, 147
Loeb, William, 250
Lord, George E., 28, 31, 37
Luce, Claire Booth, 213

M
MacArthur, Douglas, 34, 95
MacDonald, Paul, 131, 157
Magnuson, Warren G., 146
Maine Democratic Convention 1950, 91–93; 1954, 115, 122–24; 1956, 217–218; 1958, 235–36
Maine House of Representatives, 74, 77, 79, 82, 89, 94
Maine Potato Growers Association, 99, 100
Maine State Budget, 1955–57, 191–92, 196; 1957–59, 227
Malenfant, Ernest, 103, 193

Manchester Union Leader, 247
Mansfield, Jayne, *214*
Marriage to Jane Gray, 87–89
Mascianica, Francis, 68, 69
McCarthy, Joseph, 106, 123, 204–05
McKusick, Vincent, 190
McMahon, Richard, 78, 86, 88, 115, 124, 131, 139, 144–45, 153, 154, 157, 163, 176, 184, 209, 236, 244
McQuade, J. Harold, 228–29
Merrill, Gary, 223, 239
Millett, Obed F., 156, 206
Mitchell, George, 251
Mitchell, Stephen, 135, 141, 142, 143, 146, 181
Montgomery, Claude; portrait of Governor Muskie, *222*
Movies filmed in Maine: *Carousel*, 213, *214*; *Payton Place*, 230
Mudge, Raymond, 196
Muskie, Edmund S., Jr. "Ned" (son), 247
Muskie, Ellen (daughter), 98, 178, 182, 187, *204, 226*, 227
Muskie, Elizabeth (sister), 4, *17*
Muskie, Eugene (brother), 4, 15, 16, *17, 67*
Muskie, Frances (sister), 4, *17*, 65
Muskie, Irene (sister), 4, 5, 7, *17*, 18, 19, 40
Muskie, Jane Gray (wife), 80–84, *81*, 86, 98, 107, 109, 110–11, 128, 144, 157, 171, 174, *177*, 178, 179, 180, 181, 182, 189, *204*, 221, 225, *226*, 227, 250
Muskie, Josephine (mother), 1, 2, 4, 5, 9, 15, 16, *17*, 18, *189*, 215, *222*
Muskie, Lucy (sister), 4, 5, *17*, 40, 42, *43*, 44, 46, 47, 48, 49, 51, 215
Muskie, Martha (daughter), 239, 250
Muskie, Melinda (daughter), 225, *226*
Muskie, Stephen (father), 1, 2, 3, 4, 5, 6, 7, 8, 9, 13, 16, *17*, 18, 19, 21, 26, 31, 61, 64, 84, 88, 153, 180, *189*, 243; death, 215; immigration to America, 7–9; fire at his tailor shop, 40–41; political views, 13–15
Muskie, Steve, (son), 87, 109, 178, 180, 187, 188, *204, 226*, 227, 236

N

Nadeau, Blanch, 62
Narragansett-by-the-Sea hotel, 36, 42, 49, 50, 58
Nelson, Charles, 127, 129, 136, 213, 217
Newcomb, Elliot, 94, 160
New Deal, 34, 35, 50, 53, 74, 164–65
Nicoll, Donald E., 59, 107, 108, 111, 115, 117, 118, 119, 120, 125, 126, 127, 129, 130, 132, 137, *138, 140*, 141, 142, 144, 148, 151, 170, 172, 176, 184, 194, 195, 197, 219, 224, 236, 244
Nixon, Richard M., 107, 164, 172, 213, 247
Nute, Floyd "Tom," 184

O

Office of Price Stabilization, 96, 97, 98, 99, 100, 103, 105, 154
Oliver, James "Big Jim," 105, 117, 120, 126, 127, 129, 134, 149, *173*, 179, 220, 224, 236, 240
Oxford Paper Company, 1, 2, 11, 12, 13, 33, 36, 52

P

Pagoda Restaurant, 104, 163
Payne, Frederick, 101, 102, 103, 114, 148, 184, 201, 202, 234, 237–38, 239
Poland, 7–9
Pollution, 1, 20, 172, 188, 192–93, 243, 247–48, 251
Poulin, Dorothy, 29, 171
Puiia, Vito, 1, 22, 25–26

Q

Quimby, Brooks, 38, 44, 72

R

Radio's use in the campaign, 170
Rangeley, 21, 31, 88–89, 153, 165, 202
Reed, John H., 93, 242
Reid, James, 194, 220, 224
Republicans for Muskie, 156, 206
Rines, Catherine, 186, 225
Roosevelt, Eleanor, 161–62
Roosevelt, Franklin Delano, 34, 35, 50, 53, 61, 63, 90, 122

Ross, Norm, 38, 53
Rowe, Harry, 37, 38, 42, 45, 50, 51, 52
Rowe Wilson, Ruth, 44, 52
Rumford, history of, 9–13

S

Sawyer, James, 109, 115, 125
Schnurle, Harold, 194, 195, 229
Sills, Dr. Kenneth C. M. "Casey," 120,
    141
Silsby, William, 96
Sisters' Hospital, 94, 109, 112–13, 239
Sixtus, (popes I–V), 2–3
Smith, Margaret Chase, 102, 125, 126,
    127, 130, 142, 148, 149, 161, 164,
    202, 204, 213, 215; "Declaration of
    Conscience" speech, 106
Spinney Campbell, Elizabeth, 27, 171
Squire, Russell M., 84, 86
Stephens High School, 22, 23, 25, 26,
    32, 37, 54, 59, 137
Stephens, John E., 22
Stevenson, Adlai, 107
Studebaker, 65, 76, 77, 84, 87, 98

T

Taylor, Charles, 31, 39, 42, 141, 160
Television's use in the campaign,
    150–52
Temper, 198, 251

Trafton, Willis A., Jr., 209, 218, 220,
    223, 224
Truman, Harry S., 90, 95, 96, 105, 106,
    122, 203
Tupper, Stanley, 135, 174–75

U

Umbro, Vito, 26, 41, 84
United States Navy, 63–64, 66–67, 68,
    69, 70, 72, 73, 93
USS *Bracket* (DE-41), 70–71, 72, 73

V

Vallée, Rudy, 33, 41, 85
Victory Chimes, 176

W

Walsh, Adam, 223, 236
Wheeler, Milton, 97, 103, 104
Williams, Jean Gannett, 134
Williams, Maurice "Maury," 102, 184,
    227
Williams, "Vi," 70
Wilson, Woodrow, 3
Winston Levinson, Betty, 46, 47, 49, 50,
    52, 58, 182
Wong, Danny, 104
Wong, Henry, 104, 163
Wyman, William F., 202